# A+ PREPARATION COMPANION
# Semester 1

**Edited by Bonnie Yarbrough**

CISCO PRESS

201 West 103rd Street

Indianapolis, IN 46290 USA

# A+ Preparation Companion

Published by:
Cisco Press
201 West 103rd Street
Indianapolis, IN 46290 USA

Printed in the United States of America 1 2 3 4 5 6 7 8 9 0

Library of Congress Cataloging-in-Publication Number: 00-102054

ISBN: 1-57870-250-x

| | |
|---|---|
| *Publisher* | *John Wait* |
| *Executive Editor* | *Dave Dusthimer* |
| *Managing Editor* | *Patrick Kanouse* |
| *Development Editor* | *Kitty Wilson Jarrett* |
| *Senior Editor* | *Jennifer Chisholm* |
| *Proofreader* | *Erich Richter* |
| *Associate Editor* | *Shannon Gross* |
| *Team Coordinator* | *Amy Lewis* |

# TABLE OF CONTENTS

# INTRODUCTION

*A+ Preparation Companion* is a two-volume book designed as text for the A+ classroom and lab experience. This text and the classroom activities help students gain A+ certification and enter the workforce with certified skills. The text is particularly helpful when used in conjunction with the online Aries Certified Computer Technician Curriculum.

This book is designed to further train students and instructors beyond the online training materials. It closely follows a pedagogical style and format that enables students to incorporate prior content knowledge and experience into the present curriculum as they progress through each lesson. In addition, the book provides students the opportunity to reflect on and test their understanding of each lesson's content by completing exercises.

Concepts covered in the two volumes of this book include a brief history of computers, number systems, electricity, power supplies, power events, the workplace and tools, the computer case, the motherboard, the microprocessor, voltage settings, memory, drives, video displays, communication devices, networking architecture and configuration, the Internet, input devices, operating systems, network concepts, operating systems, user profiles and system policy, dial-up networking servers and services, boot files and initialization, problem avoidance, troubleshooting and recovery, and plug-and-play hardware.

## The goal of this book

The goal of *A+ Preparation Companion* is to prepare readers to take the A+ and Microsoft Certified Professional exams. It is designed for use independently or in conjunction with the online Aries Certified Computer Technician Curriculum.

## This book's audience

*A+ Preparation Companion* is for anyone who wants to prepare to take the A+ and Microsoft Certified Professional exams. The main target audience for this book is students in high schools, community colleges, and four-year institutions. Specifically, in an educational environment this book could be used both in the classroom as a text book companion and in computer labs as a lab manual companion.

This book is also for corporate training faculty and staff members. In order for corporations and academic institutions to take advantage of the capabilities of computer technologies, a large number of individuals have to be trained in computer basics, operating systems, and the use of networks.

Finally, this book is for general users. This book's user-friendly and nontechnical approach should be appealing to readers who prefer material that's less technical than that in most manuals.

# This book's features

Many of this book's features, including the following, help facilitate a full understanding of the requirements necessary to prepare for the A+ and Microsoft Certified Professional exams:

- The format of the material—Content is presented in a series of units, each comprised of five lessons. This format allows students to proceed through the material in a sequential manner and creates a solid foundation of knowledge that leads to a thorough understanding of the content.

- Review exercises—Each lesson contains focus and concept questions, as well as vocabulary exercises, that serve as end-of-lesson assessments and reinforce the concepts introduced in the lesson by helping a student test his or her understanding before moving on to new concepts.

- Glossary—Each semester contains a glossary that provides quick, easy reference. Key terms throughout the lessons are highlighted in bold and are defined in the glossary.

# This book's organization

Semester 1 of *A+ Preparation Companion* includes 14 units, each of which contains 5 lessons. Each lesson contains focus, vocabulary, and review exercises.

Unit 1 discusses computer basics, the history of computers, numbers and number systems, and a brief introduction to electricity.

Unit 2 presents power supplies, their external and internal components and functions, as well as power supply form factor. In addition, power supply specifications, implications, and potential problems are discussed.

Unit 3 describes how you can protect the power supply by testing the external environment. In addition, the qualities that determine a safe, efficient work environment are explored. Finally, the basics of a computer's interrelated core—its case, power supply, and motherboard—are discussed.

Unit 4 explores the subject of motherboard technology, how the motherboard must be configured to properly to support the components of the system, and the types of specifications contained in the motherboard manual. Finally, this unit discusses how the BIOS manages the motherboard, connected devices, and peripherals.

Unit 5 discusses how the CPU connects to the motherboard, how the CPU works, and how to match correct voltage on the motherboard.

Unit 6 introduces the many forms of memory and how it functions, in combination with permanent storage devices, to process and preserve data. RAM, floppy disks, and CD-ROMs are discussed in detail.

Unit 7 describes hard drive components, operations, interfaces, and specifications. The particular differences between two hard drive types in common use today—the IDE and the SCSI types—are discussed in depth.

Unit 8 discusses the basic components of the video adapter, how it functions, and how to choose a good video adapter. The unit also describes monitor display basics and specifications.

Unit 9 presents an overview of the different communication systems and their devices and functions, including modems, serial and parallel ports, universal serial buses, and networks.

Unit 10 introduces various types of networks and networking hardware systems. The Internet, input devices, and sound cards are also discussed.

Unit 11 covers the major printer types and how they function, as well as BIOS basics and setup.

Unit 12 refers to the online A+ labs for system assembly, motherboard preparation and assembly, motherboard installation to the chassis, and drive assembly.

Unit 13 refers to the online A+ labs for system assembly and startup troubleshooting, BIOS setup, preparation for operating systems installation, and basic Windows 95 installation.

Unit 14 refers to the online A+ labs for sound card and speaker installation, modem installation and Internet configuration, network card installation, and basic networking.

The Glossary defines the terms and abbreviations related to networking that are used throughout this book.

# SEMESTER 1, UNIT 1

- Lesson 1: An Introduction to Computer Basics
- Lesson 2: The History of Computing
- Lesson 3: Numbers and Number Systems
- Lesson 4: A Brief Introduction to Electricity
- Lesson 5: Unit 1 Exam

# SEMESTER 1, UNIT 1, LESSON 1

# An Introduction to Computer Basics

Although you know what computers do, if someone asked, you probably could not define precisely what a computer is. This book will help you understand computers from the ground up. Beginning with a brief history of computing, it will guide you through the "nuts and bolts" that make computers work: computer components and their various devices. You will discover computer technician tools and how to assemble, repair, and maintain a finely tuned computer.

## A computer's basic parts

Essentially three fundamental components make up a computer: the *system unit*, *the output device*, and the *input device*. Let's look at each of these components.

### The system unit

The **system unit** contains all the computer components for processing and storing data, and for communicating with the computer's other parts.

### Output devices

An **output device** displays data or information, either in the form of a hard copy or an image on the screen, or as an electrical signal. Some examples of output devices are

- **Dot-matrix printer**—A type of printer that creates characters and graphics by striking pins against an ink ribbon. The striking pins print closely spaced dots in the appropriate shapes of characters.

- **Inkjet printer**—A type of non-impact printer that uses liquid ink to spray characters onto the page.

- **Laser printer**—A type of non-impact printer that uses a laser to draw an image on an electrically charged drum, and then transfers the image to electrically charged paper using toner.

- **Cathode ray tube (CRT)**—The vacuum tube used in display monitors, video terminals, or televisions. CRT is also used as a general name for any type of monitor that uses cathode ray tubes and a phosphor-coated screen.

- **Liquid crystal display (LCD)**—A monitor type that uses as its display medium a polarized, molecular-structure liquid that is held between two see-through electrodes.

- **Projector**—A peripheral device that enables computer data to be displayed on a large remote screen for presentation purposes.

- **Speaker**—A device that enables you to hear sound.

## *Input devices*

An **input device** allows you to enter data into the computer to be processed. Some examples of input devices are

- **Keyboard**—An input device that allows you to type text or enter commands into the computer. It has the same keys as a typewriter keyboard, as well as special keys that are used with computer programs.

- **Mouse**—An input device that allows you to point to and select items onscreen. It is used primarily with graphical user interface (GUI) programs to select icons and menu commands. It is also used with most drawing and paint programs.

- **Trackball**—A type of mouse that features a rotating ball that you manipulate with your thumb, fingertips, or palm. A trackball's buttons are used to perform basic clicking actions such as selecting commands from a menu.

- **Scanner**—An input device that reads printed information such as pictures or text and translates it into digital data the computer can understand.

- **Touch screen**—An input device that allows you to interact with a computer by touching the display screen.

- **Graphics tablet**—An input device that has a touch-sensitive surface. When you draw on the tablet's surface using a special pen, the image that is drawn is relayed to the computer, where it can be manipulated in a graphics application. Also referred to as a computing pen.

- **Joystick**—An input device that is used to control onscreen movement. It is usually used in game applications to control the movement of some object such as an animated character.

- **Microphone**—A device that changes sound energy into electrical signals. A microphone is used to "input" sounds into a computer.

# Data

The system unit and output and input devices work together to enable the computer to process information called **data**, which you input, manipulate, store, and output to create a product or perform analyses. Computer data is written in a digital format that uses a binary number system.

## *Processing data*

When you type on the keyboard or use another method for information input, you generate data that the computer's operating system deciphers. The computer stores the typed-in data in its **random access memory (RAM)** chips. RAM manipulates data at very high speeds. From RAM, data is moved into the **central processing unit (CPU)**, sometimes called the microprocessor. Think of the CPU as the computer's brain. The CPU's job is to analyze and process instructions and perform any tasks that may have been requested. Information created as a result of CPU data processing can be displayed on the monitor.

# Peripheral devices

A **peripheral device** is any tool or mechanism that connects to a computer. Many types of peripherals can be used with computers. Some examples of peripheral devices are

- **CD-ROM drive**—A peripheral device that uses a read-only optical storage medium to access up to 682 MB of data, including text, audio, video, and graphics. This type of device can have either an IDE or a SCSI interface.

- **Speaker**—A device that enables users to hear sound.

- **Modem**—An electronic device used for computer communications via telephone lines. It allows data transfer between one computer and another. Typically, it converts digital data to analog signals, and then back into digital data.

- **External drive unit**—A peripheral device such as a floppy disk drive that attaches to the system unit and is used for input and output such as storage of data.

- **Floppy disk drive**—A type of disk drive that uses removable storage media called floppy disks. Commonly called a floppy drive.

# Concept Questions         *Semester 1, Unit 1, Lesson 1*

Demonstrate your knowledge of the concepts in this lesson by answering the following questions in the space provided.

*1.* Explain how the three fundamental components make up a computer: the system unit, the output device, and the input device.

*2.* Explain how RAM and the CPU work together to process data.

_____

_____

_____

_____

_____

_____

_____

_____

_____

_____

_____

_____

_____

_____

_____

_____

_____

# Vocabulary Exercise     *Semester 1, Unit 1, Lesson 1*

Name: _____

Date: _____    Class: _____

Define the following terms as completely as you can.

**computer**

_____

_____

**data**

_____

_____

**peripheral**

_____

_____

**RAM**

_____

_____

# Focus Questions

## *Semester 1, Unit 1, Lesson 1*

*Name:* _____

*Date:* _____   *Class:* _____

**1.** What is random access memory referred to as?

_____

_____

_____

**2.** What carries out commands, performs calculations, and communicates with all the hardware components needed to operate a computer? (It is sometimes referred to as a microprocessor.)

_____

_____

_____

**3.** Describe the three fundamental components of a computer.

_____

_____

_____

_____

**4.** Describe a dot-matrix printer.

_____

_____

_____

**5.** Describe an inkjet printer.

_____

_____

_____

**6.** Describe a laser printer.

_____

_____

_____

**7.** Describe a CRT.

_____

_____

_____

**8.** Describe an LCD.

_____

_____

_____

**9.** Describe a projector.

_____

_____

_____

**10.** Describe speakers.

_____

_____

_____

**11.** Describe a keyboard.

_____

_____

_____

**12.** Describe a mouse.

_____

_____

_____

**13.** Describe a trackball.

_____

_____

_____

**14.** Describe a scanner.

_____

_____

_____

**15.** Describe a touch screen.

_____

_____

_____

**16.** Describe a graphics tablet.

_____

_____

_____

**17.** Describe a joystick.

_____

_____

_____

**18.** Describe a microphone.

_____

_____

_____

**19.** Describe a CD-ROM drive.

_____

_____

_____

**20.** Describe a modem.

_____

_____

_____

**21.** Describe an external drive unit.

_____

_____

_____

**22.** Describe a floppy drive.

_____

_____

_____

# SEMESTER 1, UNIT 1, LESSON 2
# The History of Computing

Understanding the evolution of computers will help you make sense of the interrelationship between computers and the essential components and peripheral devices that comprise the powerful technology of today. Many people think computers are inventions of the 20th century. However, computing began when our ancient ancestors devised counting methods. Table 1-1 outlines the historical development of the computer.

**Table 1-1**    *The historical development of computers*

| Time Period | Inventor | Computing Invention |
|---|---|---|
| Ancient times | Chinese | The *abacus* is the first recorded adding machine, constructed of sliding beads on small wooden rods strung on a wooden frame. |
| 1642 | Blaise Pascal | The *pascaline* is the first recorded **calculator**. It was made out of clock gears and levers, and could solve basic mathematical problems such as addition and subtraction. |
| 1694 | Gottfried Wilhelm von Liebniz | A machine similar to Pascal's, the *stepped reckoner* could perform addition, subtraction, multiplication, and division; however, it was often inaccurate. |
| 1820 | Charles Xavier Thomas de Colmar | The *arithometer* could perform addition, subtraction, multiplication, and division with total accuracy. |
| Late 1800s | Joseph Jacquard | Jacquard used cards with holes punched in them to program fabric patterns into his weaving loom. These are the first known *punch cards*. |
| 1821 | Charles Babbage | The *Difference Engine* was the first modern computer design. It was a steam-powered adding machine that automatically solved math problems. The *Analytical Engine* was a mechanical adding machine that took information from punched cards to solve and print complex mathematical operations. Because of his work on the Difference Engine and the Analytical Engine, Babbage is considered the father of computing. |

| Time Period | Inventor | Computing Invention |
|---|---|---|
| Early 19th century | Herman Hollerith | *Punch cards* were used to tabulate U.S. census data, shortening the time required by 67%. Hollerith is regarded as the father of information processing. He went on to found the Tabulating Machine Company, which later became a part of the International Business Machines (IBM) Corporation. |
| 1941 | Konrad Zuse | The *Z3* was the first programmable computer that was capable of following instructions. The Z3 was the first computer designed to solve complex engineering equations, rather than only basic arithmetic problems. The Z3 marked the changed from mechanical calculation machines to electronic computers. |
| 1942 | John Atanasoff and Clifford Berry | *ABC* was the first all-electronic computer. It used **vacuum tubes** to help make electric computation possible. |
| 1944 | Professor Howard Aiken and IBM | The *Mark 1* strung together 78 adding machines to achieve three calculations each second, which was a computing marvel for its day. The Mark 1 was 8 feet tall and 55 feet long. |
| 1945 | Presper Eckert and John Mauchly | The *Electronic Numerical Integrator and Computer (ENIAC)* was the first operational electronic digital computer. ENIAC was developed for the U.S. Army, and it was 1,000 times faster than Mark 1 and could perform 5,000 additions per second. ENIAC had more than 18,000 vacuum tubes and 7,000 transistors, and took up to 1,800 square feet of space. In addition, the electrical current ENIAC required could power more than 1,000 modern computers. |
| 1951 through 1959 | Numerous individuals | *First-generation computers* were the first true computers, as we know them. They used electricity, vacuum tubes, and magnetic drums and tape for memory. First-generation computers were large, slow, and expensive. They produced a great deal of heat and often broke down due to burned-out vacuum tubes. |

| Time Period | Inventor | Computing Invention |
|---|---|---|
| 1959 through 1963 | Numerous individuals | *Second-generation computers* used transistors instead of vacuum tubes, which allowed second-generation computers to communicate over telephone lines. A **transistor** is a small, solid-state component designed to monitor the flow of current. Transistors were smaller, faster, and cheaper than vacuum tubes, and they required less power and produced less heat. Second-generation computers could run multiple programs, and could handle input and output at the same time. They were easier to program than first-generation computers, and they used high-level languages, as well as magnetic cores and disks for memory. |
| 1963 through 1974 | Numerous individuals | *Third-generation computers* used **integrated circuits**. An integrated circuit is a single wafer or chip that can hold many transistors and electronic circuits. Third-generation computers were faster than earlier computers, and they offered improved memory and reduced the price of computers. |
| 1975 | Micro Instrumentation and Telemetry Systems (MITS) | The Altair 8080 was the first *personal computer (PC)*. It came in kit form and was designed for computer experts. The Altair 8080 had very little memory and had to be coded by flipping switches by hand. |
| 1977 | Steve Jobs and Steve Wozniak | Jobs and Wozniak founded Apple Computer and invented the Apple II, which is generally regarded as the catalyst for the PC's sudden and dramatic popularity. |
| 1981 | IBM and Tandy | IBM introduced computers that set the standard for PCs in the business world. Tandy also began producing PCs. |
| 1984 | Apple Computer | The Apple Macintosh featured the first **graphical user interface (GUI)**. Apple's GUI included a series of icons, pull-down menus, and a mouse. |
| 1993 | Intel | Intel developed the Pentium processor, which has 3.1 million transistors. |

# Concept Questions          *Semester 1, Unit 1, Lesson 2*

Demonstrate your knowledge of the concepts in this lesson by answering the following questions in the space provided.

*1.* Draw a time line illustrating the date and occurrence of major events in the history of computers.

*2.* Explain how mathematical computation drove the development of the computer.

_____

_____

_____

_____

_____

_____

_____

_____

_____

_____

_____

_____

_____

_____

_____

_____

_____

_____

# Vocabulary Exercise       *Semester 1, Unit 1, Lesson 2*

*Name:* _____

*Date:* _____     *Class:* _____

Define the following terms as completely as you can.

**calculator**

_____

_____

**GUI**

_____

_____

**pascaline**

_____

_____

**programmable computer**

_____

_____

**programming language**

_____

_____

**punch card**

_____

_____

**vacuum tube**

_____

_____

# Focus Questions

## *Semester 1, Unit 1, Lesson 2*

*Name:* _____

*Date:* _____  *Class:* _____

**1.** What was the first known counting instrument, and how was it constructed?

_____

_____

_____

_____

**2.** Who is considered the father of computers, and what did he invent?

_____

_____

_____

_____

**3.** Who was the first person to use punch cards, and how did he use them?

_____

_____

_____

_____

**4.** Describe the ENIAC.

_____

_____

_____

_____

**5.** What technology did second-generation computers rely on, and why?

_____

_____

_____

_____

**6.** Who were the founders of Apple Computer, and what was their major contribution to the history of computers?

_____

_____

_____

_____

**7.** Describe the first PC.

_____

_____

_____

_____

**8.** Describe the first electromechanical calculator.

_____

_____

_____

_____

# SEMESTER 1, UNIT 1, LESSON 3
# Numbers and Number Systems

Early mechanical computers often used decimal numbers. However, when computers became electrical and began using electronic components, it was necessary to convert decimal numbers to a form that a computer can understand. Thus, it became essential to use a more efficient number system. Binary representation met this requirement and proved important in the design of computers that took advantage of two-state devices such card readers, electric circuits that could be on or off, and vacuum tubes.

Although the binary system is the main system used by computers, it can be cumbersome for humans to work with, because binary numbers are long. This makes it easy to make mistakes that are difficult to notice in a mass of 0s and 1s. Thus, other number systems play an important part in the use of computers as well. Notice the significance of the number 8 in the computer world. Bytes are the building blocks of computer data, and nearly all numbers associated with computers are divisible by 8. Thus, hexadecimal and octal are used. Understanding these number systems and their relationship to one another is a fundamental step toward learning how computer languages operate in conjunction with technology.

## Decimal numbers

People are most familiar with the decimal number system. The decimal number system is a base-10 system, meaning it has 10 digits (0 through 9). Decimal also has a concept of place value. The rightmost digit in a number is in the ones place, the next digit on the left is in the tens place, and so on. Each successive place on the left has a value 10 times that of the one before it. Some examples follow.

Consider the number 453. If we break it down into digits and place values, we can view the number like this: 4 is in the hundreds place, 5 is in the tens place, and 3 is in the ones place.

The total value of the number can be expressed as

$4 \times 100 + 5 \times 10 + 3 \times 1$

or

$4 \times 10^2 + 5 \times 10^1 + 3 \times 10^0$

## Binary numbers

Modern computers require a more efficient number system than the decimal system, and the **binary** system meets this requirement. The word *binary* means "two," and the binary system expresses two states (on/off or true/false). Computers recognize the "on" state as 1 and the "off" state as 0. Computers can make decisions by grouping sets of 1s and 0s together to represent characters humans can understand.

This logic is the only way in which a computer or an electronic circuit can make decisions, and from these decisions we get today's electronic world. Every bit of data entered into a computer is translated first into binary number code. Even a simple keyboard command such as typing the letter *B* is translated to the binary code—in this case 01000010—before being transported electronically to the CPU.

A single digit (in binary, a 0 or 1) is called a *bit*. Eight bits associated together are called a *byte*. Therefore, each letter of the alphabet contains eight binary digits. Multiple bytes associated together form a *word*.

# Hexadecimal numbers

**Hexadecimal** (or *hex*) is a type of code that the computer uses internally. At its simplest, hex numbers are base 16 (decimal is base 10). Instead of counting from 0 to 9, as we do in decimal, and then adding a column to make 10, counting goes from 0 to F before adding a column. The characters A through F represent the decimal values 10 through 15. Each column in a hex number represents a power of 16. (In decimal each column represents a power of 10.)

# Octal numbers

The **octal** number system is a base-8 system. The octal number system uses eight values (0 through 7) to represent numbers. One octal digit stands for 3 bits. The values possible in octal can be calculated using standard 3-bit representation, as follows:

| Octal Digit | 3-Bit Representation |
| --- | --- |
| 0 | 000 |
| 1 | 001 |
| 2 | 010 |
| 3 | 011 |
| 4 | 100 |
| 5 | 101 |
| 6 | 110 |
| 7 | 111 |

Octal is commonly used to represent very large binary numbers. For example, the binary number 0010110101010011 can be written as 000 010 110 101 010 011 in octal. The bit set at the far left has been extended to a full three digits, even though only requiring 1 bit, by writing two extra 0s. These 0s have no value and are meaningless, but are placed there for sake of formality.

## Counting in the decimal, binary, octal, and hexadecimal systems

You can count in the binary system and in other systems just like you do in the decimal system. The numbers vary due to the number of digits you can use (see Table 1-2). Although binary numbers are easy to understand, it can be inefficient for humans to use large strings of numbers to represent all computer data. Note that hexadecimal numbers contain twice as many characters as the octal system because octal is a base-8 numbering system and hexadecimal is a base-16 system.

**Table 1-2** *Number systems and characters*

| Number System | Characters Used |
| --- | --- |
| Octal | 0 1 2 3 4 5 6 7 |
| Decimal | 0 1 2 3 4 5 6 7 8 9 |
| Hexadecimal | 0 1 2 3 4 5 6 7 8 9 A B C D E F |

Table 1-3 is an example of counting to 20 in decimal, binary, octal, and hexadecimal.

**Table 1-3**     *Counting in decimal, binary, octal, and hexadecimal systems*

| Decimal | Binary | Octal | Hexadecimal |
|---------|--------|-------|-------------|
| 0 | 0 | 0 | 0 |
| 1 | 1 | 1 | 1 |
| 2 | 10 | 2 | 2 |
| 3 | 11 | 3 | 3 |
| 4 | 100 | 4 | 4 |
| 5 | 101 | 5 | 5 |
| 6 | 110 | 6 | 6 |
| 7 | 111 | 7 | 7 |
| 8 | 1000 | 10 | 8 |
| 9 | 1001 | 11 | 9 |
| 10 | 1010 | 12 | A |
| 11 | 1011 | 13 | B |
| 12 | 1100 | 14 | C |
| 13 | 1101 | 15 | D |
| 14 | 1110 | 16 | E |
| 15 | 1111 | 17 | F |
| 16 | 10000 | 20 | 10 |
| 17 | 10001 | 21 | 11 |
| 18 | 10010 | 22 | 12 |
| 19 | 10011 | 23 | 13 |
| 20 | 10100 | 24 | 14 |

# Conversion between number systems

Sometimes you need to convert a number from one system to another. If you are using Windows, you can use the calculator that's built into the system to convert decimal numbers to binary, hexadecimal and octal numbers, and so on. You use the calculator by clicking on the Start button and then selecting Programs, Accessories, Calculator. Click on the View pull-down menu, and select Scientific. You type in the decimal number you want to convert, and instantly you will have its binary, hexadecimal, or octal equivalent.

You can also convert numbers from one system to another by hand, using the methods described in the following sections.

## *Binary-to-decimal conversion*

There are several ways to convert binary numbers to the more human-recognizable decimal numbers. One way is to use a binary-to-decimal conversion table to calculate the decimal value (see Table 1-4). You use the chart to determine which position each 1 is, and substitute the decimal values for each 1 of the binary number.

**Table 1-4** *Binary-to-decimal conversion table*

| Position | 10 | 9 | 8 | 7 | 6 | 5 | 4 | 3 | 2 | 1 |
|---|---|---|---|---|---|---|---|---|---|---|
| Power of 2 | $2^9$ | $2^8$ | $2^7$ | $2^6$ | $2^5$ | $2^4$ | $2^3$ | $2^2$ | $2^1$ | $2^0$ |
| Decimal Value | 512 | 256 | 128 | 64 | 32 | 16 | 8 | 4 | 2 | 1 |

For example, take an 8-bit binary number such 10001101, and calculate using the binary-to-decimal conversion table. Note the 1s are in the 8, 4, 3, and 1 positions:

| Position: | 8 | 7 | 6 | 5 | 4 | 3 | 2 | 1 |
|---|---|---|---|---|---|---|---|---|
| Binary number: | 1 | 0 | 0 | 0 | 1 | 1 | 0 | 1 |

Therefore, the decimal value of binary 10001101 is $128 + 8 + 4 + 1 = 141$.

You can also convert from binary to decimal by using the "weight" concept. You do this by multiplying each bit value by its weight, and then adding the results to obtain the equivalent decimal value. For example, to convert the binary sequence 10010 to decimal, we do the following, moving from right to left:

$2^0$ x 0 = 0

$2^1$ x 1 = 1

$2^2$ x 0 = 0

$2^3$ x 0 = 0

$2^4$ x 1 = 16

Adding all the results, we get $0 + 1 + 0 + 0 + 16 = 17$. Therefore, the binary sequence 10010 represents the number 17 in decimal.

Yet another, similar, way to convert from binary to decimal is to use a place-value system. If the binary value is a 1, or "on," then the place value it represents is positive, or true. If it's a 0, or "off," then the value is null. Let's use the binary 10010011 as an example:

| 1 | 0 | 0 | 1 | 0 | 0 | 1 | 1 |
|---|---|---|---|---|---|---|---|

and assign place values (starting from the right at 1 and doubling until you reach the length of the desired binary):

| 1 | 0 | 0 | 1 | 0 | 0 | 1 | 1 |
|---|---|---|---|---|---|---|---|
| (128) | (64) | (32) | (16) | (8) | (4) | (2) | (1) |

Remember that if the binary digit is a 1, then the number assigned to its place value is true. So next we add together all the true values:

| 1 | 0 | 0 | 1 | 0 | 0 | 1 | 1 |
|---|---|---|---|---|---|---|---|
| (128) | (0) | (0) | (16) | (0) | (0) | (2) | (1) |

In this case, the total of the true values $(128 + 16 + 2 + 1)$ is 147. Therefore, the binary 10010011 = decimal 147.

## *Binary-to-hexadecimal conversion*

To convert a binary number to hexadecimal, we assign each part of the binary code a place value. In this example, let's use the binary number 1111. First, we start at one end, and double each number. If you are reading from right to left, the first digit in the sequence is a 1, so the value of that digit is 1. The second digit is a 1 also (remember you can only have 1s and 0s), so its value is 2. The next digit is a 1 again, so its value is 4. The last digit is 1 also, so its value is 8:

| 1 | 1 | 1 | 1 |
|---|---|---|---|
| 8 | 4 | 2 | 1 |

Adding up all these numbers we get 8 + 4 + 2 + 1 = 15. Therefore, the binary digit 1111 is hexadecimal 15.

But remember that with hexadecimal, any number over 10 is assigned an alphabetic value, as follows:

10 = A

11 = B

12 = C

13 = D

14 = E

15 = F

Therefore, 15 in hexadecimal (and binary 1111) is F 16. You include *16* in every hexadecimal number because hexadecimal consists of sets of four-digit binary (4 x 4 = 16).

Here's another example, using the binary number 1001:

| 1 | 0 | 0 | 1 |
|---|---|---|---|
| 8 | 0 | 0 | 1 |

Adding all these up you get 8 + 1 = 9. Thus in hex the binary number 1001 is 9 16.

Note that when you want to convert a longer binary number such as 101000101101, you have to break up the sequence into sets of four digits, so it becomes

1010      0010      1101

Once this number is broken up into these smaller parts all you have to do is to convert each individual part as we did earlier.

### *Binary-to-octal conversion*

Converting from binary to octal is very similar to converting from binary to hexadecimal. Let's start with binary 1011001110 as an example. First, group the binary into groups of 3 bits each, starting at the right side:

1          011       001       110

If we want to, we can always add 0s to the left of the number; just like the 0s on the left of the odometer of a car, they do not change the value of the number. We add two 0s here for demonstration purposes:

001       011       001       110

Now we look up each group of 3 bits in Table 1-3. (It is best to have some convention for this, and right to left makes the most sense to keep the groups of 3 bits in order.) So if we look up 110 in the Binary column of Table 1-3, we see that it corresponds to 6 in the Octal column. This is the ones digit in our answer. Then we look up each of the other sets of 3 bits, and come up with the following:

001       011       001       110

1          3         1         6

We add the digits $1 + 3 + 1 + 6$, and find that the result is 11. So binary 1011001110 converts to octal 11.

# Concept Questions     *Semester 1, Unit 1, Lesson 3*

Demonstrate your knowledge of the concepts in this lesson by answering the following questions in the space provided.

1.  Explain why the binary number system is ideally suited for computer languages.

2.  Explain how the decimal, binary, hexadecimal, and octal number systems are related.

_____

_____

_____

_____

_____

_____

_____

_____

_____

_____

_____

_____

_____

_____

_____

_____

_____

# Vocabulary Exercise     *Semester 1, Unit 1, Lesson 3*

*Name:* _____

*Date:* _____     *Class:* _____

Define the following terms as completely as you can.

**bit**

_____

_____

**byte**

_____

_____

**decimal number system**

_____

_____

**binary number system**

_____

_____

**hexadecimal number system**

_____

_____

**octal number system**

_____

_____

# Focus Questions

## *Semester 1, Unit 1, Lesson 3*

*Name:* _____

*Date:* _____    *Class:* _____

**1.** What are the two possible states of an electronic circuit?

_____

_____

**2.** What is the number system based on only the digits 0 and 1? Describe.

_____

_____

_____

_____

**3.** What do multiple bytes associated together form?

_____

_____

**4.** Convert the binary numbers to decimal in the following table:

| Position | 10 | 9 | 8 | 7 | 6 | 5 | 4 | 3 | 2 | 1 |
|---|---|---|---|---|---|---|---|---|---|---|
| Power of 2 | $2^9$ | $2^8$ | $2^7$ | $2^6$ | $2^5$ | $2^4$ | $2^3$ | $2^2$ | $2^1$ | $2^0$ |
| Decimal Value | | | | | | | | | | |

**5.** Convert the decimal numbers to binary in the following table:

| Decimal | Binary |
|---------|--------|
| 0 | |
| 1 | |
| 2 | |
| 4 | |
| 8 | |
| 16 | |
| 32 | |
| 64 | |

**6.** Use the Windows calculator to convert the following decimal numbers to hexadecimal:

| Decimal | Hexadecimal |
|---------|-------------|
| 5 | |
| 10 | |
| 15 | |
| 20 | |
| 25 | |
| 30 | |
| 35 | |
| 40 | |

# SEMESTER 1, UNIT 1, LESSON 4
# A Brief Introduction to Electricity

The basic unit of all matter is the atom. The atom is made of three tiny parts: protons, neutrons, and electrons. The protons and neutrons are lumped together in a small grouping called a nucleus, and the electron flows freely around the nucleus.

What does an atom have to do with **electricity**? The key to electricity lies in the difference between protons and the electrons. Protons have a positive (+) charge, and electrons have a negative (–) charge. Neutrons have no charge. The protons and the neutrons result in a positively charged nucleus. The electrons result in a negatively charged cloud around the outside of the nucleus. This creates a balanced atom.

## Electricity basics

Although the electrons may seem to eternally revolve around the nucleus, they often jump from one atom to another. **Static electricity** is stationary and occurs when electrons build up on a surface. **Dynamic electricity** results from moving charges. Where static electricity occurs, physical forces can act on two objects, causing electrons to move from one object to another. This causes an imbalance of charges between the two objects; one becomes positively charged and the other becomes negatively charged. When the two objects meet again, they create a zap of electricity as the natural balance of the atoms is returned. We use the natural movement of electrons, called a *current*, to create a flow of electricity to power computers and peripherals.

It is important to understand how basic electronic components work together with electrical current to power computers. Each time we turn on a computer, we are calling on a combination of electrical components to work in conjunction with an electrical source to operate our computer. In order to understand how this collaborative effort occurs, we must first understand each of the individual contributors.

### *Current*

*Current* is the flow of electrons in an electric circuit. Flowing water is a good analogy of electricity. When water flows through a pipe, or down a stream, there is current. Sometimes the current flows quickly, and sometimes it flows more slowly. If we were to measure how fast the current was flowing in a pipe, we might say it was so many gallons per minute. When we measure how much current is flowing through a wire, it is based on the number of electrons flowing past that point in one second. We use a unit of measure called the Coulomb to measure the amount of charge an object has. One Coulomb equals 6,240,000,000,000,000,000 (that is, 6.24 billion-billion) electrons.

One Coulomb of electrons passing through a wire in one second is one **ampere** (or **amp**) of current. Since we aren't able to actually see electrons or Coulombs, we use an ammeter to measure electric current. Table 1-5 defines common units of electricity and gives examples of each.

**Table 1-5**     *Electrical measurement*

| Unit | Definition | Example |
|------|-----------|---------|
| Amp | A measure of the rate of flow of electrical charge. | A 17-inch monitor and a small laser printer each use 2 amps, whereas a CD-ROM drive uses approximately 1 amp. |
| Ohm | A measure of the electrical resistance to the flow of charge. | The typical resistance across the terminals of a loudspeaker at home is 8 ohms. A very low resistance between two points indicates continuity. |
| Volt | A measure of electrical pressure, measured by finding the difference in electrical pressure between two points. | A PC power supply contains four voltages: +12v, –12v, +5v, and –5v |
| Watt | A measure of electrical power, calculated by multiplying volts by amps. | A power supply is rated at about 200 watts. |

There are two types of current:

- **Alternating current (AC)** is a form of electricity where the current changes direction regularly. This kind of current is produced by power stations and is used to power lights and most appliances. This normal household electricity repeatedly reverses its direction; it cycles back and forth 60 times each second. Computers and many electronic components cannot use AC, so it must be converted to DC.

- **Direct current (DC)** is a current that moves in a single direction in a steady flow around a circuit. Computers and many electronics devices require DC. Diodes are used to convert AC to DC.

## *Voltage*

*Voltage*, sometimes called electromotive force (EMF), is a measure of the energy required to move a charge from one point to another. A difference in the amount of electric charge between two points creates a difference in potential energy, measured in volts, which causes electrons to flow from an area with more electrons to an area with fewer, producing an electric current.

The basic unit of voltage is the **volt**. 1 volt could be abbreviated as 1v. If you wanted to measure how much voltage a circuit or battery had, you would use a voltmeter.

## *Resistance*

Similarly to the way that only so much water can flow down a stream or through a pipe, only so much current can flow in a circuit. Water is limited by the amount of friction it encounters as it flows. Electricity is limited by the amount of resistance it meets as it passes through a circuit. If we increased the water pressure in a pipe, more water would flow; if we turned up the voltage in a circuit, more current would also flow.

A **resistor** is a device that limits the amount of current flowing through a circuit for a particular applied voltage. That is, only so much current will flow with a certain amount of voltage and resistance. For example

- If the resistance stays the same and the voltage goes up, then the current increases.

- If the resistance stays the same and the voltage goes down, then the current decreases.

- If the voltage stays the same and the resistance goes up, then the current decreases.

- If the voltage stays the same and the resistance goes down, then the current increases.

The basic unit of resistance is the ohm. 1 ohm of resistance is defined as the resistance of a circuit in which a 1-amp current flows when 1v is applied. In order to measure the amount of resistance in a circuit, you use an ohmmeter.

There are two types of resistors:

- **Fixed resistors** are used to reduce the current by a certain amount. Fixed resistors are color-coded to identify their resistance values. When replacing a resistor, you must replace it with a resistor of the same resistance level, which you determine by reading the values of the colored bands. Each colored band represents a number. The first two bands together represent a two-digit number. The third band represents a multiplier. If a fourth band is present, it represents a margin of error.

- **Variable resistors** are most commonly used for volume and brightness control. The variable resistor does not have a single value, but rather can be changed by using a knob or slider.

## *Conductors and insulators*

A **conductor** is any type of material through which electrical charges can move under the influence of electric forces. Electricity flows through some materials easily; these materials make good conductors. Most conductors are metals, such as gold, silver, and aluminum.

The opposite of a conductor is a *nonconductor*, or an **insulator**, which is a material that does not readily allow charges to flow. Four good insulators are glass, air, plastic, and porcelain.

**Semiconductors** are solid materials whose electrical conductivity at room temperature lies between that of a conductor and that of an insulator. At high temperatures a semiconductor's conductivity approaches that of a metal, and at low temperatures it acts as an insulator. In a semiconductor there is a limited movement of electrons, depending on the crystal structure of the material used.

## *Diodes*

A **diode** is a two-terminal device that has a low resistance to electric current in one direction and a high resistance in the reverse direction. Diodes are thus useful as rectifiers, converting AC into DC. Almost all diodes today are semiconductors. In general, current flowing through a diode is not proportional to the voltage between its terminals. When the voltage applied in the reverse direction exceeds a certain value, a semiconductor diode breaks down and conducts heavily in the direction of normally high resistance; this effect can be exploited to regulate voltage.

## *Capacitors*

Electrical energy can be stored in an electric field. A good example of an electric field is static electricity and static buildup. For example, when it gets very dry in the winter months, you may have experienced the sensation of static electricity when shaking hands with someone or touching a door knob or light switch. This is electrical energy that has been built up and stored in you and your clothing. A **capacitor** is a device that stores certain amounts of static electricity, creating an electric field. *Capacitance* is the ability to store an electric field. The basic unit of capacitance is the Farad.

A capacitor looks like a small metal can or small disk with two connectors. Within a capacitor, there are two electric plates (or in some cases, a series of plates—large capacitors often have many plates hooked up together to increase the capacitance) separated by an insulating material (such as plastic, glass, or air). These two plates are hooked up to two leads that allow the current to flow in and out of the capacitor. As the current flows, electrons build up on one plate. At the same time, electrons flow out of the other plate. Eventually, the capacitor is completely "charged up," and no more current will flow. There is a positive charge on one plate and a negative charge on the other plate. No more current will flow because the voltage is not able to charge the plates any higher.

If the current is only DC, a capacitor eventually becomes charged up, and no more current can flow through the capacitor. But if the current is AC, as in a computer, and the current switches directions, the capacitor starts to "uncharge" as the current begins to flow the opposite direction.

In a computer, capacitors are used in electronic circuits to block the flow of DC while allowing AC to pass. They are used in power supplies and in timing circuits. It is important to remember that you should never touch a charged capacitor, which can retain a charge of thousands of volts, which can cause serious injury. You should also not touch a capacitor even after the power has been removed because capacitors can retain a charge for hours.

## *Integrated circuits*

**Integrated circuits** are miniature electric circuits containing large numbers of electronic devices, including transistors, resistors, capacitors, and diodes. An integrated circuit is packaged as a single unit, with leads extending from it for input, output, and power-supply connections. All electronic devices are formed by selective treatment of a single chip of semiconductor material. Integrated circuits are used as computer memory circuits and microprocessors. They are categorized according to the number of transistors or other active circuit devices they contain. An active circuit device is one that receives power from a source other than its input signal. There are different types of integrated circuits, the most common being the dual inline package (DIP), the quad small outline package (QSOP), and the single inline package (SIP).

# Concept Questions       *Semester 1, Unit 1, Lesson 4*

Demonstrate your knowledge of the concepts in this lesson by answering the following questions in the space provided.

*1.* Explain why the integrated circuit made modern computers possible.

*2.* Explain how electric components work in combination to operate a computer.

*3.* Explain how current is received into your home and converted for your computer to use.

_____

_____

_____

_____

_____

_____

_____

_____

_____

_____

_____

_____

_____

_____

_____

_____

_____

# Vocabulary Exercise     *Semester 1, Unit 1, Lesson 4*

*Name:* _____

*Date:* _____     *Class:* _____

Define the following terms as completely as you can.

**amp**

_____

_____

**capacitor**

_____

_____

**diode**

_____

_____

**electricity**

_____

_____

**integrated circuit**

_____

_____

**ohm**

_____

_____

**variable resistor**

_____

_____

**volt**

_____

_____

**watt**

_____

_____

# Focus Questions     *Semester 1, Unit 1, Lesson 4*

*Name:* _____

*Date:* _____  *Class:* _____

**1.** What type of material allows electricity to flow readily?

_____

_____

_____

**2.** What type of material inhibits the flow of electricity?

_____

_____

_____

**3.** What components are used to reduce the current by a certain amount? How does this process work?

_____

_____

_____

_____

_____

**4.** How is a resistance level determined?

_____

_____

_____

_____

_____

# SEMESTER 1, UNIT 1, LESSON 5
# Unit 1 Exam

If you have access to the online Aries A+ curriculum, contact your instructor for the Assessment System URL. If you do not have access to the online curriculum, please continue to Unit 2.

# SEMESTER 1, UNIT 2

- Lesson 6: Power Supply Basics
- Lesson 7: External Power Supply Components
- Lesson 8: Power Supply Specifications
- Lesson 9: Problem-Causing Power Events
- Lesson 10: Unit 2 Exam

# SEMESTER 1, UNIT 2, LESSON 6
# Power Supply Basics

In this lesson you will learn about basic electricity and power supplies, specifically about power supplies required by modern computers. You will study different types of power supplies and how they function, as well as the kinds of cases they fit in and their components.

## The power supply

The **power supply** provides electrical power for all the components inside the computer. The computer system plugs into a wall socket to access electrical power. The power supply converts electrical power from the wall outlet so that it can be used by the computer circuitry. The power supply is one of the most important computer components because the type of power supply restricts the type of components that can be used. For example, the type of motherboard and case are determined by the type of power supply used.

Before you continue with this lesson, it is important that you are aware that care must be taken when handling a power supply. A power supply has a caution label, usually written in several languages, cautioning the user to beware. *Do not open a power supply because capacitors hold a charge and can kill.*

### The function of the power supply

Electricity is carried to homes, schools, and offices by power lines. So that it can be transported over long distances, electricity carried by power lines is in the form of **alternating current (AC)** electricity. Most modern electronic devices, including computers, do not use AC. Instead, they generally use a form of electricity called **direct current (DC)**. The power supply converts AC to DC.

### Types of power supplies and form factors

There are several different types of power supplies, varying in size and design. The type of power supply you use influences the choice of computer form factor, or physical dimensions. There are six types of power supplies in the personal computer (PC) industry. Four are associated with older technology: **PC/XT**, **AT Desk**, **AT Tower**, and **Baby AT**. Two are associated with current technology: **Slimline** and **ATX**. Table 2-1 gives more information about these form factors. The four older power supply types are generally found on PCs built prior to the mid-1990s. Generally, they are no longer used in new systems, and they are easily distinguished by their large size and by the kind of power on/off switch they use. An older power supply form factor's power switch is a lever or rocker attached directly to the back or side of the power supply itself. Because many of the PCs built through the early 1990s are still in operation today, information about older form factors is included in the materials for this course.

**Table 2-1**     *Form factors*

| Form Factor | Dimensions (length x width x height, in inches) | Product Usage | International 220v Use | 110v/220v Switch |
|---|---|---|---|---|
| PC-XT | 8.8 x 5.6 x 4.75 | Obsolete | No | Rocker switch |
| AT Desk | 8.35 x 5.9 x 5.9 | Current | Yes | Rocker switch |
| AT Tower | 8.35 x 5.9 x 5.9 | Current | Yes | Rocker switch |
| Baby AT | 6.5 x 5.9 x 5.9 | Current | Yes | Rocker switch |
| Slimline | 6 x 5.56 x 3.38 | Current | Yes | Rocker switch |
| ATX | 6 x 5.56 x 3.38 | Current | Yes | Rocker switch |

The Slimline (whose name refers to the form factor's low height) and ATX form factors have been used on most new systems since the mid-1990s. Slimline and ATX power supplies are easily distinguished from the earlier types by their smaller size and lack of a built-in power on/off switch. On Slimline models, the switch attaches to the case and connects to the power supply via a cable. An ATX power supply attaches to the motherboard, and the on/off switch attaches to the front panel connections on the motherboard. This allows for "automatic" shutdown. The AT power supply attaches to the on/off switch and must be turned off.

The Slimline power supply is often used to replace earlier types of form factors. The Slimline and ATX power supplies share the same form factor, but they differ in their external connectors to the motherboard cooling system.

Designed by Intel in 1995, the ATX is the newest form factor on the market. It has a new motherboard shape, as well as a new case and power supply form factor. The form factor is based on the Slimline. The ATX uses a reverse flow cooling, which forces the air over the hottest components of the board, reducing the need for unreliable CPU fans. Reverse cooling also helps the system remain cleaner and free from dust and dirt.

The ATX form factor has solved some problems that occurred with the earlier form factors like the Baby AT and the Slimline. One problem was that the traditional PC power supply had two connectors that plugged into the motherboard. A user inserting these two connectors out of sequence would damage the motherboard. The ATX form factor solved this problem by including a new power plug that features 20 pins, and is a single-key connector. Since there is only one unipolar connector, out-of-sequence plugging in is not possible.

# Power supply components

The power supply contains two major components:

- Fan

- AC/DC converter, including the regulator, the rectifier, resistors, capacitors, and the transformer

These components are discussed in the following sections.

## *The power supply fan*

When the power supply converts AC to DC electricity, it generates a lot of heat. In addition, all the other electrically powered components inside the system unit generate heat during operation. As computers have become faster, the more heat they have generated. If a computer overheats, its components can cease functioning correctly or be damaged, and data can be corrupted. Microprocessor designers strive to use processors that require less voltage to reduce the heat inside the chip.

The power supply fan is the first defense in the battle to control the overheating problem. The power supply's fan supplies air and keeps a constant and bearable temperature inside the computer's case by promoting airflow. This flow of air inside the case also provides a secondary benefit: keeping dust from settling on and coating components. Dust can cause heat containment and can short out electrical connections.

To operate best, the computer needs a good supply of air. On all types of power supplies (except the ATX, as discussed shortly), as the power supply fan turns, it pulls unfiltered air through the vent located at the front of the system unit's case and across the CPU. Then the air is pulled through the power supply and out the back of the case. This type of fan operation has a couple disadvantages. First, the relatively weak airflow can cause dust to settle on internal components. Second, this type of airflow pattern does not result in optimal cooling of the most heat-sensitive internal component, the silicon CPU chip.

The ATX form factor uses a different airflow pattern. This is due in part to the ATX CPU's location, just beneath the power supply inside the case. In an ATX, air is pulled into the case by the power supply fan and then is blown directly onto the CPU. Because of direct airflow onto the CPU, dust does not tend to settle on it. In addition, this direct airflow pattern is more effective and dissipates heat better from the CPU. The ATX form factor also uses a second fan, in addition to the power supply fan, because the CPU generates so much heat that the power supply fan alone cannot provide sufficient cooling.

It is possible for a computer to operate outside its case. However, to ensure proper airflow from the power supply fan, the case should be on while the PC is turned on and operating. The computer case, which is scientifically designed to allow proper airflow, is the second level of defense against heat problems. Dust can also interfere with proper fan operation. Therefore, a **dust plate** should always cover each computer-back hole that is not being used by an expansion card.

## *The power supply's AC/DC converter*

The AC/DC converter is the heart of the power supply. The job of the AC/DC converter, as its name implies, is to change the 120v AC electricity as it comes from the wall socket to the 5v and 12v DC electricity used by the computer's components. Generally, 5v power is used by **logic boards**, and 12v power by drive motors. Logic boards are circuit boards, like the motherboard expansion cards.

The power supply converts external 120v AC power to different DC power voltages for internal components. In general, there are two basic types of power supplies: linear supplies and switching supplies. Linear supplies are typical of older designs, where the 60-Hz AC wall current is converted to lower AC voltages via a large, inefficient 120v transformer to the desired DC voltages.

Conversely, in a switching power supply, the 60-Hz wall power is "chopped" to produce a much higher frequency (greater than 60 Hz) signal, which can be more efficiently converted to the desired DC voltages, using a smaller transformer. A transformer allows voltage to be stepped up or stepped down. The output from a transformer would still be AC; the voltage must go through a diode bridge to convert it to DC. Other internal components of a switching power supply (such as filtering capacitors) are also smaller than their linear counterparts, resulting in a more compact and efficient overall design.

Let's can compare a PC power supply to a car stereo. There is a noticeable difference between a $60 car stereo and a $200 car stereo. Usually the number of filtering capacitors and inductance coils in the power supply design allows for better, less static sound. The same principle applies to a PC power supply. The better the electronic circuit design, the better the quality of voltage.

One drawback of the switched power supply is that it requires a load to function. Voltage does not flow unless something asks for the voltage. You can use a **load resistor** and a **fuse** to address this problem. The load resistor provides the needed load to test a power supply and maintains the power flow (or load) at a predetermined minimum operating limit. When a predetermined maximum current has been exceeded, the fuse burns out. This protects the power supply from short-circuiting.

# Concept Questions          *Semester 1, Unit 2, Lesson 6*

Demonstrate your knowledge of the concepts in this lesson by answering the following questions in the space provided.

*1.* Explain how the power supply is one of the most important computer components.

*2.* Explain how a fan contributes to the overall function of a computer, and describe the factors that can hinder its operation.

_____

_____

_____

_____

_____

_____

_____

_____

_____

_____

_____

_____

_____

_____

_____

_____

_____

# Vocabulary Exercise

## *Semester 1, Unit 2, Lesson 6*

*Name:* _____

*Date:* _____  *Class:* _____

Define the following terms as completely as you can.

**AC**

_____

_____

**DC**

_____

_____

**form factor**

_____

_____

**load resistor**

_____

_____

**logic board**

_____

_____

# Focus Questions

## *Semester 1, Unit 2, Lesson 6*

*Name:* _____

*Date:* _____    *Class:* _____

1. Why is it important not to open a power supply?

   _____

   _____

2. Describe the different types of power supplies and how they vary in size and design.

   _____

   _____

   _____

3. Describe the function of the power supply's AC/DC converter.

   _____

   _____

   _____

4. What are the two major components of the power supply?

   _____

   _____

   _____

5. What are the components of the power supply's AC/DC converter?

   _____

   _____

   _____

**6.** Describe the ATX power plug.

_____

_____

_____

**7.** Describe how airflow for the ATX power supply differs from other power supplies.

_____

_____

_____

**8.** Why is a second fan required in the ATX form factor?

_____

_____

_____

**9.** What is the purpose of a fuse?

_____

_____

_____

# SEMESTER 1, UNIT 2, LESSON 7
# External Power Supply Components

In this lesson, you will learn about the power supply's external components and their functions. You will also learn how these components differ from one form factor to another.

## The power supply's leads

Leads connect the power supply to the computer's internal components, such as the **motherboard** and **drives**. In some instances you see the term **connector** used for leads. Each power supply connector wire is attached to a female pin or male pin that mates with its counterpart on the drive or motherboard. The lead wires are color-coded to signify specific voltages. The following are some of the common colors used and their meanings:

- Black is for ground.

- Red is for +5v.

- White is for –5v.

- Yellow is for +12v.

- Blue is for –12v.

- Orange is for **Power_Good**.

The number of leads in a power supply varies from three to five. There are three types of power supply leads: **motherboard connectors**, **large drive connectors**, and **small drive connectors**. The large drive connectors are called molex and the small drive connectors are called berg.

### *Motherboard connectors*

Motherboard connectors come in two kinds: ATX and all others. For the Slimline and AT motherboard connectors, there are two 6-pin connectors, usually marked P8 and P9.

Some motherboard connector pins are used for signaling. Older-style and Slimline form factor computers use a pair of female 6-pin connectors marked P8 and P9.

A pinout is a diagram of the pins of a chip or connector. On some power supplies, P8 and P9 connectors are not keyed directionally for placement. Color schemes help verify the proper pinout connection sequence. A good rule of thumb for installation is to pair the black pinouts back-to-back to ensure proper placement.

A P8's six pins are three pinouts for power (+5v, +12v, –12v), one ground for each of the two + volts, and one pinout for **Power_Good signal**. A **Power_Good** signal is a +5v signal sent by the power supply after it has passed a series of internal self-tests. It is sent to the motherboard, where it is received by the processor timer chip controlling the reset line to the processor. Since the early 1990s, motherboards have used only +5v and +12v current. The −12v pinout is provided only for backward compatibility on older systems.

A P9's six pins are four pinouts for power (three for +5v, one for −5v) and two grounds. The −5v power pinouts are no longer used on newer motherboards; again, they provide backward compatibility.

The ATX power supply's single 20-pin motherboard connector includes standard 5v and 12v power and additional pins for 3.3v DC power. Two additional ATX signaling pinouts— Power_On and 5v_Standby signals—provide power management capabilities for more advanced **operating systems**, such as **Windows 95** and **Windows NT**.

### *Large and small drive connectors*

Small and large drive leads are identified by four pins. But large drive leads are, as you may have guessed, much larger than small drive connectors. Although the size difference is significant and makes it easier to distinguish the difference between them, the size difference is not conclusive. The larger molex connectors are "keyed" and cannot be easily inserted incorrectly. However, care should be used with the smaller berg connectors because they can be connected incorrectly, which can damage a floppy drive.

Large drive connectors operate 12v motors, like the computer's drive motors. Typically, small drive connectors transmit power to 5v computer mechanisms such as logic boards and floppy drives.

Drive connectors share a standard 4-pin scheme for delivering power. Male and female connectors are keyed by shape to fit only one way. Usually the female lead connects to the appropriate male drive, such as a CD-ROM or hard disk drive. A color scheme helps verify correct connection sequence: red to red, black to black, yellow to yellow, and so on. Most components, CD-ROMs, hard drives, and so on also have the colors printed or labeled.

## Types of power cord sockets

Generally, two types of power cord sockets are found on the power supply: One of these sockets is required, and the other is optional. The following sections give more details.

### *The required power cord socket*

The required power cord socket connects the computer to an external power source, such as a wall outlet. Wall unit types vary from country to country, and it is necessary to use the power cord suited to the country where the computer is used. In the United States, for example, a three-pronged power cord provides the AC input voltage to the power supply.

On the back of the computer, a small switch permits the power supply to operate on 220v AC when outside the United States. When this switch is on the 220 position, the voltage to the power supply's monitor will also be 220.

### *The optional power cord socket*

In most cases a power supply has a second power cord socket: the optional power cord socket. The optional socket is often used to provide power to the computer's monitor. An easy way to identify this type of socket is to look for the socket that uses a three-pronged female connection. However, is it now considered unwise to use this monitor plug due to wattage demands.

## The voltage switch

In the United States and some other countries, appliances such as computers operate on 120v current. In European countries, appliances operate on 220v current. The computer's voltage switch allows the user to select either 120v or 220v, whichever is the voltage level most closely compatible with the country's electrical source. This is usually the first place a smart teacher looks when a computer will not boot. This selector switch is very important. Table 2-2 lists types of power used in different countries.

**Table 2-2**   *Types of power used in different countries*

| Country | Type of Power |
| --- | --- |
| United States | 120v/60 Hz |
| Bahamas | 115v/60 Hz |
| Brazil | 110v–127v–220v/60 Hz |
| Canada | 120v/60 Hz |
| Costa Rica | 120v/60 Hz |
| Mexico | 120v/60 Hz |
| Panama | 120v/60 Hz |
| Peru | 220v/60 Hz |
| United Kingdom | 220v/50 Hz |
| France | 220v/50 Hz |
| Germany | 220v/50 Hz |
| Saudi Arabia | 127v–220v/50 Hz or 60 Hz |
| Vietnam | 120v/50 Hz |

| Country | Type of Power |
|---------|---------------|
| Taiwan | 110v/60 Hz |
| Japan | 100v–200v/50 Hz or 60 Hz |
| China | 220v/50 Hz |
| Uganda | 240v/50 Hz |
| Kuwait | 240v/50 Hz |
| Australia | 240v–250v/50 Hz |
| Philippines | 110v–220v/60 Hz |
| Lebanon | 110v–220v/50 Hz |

## The power on/off switch

The power on/off switch is also called the **power switch connector**. There are two kinds of power on/off switches: the **external lever switch** (connected directly to the older AT styles), and the **remote button switch** (connected to the Slimline and ATX switches via a 4-wire cable). The remote button switch, mounted on the case, has been used on all modern computers since the mid-1990s.

The power on/off switch controls the AC from the power supply to the system. The switch wires are color-coded and work in two pairs. The brown and blue wires provide the live and neutral feeds; the black and white wires return the AC feeds back to the power supply.

# Concept Questions          *Semester 1, Unit 2, Lesson 7*

Demonstrate your knowledge of the concepts in this lesson by answering the following questions in the space provided.

1. Why are lead wires color-coded? What does each color specify?

2. Why does a computer's voltage switch allow the user to select different voltages, and how does that relate to a country's electrical source?

_____

_____

_____

_____

_____

_____

_____

_____

_____

_____

_____

_____

_____

_____

_____

_____

_____

# Vocabulary Exercise

## *Semester 1, Unit 2, Lesson 7*

*Name:* _____

*Date:* _____    *Class:* _____

Define the following terms as completely as you can.

**large drive connector**

_____

_____

**motherboard connector**

_____

_____

**power switch connector**

_____

_____

**remote button switch**

_____

_____

**small drive connector**

_____

_____

# Focus Questions

## *Semester 1, Unit 2, Lesson 7*

*Name:* _____

*Date:* _____    *Class:* _____

**1.** What is the function of leads in a power supply, and how many are there?

_____

_____

_____

_____

**2.** What do drive connectors look like?

_____

_____

_____

**3.** What do motherboard connectors look like?

_____

_____

_____

_____

**4.** How do large and small drive connectors operate?

_____

_____

_____

_____

**5.** Describe the pin connectors and motherboard connectors that older-style and Slimline form factor computers use.

_____

_____

_____

_____

**6.** What are the P8's six pins used for?

_____

_____

_____

_____

**7.** What are the P9's six pins used for?

_____

_____

_____

_____

**8.** What is the ATX power supply's single 20-pin motherboard connector used for?

_____

_____

_____

_____

**9.** How many types of power cord sockets are on the power supply? Why?

_____

_____

_____

_____

**10.** Describe the function of the required power cord socket.

_____

_____

_____

_____

**11.** Describe the function of the optional power cord socket.

_____

_____

_____

_____

**12.** Describe the function of the power on/off switch and how it operates.

_____

_____

_____

_____

# SEMESTER 1, UNIT 2, LESSON 8
# Power Supply Specifications

The **booting process** takes place between the time you turn on your computer and the time the computer is ready to receive your commands. Once in a while, this process gets stuck: You type on the keyboard and you click on the mouse, but to your great frustration, nothing happens. You are experiencing a **lockup**, and it might be caused by an insufficient power supply.

An unstable or inadequate power supply can cause other problems besides lockups; for example, devices might take too long to power up, or your computer might spontaneously reboot.

To avoid frustration and the problems that can result from an insufficient power supply, make sure the power supply specifications meet your computer's needs. *Specifications* are technical descriptions of a power supply's capabilities. The power supply's vendor attaches specification stickers to the power supply. Specification stickers tell you most of what you need to know to assure a fully functioning, smoothly operating computer. You can also find power supply specifications in the power supply's manual. The power supply's vendor might also have a Web site providing specification information.

Specifications vary from manufacturer to manufacturer. A Slimline form factor could be just the thing for one power supply, whereas another power supply might really need an ATX form factor. One power supply might provide 250 watts output, and another 300 watts.

## AC input specifications

Generally, there are five AC input specifications:

- Operating range

- Frequency

- Current

- Efficiency

- EMI

These specifications are discussed in detail in the following sections.

### *The operating range specification*

The operating range specification tells the electrical current span what the power supply requires to operate. Power supplies in the United States use 110v or 120v AC power. Power supplies in most other countries use 220v or 230v AC power. Make sure the power supply you are choosing works with the AC electrical power in the country where you're located.

## *The frequency specification*

The frequency specification tells the range within which the power supply operates. Because most power supplies operate at 60 Hz, the range should include that frequency.

## *The current specification*

The current specification cites how much electrical current a power supply will draw from the wall outlet power source. This specification is usually given as X amps at 110v/120v and X amps at 220v/230v. The power supply draws a specified amount of amperage from the external circuit for that voltage.

Your computer's power supply isn't the only electricity-hungry device hooked up to your wall outlet power source. Your printer, modem, scanner, and monitor probably run from that same power source. An average 120v electrical wall outlet power source is limited to devices that use no more than a total of 20 amps. The fewer amps drawn by your computer power supply, the more that remains available for other devices. The lower the number of amps used by a computer's power supply, the more computing devices that can be attached to a wall outlet circuit.

## *The efficiency specification*

How effectively a power supply works—that is, how much energy it puts out relative to how much energy it takes in—is referred to as its **efficiency** specification. Generally speaking, the higher the efficiency rating, the better.

## *The EMI specification*

Power supplies try to suppress **electromagnetic interference (EMI)**, or **noise**. Noise is electrical noise, like static on a radio. Too much EMI can cause devices attached to the power supply to function incorrectly. In the worst cases, such EMI can actually devices attached to the power supply.

The AC input specification should indicate that a power supply meets the guidelines for filtering EMI. You should make sure the power supply uses an EMI filter that conforms to **Federal Communications Commission (FCC)** Class B standards.

# DC output specifications

DC output specifications include information about

- Total power

- Output

- Load regulation

- Line regulation

- Ripple

- Hold time

- **Power_Good** delay

These specifications are described in the following sections.

## *The total power specification*

You can't run a lot of devices on a power supply meant for a limited number of devices. Your power supply has to provide enough electricity to run every single device you have on your system. The total power the power supply can provide is expressed in watts. If watts are not listed in the specifications, you can calculate the approximate output by using the formula

output in watts = voltage x amperage

When you upgrade your computer by adding devices such as drives, cooling fans, or **Industry Standard Architecture (ISA)** cards, you might have to upgrade the power supply. Check all power requirements for all devices you add to your system. If the total amount of power needed to accommodate your devices exceeds what the current power supply's total power can provide, you need to upgrade to a power supply that accommodates all your devices' electrical needs.

## *The output specification*

The output specification indicates the amps available to be used for each type of DC voltage. As you learned earlier, devices that attach to the power supply use +5v, +12v, and +3.3v DC power. Only older devices (PC/XT and early AT) also use –5v and –12v DC power. Therefore, when you upgrade your system, you must not only calculate the wattage that will be used, but you must also make sure that no more amps are drawn for each type of DC voltage than are available. You should list all the +5v devices that will be attached to the power supply, and show how many amps will be used by each device. Usually, manuals for devices indicate how many amps are used. If you are unsure how many amps are used by a particular device, you can contact the vendor to find out.

## *The load regulation specification*

Usually, power supply specifications list a load regulation for each type of voltage used. The load regulation for devices using +5v and +12v power is 5%. This means that the power supply will keep the power it is sending to devices using those voltages within a 5% range above or below +5v and +12v, respectively. The load regulation shown for devices using +3.3v power is 1%. This means that the power supply will keep the power it is sending to devices using that voltage within a 1% range above or below the +3.3 voltage. Generally, the lower the range, the better.

## *The line regulation specification*

As you learned earlier, AC power comes into the power supply, where it is converted to DC power for use by devices attached to the power supply. From time to time, there may be fluctuations in the level of AC power. These fluctuations can vary greatly. The line regulation specification indicates the amount of variation that will be passed on by the power supply to devices connected to it, in DC power voltages.

## *The ripple specification*

**Ripple** is another term for EMI. Too much ripple can cause devices working from your power supply to function improperly. The worst case is that EMI can damage devices. The ripple specification shows how much noise is allowed by the power supply from one peak of an electrical cycle to the next.

## *The hold time specification*

The hold time specification indicates the amount of time during which a power supply's DC output voltage can remain within acceptable specifications if there is a loss of AC input power into the system.

## *The Power_Good delay specification*

When you start up your computer, your power supply checks itself out, running a series of internal self-tests. When the power supply passes these internal self-tests and determines that its outputs have stabilized, it sends out a +5v signal to the motherboard. Called the **Power_Good** signal, this signal is delayed until all voltages have stabilized. Normally, the **Power_Good** delay is from 0.1 to 0.5 seconds.

# Power supply safety specifications

Three safety specifications are usually listed for power supplies:

- Overvoltage protection

- Overload protection

- Safety certifications provided by recognized testing agencies

These specifications are described in the following sections.

## *The overvoltage and overload protection specifications*

**Overvoltage protection** is a power supply feature that shuts down the supply, or clamps down on the output, when its voltage exceeds a preset level. **Overload protection** is protection provided against short-circuits. It is provided on all outputs.

## *The safety certification specification*

In the United States, a good power supply should be certified by the appropriate and relative organization, such as **Underwriters Laboratories (UL)**. Other certification marks that may also be included are from the **Canadian Standards Association (CSA)**. CSA is a nongovernment, not-for-profit agency founded in 1919, that today is Canada's largest standards development and certification organization. Originally concerned only with German safety standards, today, **TUV** product service certification and testing provides proof that products meet all requirements of relevant European Union directives. Marks from these three major testing organizations certify that a device meets the power rating specifications properly without cutting corners.

# Environmental factors listed in the specifications

Three environmental factors are usually included in power supply specifications:

- Temperature

- Humidity

- Fan rating

Usually the specifications for temperature and humidity are presented as a range within which the equipment can be operated safely. The fan rating indicates how many cubic feet of air per minute (cfm) are circulated through the case by the power supply's fan.

# Other factors listed in the specifications

Other factors that may be listed in the specifications include the form factor, the number of motherboard connectors, the number of drive connectors, the **mean time between failures (MTBF)**, and the amount of time covered by the warranty. It is important to know the number of drive connections that are possible because it might limit future expansion or upgrades of the system. The MTBF is the average failure rate of a power supply, expressed in hours.

# Concept Questions     *Semester 1, Unit 2, Lesson 8*

Demonstrate your knowledge of the concepts in this lesson by answering the following questions in the space provided.

1. Explain why when you upgrade your system, you must not only calculate the wattage that your computer will use, but also what each optional device will require. Also describe what modifications, if any, the power supply might require based on the above calculation.

2. Describe typical problems resulting from an insufficient power supply and explain how to correct for the problem.

_____

_____

_____

_____

_____

_____

_____

_____

_____

_____

_____

_____

_____

_____

_____

# Vocabulary Exercise       *Semester 1, Unit 2, Lesson 8*

*Name:* _____

*Date:* _____        *Class:* _____

Define the following terms as completely as you can.

**current specification**

_____

_____

**EMI**

_____

_____

**frequency specification**

_____

_____

**operating range specification**

_____

_____

**output specification**

_____

_____

# Focus Questions                    *Semester 1, Unit 2, Lesson 8*

*Name:* _____

*Date:* _____    *Class:* _____

**1.** What are power supply specifications?

_____

_____

_____

**2.** How many watts does a power supply provide?

_____

_____

_____

**3.** Describe how to calculate the total power the power supply can provide and what units it is given in.

_____

_____

_____

_____

_____

**4.** When do you need to upgrade the power supply?

_____

_____

_____

_____

**5.** What are the functions of the load regulation and the line regulation specifications?

_____

_____

_____

**6.** What is the hold time specification?

_____

_____

_____

**7.** What is the **Power_Good** signal?

_____

_____

_____

**8.** What are power supply safety specifications?

_____

_____

_____

**9.** What is overvoltage protection?

_____

_____

_____

# SEMESTER 1, UNIT 2, LESSON 9
# Problem-Causing Power Events

Several external power problems or disturbances can cause trouble in a computer's operation. A power disturbance, or unwanted variance in electrical supply power, can have major or minor implications for your computer.

Minor external problems include

- Electrostatic discharge

- Line noise

Major external events include

- Improper grounding

- Surges

- Spikes

- Sags (also called brownouts)

- Oscillations

- Blackouts

These problems are described in the following sections.

## Electrostatic discharge

**Electrostatic discharge (ESD)** occurs when a material carrying an electrostatic charge transfers that charge to an electrostatic-sensitive device. Almost any material can generate static electricity. When static electricity is present, ESD can result from a simple action such as walking across a carpet and then touching a doorknob. ESD can damage internal system components. For example, a person can build up a static charge of 20,000 volts, and a voltage of only 100 volts can cause real damage to the very important CMOS chip.

## Line noise problems

Two types of line noise can cause computing problems: EMI and **radio-frequency interference (RFI)**.

Electricity reaching schools, homes, and offices is transported through wires hidden behind walls, under floors, and in ceilings. So in any building where computers are used, there is AC power line noise. EMI is magnetic distortion created as electrical current travels in wires.

Strong vibrations from nearby appliances' electric motors add to line noise. In some cases, line noise can distort data traveling over computer networks, creating errors in the way this data is read or understood by computers.

The other type of noise, RFI, occurs when electrical wires function like a radio antenna, picking up radio waves and microwaves. RFI coming from a video monitor or hard disk drive can be enough to create errors in a computer system. However, RFI seldom permanently damages internal computer components.

You might wonder how EMI and RFI can create computing errors. As you know, computers operate using a binary number system. The computer reads the presence of an electrical **signal** as a 1 and the absence of an electrical signal as a 0. Everything that is entered into a computer is transformed into this binary code. The computer understands binary code and manipulates it easily and rapidly. So that the computer can recognize one binary number from the next, each signal is timed. This means that each signal lasts for a specific duration. In addition, electrical impulses representing binary numbers are digital, which means that the leading and trailing edges of each signal are square. If line noise is present, it can create data errors by burying the desired square signals, thus preventing a computer from detecting their leading and trailing edges.

# Improper grounding

AC power cables typically have three wires, so you usually find three prongs in the typical power outlet. The power cable's three wires are the **safety ground wire**, the **hot wire**, and the **neutral wire**.

An improper ground occurs when the ground and neutral wires are not properly tied together at the circuit panel. Electrical current flows on the ground circuit to the system. Electrical power on the ground wire can bypass the normal power supply protections and go directly through the case. Improper grounding can cause inside computer component disruption or burnout.

# Surges

A surge is a voltage increase above 110% of the normal voltage carried by a typical 120v, 20-amp electrical circuit. Power surges are a major cause of hardware damage because most computer power supplies built to run at 115v and120v cannot handle 260v for any length of time.

Surges are often caused by malfunctions at the local power utility company. In most instances, power supplies alone do not provide adequate protection against such high-power problems.

Consequences of electrical surges can be severe, including lockups, loss of memory, problems in retrieving data, altered data, and garbling.

# Spikes

Also called a **transient**, a spike is an impulse that produces a voltage overload on the power line. Spikes generally last between .5 and 100 microseconds. When a spike occurs, the power line has been hit with at least 240v, and possibly up to several thousands volts. Spikes are most commonly caused by lightning strikes. Power supplies alone are usually not adequate protection against spikes.

As with surges, the consequences of spikes can be severe. They can include lockups, loss of memory, problems in retrieving data, altered data, garbling, and possibly catastrophic failure.

# Sags

Also called **brownouts**, **sags** occur when voltage on the power line falls below 80% of the normal voltage. Sags are commonly caused by overloaded circuits or by utility companies trying to reduce power during peak demand periods. Usually, when your lights flicker faintly, a sag has occurred.

Such momentary interruptions in the power supply can be devastating to data on a computer; for example, open files can be lost. Power supplies alone usually do not provide adequate protection against sags.

# Oscillations

Sometimes called **harmonic distortion**, **oscillations** are secondary signals that occur on top of the 60-Hz **waveform**. These secondary signals raise signal voltage levels anywhere from 10% to 100% above normal. Oscillations are actually a variety of line noise. Severe cases of oscillations can disrupt the operation of a computer system. In most instances, power supplies alone do not provide adequate protection against oscillations.

# Blackouts

Also called **outages**, **blackouts** occur when electrical power is cut to a circuit, thus causing complete loss of power to connected equipment. Loss of power during computer operations can easily lead to loss or corruption of data. As with sags, files that are open at the time of a power outage can be lost. In most instances, power supplies alone do not provide adequate protection against blackouts.

# Concept Questions     *Semester 1, Unit 2, Lesson 9*

Demonstrate your knowledge of the concepts in this lesson by answering the following questions in the space provided.

1. How do EMI and RFI cause computing errors?

2. What is a power disturbance, and what problems can it create for a computer system? How can you resolve or avoid these problems?

_____

_____

_____

_____

_____

_____

_____

_____

_____

_____

_____

_____

_____

_____

_____

_____

_____

_____

# Vocabulary Exercise       *Semester 1, Unit 2, Lesson 9*

*Name:* _____

*Date:* _____    *Class:* _____

Define the following terms as completely as you can.

**blackout**

_____

_____

**ESD**

_____

_____

**line noise**

_____

_____

**oscillation**

_____

_____

**safety ground wire**

_____

_____

**sag**

_____

_____

**spike**

_____

_____

**surge**

_____

_____

# Focus Questions

## *Semester 1, Unit 2, Lesson 9*

Name: _____

Date: _____     Class: _____

**1.** What are the potential consequences of improper grounding?

_____

_____

_____

**2.** What are the potential consequences of surges?

_____

_____

_____

**3.** What are the potential consequences of spikes?

_____

_____

_____

**4.** What are the potential consequences of improper grounding?

_____

_____

_____

**5.** What are the potential consequences of sags?

_____

_____

_____

**6.** What are the potential consequences of oscillations?

_____

_____

_____

# SEMESTER 1, UNIT 2, LESSON 10
# Unit 2 Exam

If you have access to the online Aries A+ curriculum, contact your instructor for the Assessment System URL. If you do not have access to the online curriculum, please continue to Unit 3.

# SEMESTER 1, UNIT 3

- Lesson 11: Protecting the Power Supply
- Lesson 12: Outlet Tester and Digital Multimeter Lab Exercises
- Lesson 13: The Workplace and Tools
- Lesson 14: Computer Cases
- Lesson 15: Unit 3 Exam

# SEMESTER 1, UNIT 3, LESSON 11
# Protecting the Power Supply

In Unit 2 you learned that external power sources have the potential to exceed safeguards provided by the computer's power supply. You also learned about some of the potential consequences of power events such as electrostatic discharge, line noise, improper grounding, surges, spikes, sags, brownouts, oscillations, and blackouts.

In this lesson you will learn how you can protect the power supply by testing the external environment. You will learn about different kinds of external protection equipment, as well as how each functions and what to look for when selecting protection equipment.

There are two types of measures to take in preventing or minimizing the occurrence and damaging consequences of power disturbances. First, you can certify the external circuit that the computer system is plugged into. Second, you can identify and use the right kind of power protection equipment.

## Certifying the external circuit

To certify the external electrical circuit, you need to test it to ensure that it works within the acceptable limits of its operation. You should follow these steps when testing and certifying circuits:

1.  Isolate and identify the external circuit that provides electricity to the power supply and computer. In order to do this you need to find the building electrical diagram and trace the circuit back from the wall socket to the circuit breaker or fuse panel.

2.  Determine the total amperage of the electrical circuit.

3.  Check the circuit breakers or fuses to determine their ratings. This provides the baseline for minimum protection in the external protection equipment.

4.  Find the average variance in the power supply over the circuit. If the variance averages above or below an acceptable limit (for example, 110 volts plus or minus 10%), then you need to consider using another electrical circuit that has less variance. Another option is to determine the average variance on the circuit and use it as a secondary specification to determine what external protection equipment should be used. The device used to test electrical circuit variance is called a **digital multimeter (DMM)**.

5.  Determine whether the three-wire wall outlet is properly grounded. You can do this with an outlet tester, which is an inexpensive device that can be purchased at most hardware stores. To use it, plug it into a wall socket, and it indicates the status of the wiring via **light-emitting diode (LED)** readouts.

6.  Identify what other devices are connected to the circuit, their number, and their total power draw on the circuit. To do this, you need to trace the electrical circuit from the wiring diagram to identify the other outlets on the line.

*7.* Examine the power draws on the devices attached to these outlets. The rating for most electrical circuits is 20 amps. You need to check the wiring diagram to determine whether the rating is the same for the circuit you are certifying.

If the circuit examination reveals any deficiencies, you can use one of the following three options to remedy the problem:

- You can rewire the circuit to correct it before the equipment is installed.

- You can relocate the computing devices or other electrical devices to another circuit.

- You can use the deficiencies you have identified for the external electrical circuit to determine what types of external protection equipment should be used.

# Identifying and using power protection equipment

There are three types of power protection equipment:

- Surge suppressors

- Line conditioners

- Uninterruptible power supplies

Each provides specific kinds of protection to deal with the power disturbances. The following sections discuss each type of protection equipment in more detail.

## *Surge suppressors*

A **metal oxide varistor (MOV)** is one type of **surge suppressor**; it is inexpensive and works with most computers. The MOV provides several plug sockets for system power cords, and contains a circuit monitor that shunts electrical overloads, such as those caused by surges and spikes, to the safety ground wire.

An MOV surge suppressor may not be an effective means of protecting the computing device attached to it. This is especially true with networked computers because the ground also serves as the common reference point for digital signals going into and out of the computer. Therefore, dumping excess voltages into the power line near the computer can avoid damage to the power supply; however, it can still result in garbled data and damaged circuits. In addition, this type of surge suppressor has a limited lifetime that is dependent on heat and usage.

The commercial-grade surge suppressor is another type of surge suppressor, which is typically used with a LAN. When a commercial-grade surge suppressor is used, it should be located near the power distribution panel rather than next to each individual computing device. Because a commercial-grade surge suppressor is located near the power panel rather than next to the computer, the impact of voltage surges and spikes when diverted to ground can be reduced.

## *Selecting a surge suppressor*

Just like power supplies, surge suppressors are also tested and certified by testing bodies. If Underwriters Laboratories has done the testing on the device, it should show rating UL 1449. This shows that the surge suppressor has met a 330v rating, which means that in the event of a large surge or strike, the surge suppressor will let 330v pass through the circuit. If a surge suppressor product does not indicate that it meets this rating, then its quality is suspect.

Other indicators of quality are the Joule and surge amp ratings. **Joules**, like amps, are a way of measuring energy. A good rule of thumb is the higher the rating, the better the unit; for example, a rating of 400 to 600 joules indicates that the product is a high-quality unit.

A good surge suppressor provides a warranty that covers attached equipment in case the suppressor fails. It should also have a status indicator light that indicates when the unit is not functional: When large surges of voltage or massive spikes such as those caused by lightning strikes burn out the surge suppressor unit, the light is lit when the unit is turned on. When this light is lit, the unit should be replaced. Finally, good-quality suppressors often include phone line plug-in sockets to also provide surge protection to modems.

## Line conditioners

A **line conditioner** filters power disturbances to provide a clean and stable current to the computer system. The internal circuitry of a line conditioner functions to provide a buffer between the external current variances and the system.

This buffering includes noise suppression and voltage correction. Noise suppression is the elimination of line noise, and voltage correction is the maintenance of constant AC voltage to even out the voltage variances that result from power disturbances on the circuit.

Although surge suppressors protect the computer system from surges, they do not protect from other types of power disturbances such as excessive line noise, sags or brownouts, and other types of power oscillations. Electrical circuits with such variances require a protective device that can manage these power disturbances in addition to basic surges or spikes. A line conditioner provides this function.

## *Selecting a line conditioner*

Line conditioners should meet the same UL 1449 certification as surge suppressors. In addition, various ratings indicate the quality of the unit. Line noise suppression ratings indicate the standard of filtration achieved for the unit. These ratings are expressed as a **decibel (dB)** level at a specific frequency, expressed in either KHz or MHz.

A good rule of thumb is the higher the dB level, the greater the protection. Good units provide rated voltage correction between 87v and 140v for typical 115v AC American and 168v to 278v volts for typical 230v AC international circuits.

## *Uninterruptible power supplies*

An **uninterruptible power supply (UPS)** provides a backup power supply when the AC current fails. A UPS does everything a surge suppressor and line conditioner does, and it provides an additional power source for the computer system that cannot be interrupted by external line conditions. How this is accomplished depends on the type of UPS selected.

There are two types of UPS:

- The standby UPS, or offline UPS

- The online UPS, or line-interactive UPS

Both types of UPS use a battery to provide AC power during power outage conditions. However, the standby UPS uses the battery only during outage periods. It operates by means of a special sensor that monitors the external circuit AC power.

When it senses loss of power, the standby UPS switches or transfers to the standby battery and uses a power converter to produce the needed AC power from battery storage. The period of switchover is often called the **transfer time**. This type of UPS represents older technology and is being replaced by the online type of UPS for critical system use. This switchover is due to the delay inherent in a switchover. Standby UPS units are increasingly being relegated to lower-end models by most vendors.

The online UPS bypasses the standby approach by using the battery to entirely power the connected system. The battery itself is charged by an internal battery charger that is plugged into the external power circuit. A voltage inverter supplies the full-time AC power by converting from the battery DC current. This effectively isolates the system from variance on the external circuit. Generally, this newer type of device also has surge suppression, noise suppression, and line conditioning capabilities in addition to power backup protection.

## *Using a UPS*

You generally use a UPS where there is a significant danger of blackouts or outages. If a power blackout occurs, a UPS can provide power to the system long enough for it to shut down in an orderly fashion, thus preventing data loss or corruption. Or, if the blackout is relatively brief, the system continues to operate from UPS battery reserves and the battery recharges when power returns.

## *Selecting a UPS*

Picking a good UPS involves obtaining one with enough capacity for the system it will support and meeting the standards. The amount of UPS battery power must be adequate to provide all the system power needs for a desired length of time or for the minimum amount of time necessary for an orderly shutdown in the event of extended power outage.

To determine what UPS is suitable for your needs, you need to look at the specifications provided by the vendor. If a vendor provides information or a specification that you are not familiar with or do not understand, contact the vendor for an explanation.

To select the right UPS model, you must determine the total power load of the computer system and then find a model with an appropriate output rate that can run for the desired minimum length of time. This specification is called the **load runtime**. A good rule of thumb is that a UPS should be able to sustain the output at the rated level for at least 5 minutes. An important limitation is that the longer the load runtime, the larger the battery size and supporting circuitry, and the greater the expense.

A good-quality surge suppressor also has specifications for surge suppression and noise reduction. In addition to these, for the standby UPS, the transfer time, measured in milliseconds, is the critical indicator of quality. If the switchover time is too long, the connected system could potentially reboot or power cycle. For both standby and online UPSs, the specification of the power signal waveform produced by the power inverter should approximate a sine wave for both online and on-battery power conditions. The more sinusoidal the waveform, the easier the transition on the computer system. Finally, make sure the UPS has a UL 1778 rating.

# Concept Questions     *Semester 1, Unit 3, Lesson 11*

Demonstrate your knowledge of the concepts in this lesson by answering the following questions in the space provided.

1.  Explain what two measures you can take to prevent or minimize the occurrence and damaging consequences of power disturbances.

2.  Explain what types of power protection equipment are available and when you use each type.

_____

_____

_____

_____

_____

_____

_____

_____

_____

_____

_____

_____

_____

_____

_____

_____

_____

# Vocabulary Exercise     *Semester 1, Unit 3, Lesson 11*

*Name:* _____

*Date:* _____     *Class:* _____

Define the following terms as completely as you can.

**load runtime**

_____

_____

**outlet tester**

_____

_____

**standby UPS**

_____

_____

**transfer time**

_____

_____

**UPS**

_____

_____

# Focus Questions

## *Semester 1, Unit 3, Lesson 11*

*Name:* _____

*Date:* _____   *Class:* _____

**1.** What are the first steps you follow to certify the external circuit?

_____

_____

_____

_____

**2.** How do you select a good surge suppressor?

_____

_____

_____

_____

**3.** What is a line conditioner, how does it function, and when do you use it?

_____

_____

_____

_____

**4.** How do you select a good line conditioner?

_____

_____

_____

**5.** What is a UPS, how does it function, and when do you use it?

_____

_____

_____

_____

**6.** Describe the two types of UPS.

_____

_____

_____

_____

**7.** How do you select a UPS?

_____

_____

_____

_____

# SEMESTER 1, UNIT 3, LESSON 12
# Outlet Tester and Digital Multimeter Lab Exercises

If you have access to the online Aries A+ curriculum, go online to follow along with this lab exercise. If you do not have access to the online curriculum, please continue to the next lesson.

# SEMESTER 1, UNIT 3, LESSON 13
# The Workplace and Tools

In this lesson you will learn about the qualities that determine a safe, efficient work environment:

- Workspace attributes

- System maintenance and repair tools

- Cleaning equipment and materials

- Testing equipment

- Diagnostic software

## Workspace attributes

The following are some attributes of a good workspace:

- The workspace should be large enough to accommodate the system unit, the needed tools, the testing equipment, and the electrostatic discharge (ESD) prevention equipment. Near the workbench, at minimum, power outlets should be available to accommodate the system unit power plug-in and other electrical devices' power needs.

- The workspace should be distant from areas of heavy electrical equipment or concentrations of electronics.

- The workspace should be free of dust. Dust can contaminate the workspace, causing premature damage to computer components. The work area should have a filtered air system to reduce dust and contaminants.

- Lighting should be good enough that you can see small details. Two different illumination forms are preferred: an adjustable lamp with a shade and fluorescent lighting.

- Extreme variations of temperature can affect a computer's components. Therefore, workspace temperatures should be maintained consistent with the components' specifications.

- Properly grounded AC electrical current is essential. Power outlets should be tested with an outlet tester for proper grounding.

- Using an ionizer reduces the occurrence of ESD. An **ionizer** produces positive and negative ions that help workplace objects dissipate electrostatic charges.

- The workspace should maintain a humidity level of at least 50% to reduce the likelihood of ESD.

- The workbench should be well grounded, and have a flat, cleanable surface.

The following are some helpful workspace organizational aids:

- A parts organizer to keep track of small parts such as screws and connectors.

- Athletic or masking tape to make labels that identify parts.

- A small notebook to keep track of your assembly and/or troubleshooting steps.

- A place for quick references and full-blown troubleshooting texts.

- A place for extra screws.

- A clipboard for paperwork.

## *Workspace tools*

Most computer-repair and maintenance tools used in the computer workplace are small hand tools. They are included as part of PC toolkits that can be purchased at computer stores. Also, if you are working on laptops, then you need to be sure you have a small torx screwdriver, which is normally not included in a PC toolkit.

## *Workspace practices that help reduce ESD potential*

The workspace should be situated away from carpeted areas because carpets facilitate the buildup of electrostatic charges. If distance from carpeting is not possible, the carpeted surface should be covered with a plastic antistatic mat such as those commonly used under desk chairs.

ESD danger can largely be eliminated by using ESD protection tools, such as a wrist strap and a mat that are commonly sold in kits. The wrist strap is usually clipped to the metal system chassis on which you are working; this provides a ground to prevent ESD damage. The mat is usually laid on the workspace next to the system case. The mat is then clipped to the case to provide a grounded surface on which you can place parts removed from the system. Caution must be taken to ensure that the case is plugged into the AC outlet. Clipping the wrist strap to the case is useless unless the case is plugged into the AC outlet to allow for a ground.

After putting the wrist strap on, you should wait 15 seconds before touching any sensitive electronic components with your bare hands. This pause allows the wrist strap to neutralize static electricity that already exists on your body. A wrist strap can only protect from ESD voltages carried on the body. ESD charges on clothing can still cause damage. Therefore, you should avoid contact between electronic components and clothing and avoid wearing clothing that tends to build static charges, such as that made of silk, polyester, and wool. If you find yourself still receiving static shocks in the workspace while working near a computer, try using a fabric softener or using an antistatic spray on your clothing. Be certain to spray your clothes and *not* the computer. A wrist grounding strap does not discharge electrostatic charges that have built up on hair, so if you have long hair, you should take precautions to ensure that your hair cannot rub across any of the components.

There is one exception to wearing a wrist strap to provide a safe ground. You should never wear a wrist strap when working on a monitor. As a rule of thumb, most individuals should never even attempt to open a monitor's case. However, if you find yourself in a situation where you absolutely must open a monitor's case, you should make an effort *not* to ground your body. Components inside a monitor can hold a charge for a long time—even after the monitor has been unplugged from its external power source. The amount of current that a monitor can contain even when turned off and unplugged, is enough to kill you. Wearing a wrist strap helps heighten your risk of contacting the monitor's dangerous electric current.

Electronic components or circuit boards should be stored in a shielded antistatic bag, easily recognized by a shielding characteristic, which is usually a silvery, transparent appearance. Shielded antistatic bags keep static electricity out. Shielded antistatic bags need to be in good condition, without crinkles or holes. Even tiny openings from crinkles limit a bag's ability to provide protection from electrostatic discharges.

When original packaging is not available, circuit boards and peripherals should be transported in a shielded antistatic bag. However, never put a shielded antistatic bag inside a PC. And never plug in a motherboard while it is sitting on top of an antistatic bag. Remember that antistatic bags are antistatic because they are partially conductive. A motherboard could easily be shorted out when started up if several hundred pins from its components were touching the conductive bag. If computer components will be stored in plastic bins, the bins should be made of a conductive plastic. Nonconductive plastic bins tend to build up an electrostatic charge.

Handle all components by their edges. By avoiding touching pins, chips, or anything else made of metal, you can greatly decrease the chances that you will produce an ESD, and reducing the potential for ESD reduces the likelihood of damage to delicate circuits or components. Avoid touching the computer screen for any reason while it is turned on. Even brief touches to an active screen can put an electrostatic charge in your hand that can discharge through the keyboard.

## System maintenance and repair tools

Other workspace tools essential for system maintenance and repair include a duster and a computer vacuum. Computer systems gather dust over time, despite the best efforts of their designers. Dusters can help alleviate the dust collection problem. Dusters are cans of compressed air or carbon dioxide used to blow dust off system components.

In systems that have not been cleaned for a long time, lint and dust buildup in the case can be so significant that simply blowing the dust out may not be possible. Heavy lint and dust buildup should be removed with special vacuum cleaners designed expressly for this purpose. Computer vacuum cleaners use multiple nozzles for different purposes and generate low ESD. These vacuum cleaners use plastic nozzles instead of metal.

# Cleaning equipment and materials

The dust particles that computer systems gather over time may contain chemical residues that can degrade or short-circuit chips, contact surfaces, and wire contacts. Oil from human fingers can contaminate or corrode a sensitive electrical connection. Even perspiration from your skin contains chemical salts that can corrode electrical connections. This is another very good reason to hold all electronic boards by their edges, but not where the metal contacts are located.

In any case, a computer's component surfaces need to be cleaned periodically, more than just blowing off or vacuuming out dust and lint. Commonly used cleaning products include spray contact cleaner, solvents, swabs, and cleaning pads. Most vendors provide guidelines for the cleaning supplies that should be used with their equipment. You should be familiar with them and stock the recommended supplies.

Spray contact cleaner contains a mixture of a solvent and a lubricant. It is used to get into a very small area like a contact point. The cleaner can usually has a long thin plastic nozzle inserted into the head so it can discharge the solution in pinpoint fashion. Spray contact cleaner is useful when removing corroded electrical contacts or loosening adapter boards with gummy connection points.

Solvents are used with swabs to remove residues that stick to circuit boards or contacts, especially when boards or contacts cannot be easily reached with regular cleaning pads. A reliable and frequently used solvent is **isopropyl alcohol**, commonly sold in drugstores. (Make sure you should not confuse isopropyl alcohol with rubbing alcohol. Rubbing alcohol is relatively impure and can contaminate electrical connections.) Swabs resembling typical cotton swabs, but having foam or chamois cloth on the end, should be used together with isopropyl alcohol. Prepackaged cleaning pads are used for open, flat, easily accessible surfaces—those places where getting to the area is not difficult. Be sure to use these types of swabs and cleaning pads, which can be easily obtained at any electronics supply store.

# Workplace testing equipment

Computer system repair often requires diagnosing problems by testing electrical signals on a motherboard or its components. In addition, testing the external power environment is often necessary: A troublesome power source can cause difficulties for computer systems plugged into it. Earlier in this unit you learned about two common testing instruments that belong in every technician's toolkit: the outlet tester and the DMM. In addition to these two testers, a third should be part of the standard equipment kept in the workspace: wrap plugs.

**Wrap plugs**, also called **loopback connectors**, test signaling ports located on the back of the computer. The wrap plugs are wired so that they loop, or send the signals back themselves. The looping tests the signaling port.

# Diagnostic software

Sometimes computer systems that need repair are completely inoperable. Such systems may require troubleshooting and diagnosis with instruments. However, most systems brought into the workspace for repairs are at least partially operable.

When computer systems are partially operable, diagnostic software is used to conduct general system testing. Testing software is usually available on floppy disk. Three types of disk software should be kept in the workspace: an operating system boot disk, a virus scanning and repair disk, and a diagnostic software disk.

# Concept Questions        *Semester 1, Unit 3, Lesson 13*

Demonstrate your knowledge of the concepts in this lesson by answering the following questions in the space provided.

1.  What is a wrist strap, and when should you and should you not use it?

2.  What are some of the essential system maintenance and repair tools, and how should they be used?

_____

_____

_____

_____

_____

_____

_____

_____

_____

_____

_____

_____

_____

_____

_____

_____

_____

_____

# Vocabulary Exercise    *Semester 1, Unit 3, Lesson 13*

*Name:* _____

*Date:* _____    *Class:* _____

Define the following terms as completely as you can.

**computer vacuum cleaners**

_____

_____

**ESD**

_____

_____

**ionizer**

_____

_____

**isopropyl alcohol**

_____

_____

**loopback connector**

_____

_____

# Focus Questions     *Semester 1, Unit 3, Lesson 13*

*Name:* _____

*Date:* _____     *Class:* _____

**1.** What factors are important for a successful workspace?

_____

_____

_____

_____

**2.** List some workspace organizational aids.

_____

_____

_____

_____

**3.** Describe the tools used in the workspace.

_____

_____

_____

_____

**4.** Describe why you use an anti-static wrist strap and how it is used.

_____

_____

_____

_____

**5.** Describe how you should handle components.

_____

_____

_____

_____


**6.** What cleaning supplies should be kept in the workspace, and why are they necessary?

_____

_____

_____

_____


**7.** What type of workplace testing equipment is needed?

_____

_____

_____

_____

# SEMESTER 1, UNIT 3, LESSON 14
# Computer Cases

The computer case, the power supply, and the motherboard are almost always sold as a unit. This section explains you the basics of your computer's interrelated core: its case, power supply, and motherboard.

## Common computer case form factors

Computer system cases come in several different form factors: desktop, Slimline, and various types of towers. Your form factor choice affects whether you can expand your computer's function in the future.

The **desktop** form factor of IBM's first AT computer was generally adopted by other computer manufacturers during the 1980s. But desktop form factors have been losing favor gradually among computer vendors since the mid-1990s and have been replaced by Slimline and tower case designs.

The **Slimline** form factor, also called low profile, evolved in recent years from the desktop. Since the early 1990s, the Slimline has become very popular among makers of inexpensive mass-produced systems.

Because some Slimline motherboard components are integrated onto the motherboard, failure of one component requires replacing the entire motherboard. Another factor limiting the Slimline's popularity is its limited expansion and upgrading potential due, of course, to its uniquely small case size. For these reasons, the Slimline does not enjoy high visibility among today's leading computer manufacturers.

**Tower** form factors come in three sizes: mini-tower, mid-tower, and full tower. The key difference among them is height. The greater heights provide more room for drive expansion. In general, tower form factors provide more expansion capability than desktops or Slimlines. The tower form factor design also provides better access to internal components. As a result, it is much easier to work on a tower form factor system. Today, the tower form factor is the most frequently used computer system case.

## Typical parts of a computer system case

Despite differences in design, desktop, Slimline, and tower cases share the same basic structure. System cases for all three of these form factors all have the following structural design elements:

- Chassis
- Cover
- Front bezel

- Motherboard mounting plate

- Drive brackets

- Power supply mount point

To provide proper grounding, the chassis is metal. The cover is secured to the chassis with screws, and is the closing, sealing lid of the chassis. It helps protect the internal components and promotes cooling airflow.

The front bezel, usually attached by screws, clips, or snaps, is the faceplate that helps seal the chassis. The front bezel provides attachment points for standardized components, including the power button, reset button, drive status light, and **keylock** buttons and indicators usually attached to the motherboard, expansion adapters, and power supply by wires. Other indicators that are now obsolete may be found on older models. The front bezel also provides front openings for disk drives that users need to access.

The **motherboard mounting plate** is also called the **motherboard mounting pan**. It provides a surface for attaching the motherboard. Tower case motherboard mounting pans are removable and held in place by screws, clips, or snaps. Some motherboard mounting plate models are spring-loaded: They stay in place by means of tension springs. The motherboard is attached to the plate by small hardware parts called stand-offs and motherboard ground screws. (You'll learn more on stand-offs and motherboard ground screws later in this lesson.)

**Drive brackets** are attached to the front of the chassis to provide **mounting bays** for the disk drives. Although usually attached with screws, sometimes drive brackets are permanently riveted to the chassis. Drive brackets commonly come in two sizes—3.5-inch and 5.25-inch—to accommodate different physical dimensions of common drives.

**Adapter brackets** are structural units screwed into the rear of the chassis. Adapter brackets provide mounting points where expansion cards attach to the case. An expansion card, inserted into the motherboard, is secured by screws to an adapter bracket. There are holes in the adapter bracket so that external expansion card cables or wires can access the card inside the case.

Adapter bracket holes are covered with small metal covers called **adapter plates** or **dust plates** when the holes are not filled with an expansion's card securing screw. As their names indicate, dust plates help keep dust out of the case. They also help maintain good airflow inside the case.

The **power supply mount point** is where the power supply attaches to the computer. In the tower case, the power supply mount point is almost always located in the upper rear and may have a small shelf for support. Several screws usually anchor it to the outside rear of the chassis.

# Case design differences

A few differences characterize tower, desktop, and Slimline designs. For example, the motherboard mounting plate can be removed from the tower chassis. However, it cannot be removed in a desktop or Slimline chassis.

In addition, because tower cases are designed with more room for expansion, when extra devices have been added, they can also create more heat. To help solve this potential problem, a second fan is often provided in the tower's lower front chassis to promote greater airflow and cooling.

# Hardware for attaching components to the chassis

Basic hardware used to attach and secure major components to the chassis of the computer system case are screws, motherboard ground screws, and stand-offs. These are described in more detail in the following sections.

## *Screws used to attach and ground components to the chassis*

Various types of screws are used in computers. Generally, all screws used in computers serve two basic functional purposes: They secure the components to the chassis and they ground them to the chassis, protecting delicate electronic components from stray electrical current. There are essentially four types of screws, classified by their types of heads: slotted, Phillips, torx, and nut or hexagonal-head screws.

Nut or hexagonal-head screws usually attach major structural parts to the case chassis. The adapter bracket, drive brackets, and power supply all accept nut or hexagonal-head screws. Their head design allows the technician to apply more force to tightly secure these parts. Two common hexagonal screw sizes are 1/4-inch and 3/16-inch. These require the use of hexagonal-nut screwdrivers.

Phillips and slotted screws are commonly used to secure components inside the chassis. They come in different sizes, and are used to secure the motherboard to the motherboard mounting plate, the mounting plate to the chassis, the bezel to the chassis front, and drives to the drive brackets. Phillips and slotted screws require typical flat-head and Phillips screwdrivers.

Torx screws have star-shaped holes on top and provide no special advantages over other types of screws. However, torx screws are used by a few large manufacturers of computer systems such as Compaq. They are sized primarily according to a T-size standard (T-8, T-9, T-10, and so on).

## *Motherboard ground screws*

**Motherboard ground screws** are special hexagonal screws used to ground the motherboard to the mounting plate at specific points. Small Phillips screws are additionally used to secure the board to the motherboard grounds. The Phillips screws pass through special holes and into the female thread holes of the motherboard ground.

## *Stand-offs*

**Stand-offs** are special connectors—sometimes plastic, sometimes metal—that snap into holes in the motherboard. Their purpose is to hold the motherboard off the motherboard mounting plate. The bottoms of these plastic connectors slide into special slots in the motherboard mounting plate allowing it to be easily installed or removed. Stand-offs keep the motherboard circuitry isolated from the metal chassis, thereby preventing short-circuits.

There are two different types of stand-offs. Each is used for a different type of motherboard form factor. One, usually metal, is used with the ATX motherboard; the other, usually plastic, with the Baby AT motherboard.

# Concept Questions        *Semester 1, Unit 3, Lesson 14*

Demonstrate your knowledge of the concepts in this lesson by answering the following questions in the space provided.

*1.* Explain how screws are used to attach and ground components to the chassis.

*2.* Explain what the case design differences are among the tower, Slimline, and desktop form factors.

_____

_____

_____

_____

_____

_____

_____

_____

_____

_____

_____

_____

_____

_____

_____

_____

_____

# Vocabulary Exercise    *Semester 1, Unit 3, Lesson 14*

*Name:* _____

*Date:* _____    *Class:* _____

Define the following terms as completely as you can.

**chassis**

_____

_____

**drive bracket**

_____

_____

**front bezel**

_____

_____

**motherboard mounting plate**

_____

_____

**mounting bay**

_____

_____

**nut screw**

_____

_____

**power supply mount point**

_____

_____

**slotted screw**

_____

_____

**torx screw**

_____

_____

# Focus Questions

## *Semester 1, Unit 3, Lesson 14*

*Name:* _____

*Date:* _____   *Class:* _____

*1.* Describe the original form factor used by IBM for the AT computer.

_____

_____

_____

_____

*2.* Describe the Slimline form factor.

_____

_____

_____

_____

*3.* Describe the tower form factor.

_____

_____

_____

_____

*4.* What types of hardware are used to attach components to the chassis?

_____

_____

_____

_____

**5.** Describe the motherboard grounds and what they are used for.

_____

_____

_____

_____

**6.** Describe what stand-offs are and what they are used for.

_____

_____

_____

_____

# SEMESTER 1, UNIT 3, LESSON 15
# Unit 3 Exam

If you have access to the online Aries A+ curriculum, contact your instructor for the Assessment System URL. If you do not have access to the online curriculum, please continue to Unit 4.

# SEMESTER 1, UNIT 4

- Lesson 16: The Basics of Motherboards
- Lesson 17: The Motherboard Manual
- Lesson 18: Motherboard Configuration
- Lesson 19: Motherboards and the BIOS
- Lesson 20: Unit 4 Exam

# SEMESTER 1, UNIT 4, LESSON 16
# The Basics of Motherboards

This lesson explores the subject of motherboard technology. Knowledge of the **motherboard**, also called the *system board* or *main board*, is essential because the motherboard is the nerve center of the computer system. Everything else in the system plugs into it, is controlled by it, and depends on it to communicate with other devices on the system. The motherboard is the main **circuit board** containing the primary components of the computer system.

The motherboard has changed physically over time, but its basic structure has primarily remained the same. The motherboard contains the microprocessor, support devices, primary memory units, and expansion slots. If you need to change a motherboard, it is usually for one of the following three reasons: new microprocessors, new expansion slot types, or reduced chip counts resulting from improved microprocessor support chipsets.

The major components on the motherboard are

- The chipset

- The CPU socket

- Expansion sockets

- I/O support

- The BIOS

- The RAM socket

- The power supply socket

- The CMOS chip

- Dip switches and jumpers

- Memory cache

The following sections describe these components in detail.

## The chipset

A **chipset** is a collection of chips on the motherboard that functions as a unit to perform a task. A chipset typically fits on one chip, and its functions include control over the memory cache, external **buses**, and some peripherals. The chipset must operate at the speed of the **bus** to which it is connected. A **heat sink** attached to the chipset absorbs and dissipates heat generated by the chipset.

Intel makes the most common chipsets, such as the Triton I, Triton II, Triton III, Natoma, and Orion. Intel's strongest competitors for chipsets are VIA and SiS. Both of these companies have produced chipsets that support the higher bus speed of the Cyrix chips.

## The CPU socket

The CPU resides in the **CPU socket**. Motherboards provide different types of sockets to accommodate the variety of CPUs. For example, Socket 1 is an old slot that is used in 486 motherboards and supports 486 chips. Sockets 2 through 7 are all Intel sockets, with Socket 7 being the most popular and widely used socket. Socket 8 is the only socket that will fit the Pentium Pro. The newest Intel processors, the Pentium IIIs, fit into either Slot 1 or 2. Special Pentium Xeon processors fit only into Slot 2. (Be careful not to confuse slots with sockets.)

## Expansion sockets

**Expansion sockets**, or slots, are receptacles inside the computer that accept printed circuit boards. Some examples of expansion cards that fit into the expansion sockets are video cards, I/O cards, and sound cards. The number and types of expansion slots in the computer determines future expansion. In PCs, expansion slots are connected to the bus. A bus is like a shared highway that connects the components, such as the microprocessor, memory, and input/output (I/O) ports. The bus makes it possible to transfer data.

The **industry standard architecture (ISA) bus** was the original bus, designed to allow expansion cards to be plugged into the motherboard's expansion slots. The first ISA bus used only 8 bits. Remember that a bit is an on or off signal. An 8-bit card allowed 8 bits of information at a time, which is very slow data transmission capability. Later, IBM developed a 16-bit bus, which combined two separate 8-bit slots mounted end-to-end so that a 16-bit slot would fit into both slots. In 1987 IBM came out with the 32-bit bus, which accommodates the Pentium chip and has become very popular.

The **peripheral component interconnect (PCI) bus** was developed by Intel and is faster than the ISA. With the PCI bus, each add-on card contains information that the processor uses to automatically set up the card's configuration. The PCI bus is one of the three components necessary for plug-and-play. The main purpose of the PCI bus is to have direct access to the CPU for devices such as those for memory and video.

The **accelerated graphics port (AGP)** is the newest type of bus. The AGP is a high-speed bus that is used for the high demands of graphical software.

## I/O support

I/O circuitry is often integrated onto the motherboard. There are three main external methods of connecting to the motherboard:

- Through the keyboard, or mouse, which plug into connectors built into the motherboard.

- Through the expansion slots on the motherboard. Expansion cards are plugged into the slots and contain cables to their respective devices. These cards provide control circuitry for disk drives, the video display, and CD-ROM drives.

- Through serial and parallel ports, which are I/O pathways built into the motherboard. On the back of the PC, there are typically two serial ports, which are called COM1 and COM2, and a parallel port called LPT1. The serial ports are typically used for modems or mouse devices. The parallel port is generally used for a printer.

# The BIOS

The **basic input/output system (BIOS)** is easy to locate because it is the shiniest chip on the motherboard. It often has a shiny plastic label on it, containing the manufacturer's name, the serial number of the chip, and the date the chip was manufactured. This information is vital when it's time to select the correct upgrade for the chip.

# The RAM socket

There are two types of RAM sockets used to connect memory modules:

- A **single inline memory module (SIMM)** is a narrow printed circuit board that holds memory chips and plugs into a RAM socket on the motherboard.

- The **dual inline memory module (DIMM)** evolved from the SIMM. DIMM modules can be added one at a time on a Pentium motherboard, whereas SIMMs are generally used in pairs and in groups of four on older computers.

SIMM pins contain the same circuit path on both sides of the edge connector, whereas DIMM pins are different on each side, thus providing double the circuit paths.

# The power supply socket

The **power supply socket** is used to connect the power supply to the motherboard.

# The CMOS chip

The setup configuration for a computer's BIOS is stored in a chip called the **complementary metal-oxide semiconductor (CMOS) chip**. The CMOS memory keeps track of the amount of memory, the types of drives and video cards installed, and the date and the time. A small battery prevents CMOS settings from being lost when the computer is shut off.

# DIP switches and jumpers

A **DIP switch** is a small switch used to select the operating mode of a device. DIP switches can be either sliding or rocker switches, and are typically grouped together for convenience.

A **jumper** is a plastic cap with metal inserts. You can move the jumper to cover different pairs of pins. When the jumper is connected to any two pins, it completes the circuit between those pins, telling the computer the possible configuration options for that device. Different components may require different jumper settings in order to ensure that the correct circuit is used.

# The memory cache

A **memory cache**, also known as a CPU cache, is a memory bank that links the CPU and main memory. It temporarily stores data and instructions the CPU needs to execute commands and programs. It is faster than main memory and allows instructions to be performed and data to be read at a higher speed. This cache is almost always located very near the CPU, and is often located inside the CPU to allow faster transfer rates.

# Concept Questions     *Semester 1, Unit 4, Lesson 16*

Demonstrate your knowledge of the concepts in this lesson by answering the following questions in the space provided.

1. Explain why DIMMs can be added one at a time on a Pentium motherboard, whereas SIMMs are generally used in pairs and in groups of four on older computers.

2. Explain why the chipset must operate at the speed of the bus to which it is connected and how a heat sink attached to the chipset absorbs and dissipates heat generated by the chipset.

_____

_____

_____

_____

_____

_____

_____

_____

_____

_____

_____

_____

_____

_____

_____

# Vocabulary Exercise      *Semester 1, Unit 4, Lesson 16*

*Name:* _____

*Date:* _____      *Class:* _____

Define the following terms as completely as you can.

**BIOS**

_____

_____

**bus**

_____

_____

**chipset**

_____

_____

**CMOS chip**

_____

_____

**CPU socket**

_____

_____

**DIMM**

_____

_____

**DIP switch**

_____

_____

**expansion socket**

_____

_____

**jumper**

_____

_____

**motherboard**

_____

_____

**parallel port**

_____

_____

**power supply socket**

_____

_____

**SIMM**

_____

_____

# Focus Questions

## *Semester 1, Unit 4, Lesson 16*

*Name:* _____

*Date:* _____   *Class:* _____

**1.** For what reasons might a motherboard need to change?

_____

_____

_____

_____

**2.** What is an ISA bus, and how does it function?

_____

_____

_____

_____

**3.** What is a PCI bus, and how does it function?

_____

_____

_____

_____

**4.** What is an AGP bus, and how does it function?

_____

_____

_____

_____

**5.** What is an I/O support, and how does it function?

_____

_____

_____

_____

**6.** What is a memory cache, and how does it function?

_____

_____

_____

_____

**7.** Describe two types of RAM sockets.

_____

_____

_____

_____

**8.** How many serial ports are typically located on the back of a PC? What are they called, and what are they used for?

_____

_____

_____

_____

# SEMESTER 1, UNIT 4, LESSON 17
# The Motherboard Manual

Thus far, you have learned a little about the motherboard and how it functions. Because the motherboard is the nerve center of the computer, it must be configured properly to support the components of the system. For example, the pins and jumpers that control the circuits must be set correctly, or the system components will not be able to function properly. External devices that connect to the motherboard must also be attached to the right connectors in order to function properly. This section covers the kinds of basic information you can expect to find in the **motherboard manual**.

When you purchase a motherboard, it should come boxed with a manual. The manual is important because it provides all the basic information needed to properly identify and configure the components on the motherboard. Most, if not all, good motherboards have coded information about the jumpers, connectors, and other labels inscribed on the board. These inscriptions are often referred to as *silk-screened* and *match codes*. The manual provides instructions for their configuration.

Not all motherboards are alike. Each motherboard has its own set of specifications for proper configuration, so motherboard manuals are not interchangeable. So before you do anything else, you should make sure the manual you have is the correct one for the motherboard you are working on. Check to make sure the model number on the manual is exactly the same as the number silk-screened on the motherboard. It is very important that these numbers match because motherboard specifications are so exact that even a minor model difference will render the manual information useless.

## Motherboard specifications

Most motherboard manuals include a features page, sometimes referred to as a specifications section. You should refer to the specifications section first, before you assemble your system, to make sure the components you want to use are correct for the motherboard. By consulting the specifications first, you will avoid surprises when you begin assembling the system.

The specifications section usually includes information about the types of processors supported, the chipsets used, the types and amount of memory (RAM) supported, the kinds of internal and external I/O connectors used, the kind and number of expansion slots there are, and what type of form factor should be used with the motherboard.

### The CPU specifications

One of the specifications describes the models of CPU supported by the motherboard (for example, Intel Pentium II running at 233, 266, and 300 MHz). Later, you will need to set the correct speed for the CPU model by changing the jumper settings.

## The chipset specifications

Next, you need to look at the chipset specification, which tells what types of logic chipsets are used to control the major subsystems of the motherboard, the internal and external I/O connectors, and the bus systems. The make and model of these chipsets usually indicates the quality of the motherboard. Check to make sure the numbers listed in the manual specifications match those of the chips on the motherboard.

## The main memory specifications

The main memory specification indicates what kind of memory and how much of it can be supported by the motherboard. For example, the motherboard might support DIMM type memory up to a total of 512 MB. In addition, the memory specification tells you whether the DIMM memory must be of the **synchronous DRAM (SDRAM)** or **extended data output (EDO)** type. By reading the memory specification, you also learn whether the other type of memory, SIMM, is supported by this motherboard model.

## The I/O specifications

The multi I/O specification tells you how many and what kind of internal and external I/O connectors are available. For example, the external I/O connectors might be two serial ports, one parallel port, and two **mini-DIN (Deutsche Industries Norm) connectors**, commonly referred to as **PS/2 connectors**. One PS/2 connector is for the mouse, and the other is for the keyboard. The internal I/O connector might be the **floppy drive controller**. The I/O specification tells which type of motherboard connector fits on a particular motherboard, DIN or mini-DIN. The I/O specification also specifies the type of mouse.

The multi I/O specification indicates support for other new technology options such as **infrared connections** and **universal serial bus (USB)** connections. The **peripheral component interconnect and integrated drive electronics (PCI IDE)** specification tells what other internal I/O connectors are on the motherboard (for example, two hard drive controllers on a high-speed I/O bus). Up to two drives are possible for each controller. The PCI IDE specification also refers to the speed at which these drives exchange data.

## The system BIOS specifications

The system BIOS specification tells what type of BIOS is installed (for example, erasable programmable ROM [EPROM]). The specification also tells you whether the ROM can be upgraded with software. This is a sign of quality—it means the BIOS can be easily updated by the manufacturer if problems are discovered or enhancements added.

### *The slot specifications*

The slot specification details how many and what kinds of card expansion slots are available for the system. This tells you the ultimate expandability of the system board; it tells how many expansion boards can be installed in this system (for example, four slots available for PCI bus cards, three for ISA bus cards, and one for a special high-speed AGP video card).

### *The form factor specifications*

The form factor is one of the most important specifications given. The motherboard, power supply, and case all have a common form factor that governs the compatibility of these core components. For example, the form factor for a motherboard might be ATX. This means that its footprint will only match an ATX case. The Slimline (AT) and ATX power supplies have different motherboard power connectors.

## If components don't match the specifications

As you are looking through the motherboard manual specifications, you may discover that some of the components do not match the specifications. Or, for example, you might discover that the chipset on the board does not match what is specified in the manual. If this occurs, it's time to stop and sort this out before proceeding. Otherwise, your system probably won't work.

# Concept Questions        *Semester 1, Unit 4, Lesson 17*

Demonstrate your knowledge of the concepts in this lesson by answering the
following questions in the space provided.

**1.** Explain what the motherboard manual provides and why you should begin with
the specifications section.

**2.** Explain what you should do if the motherboard manual you have does not seem
to be the correct manual for the motherboard you are working on.

_____

_____

_____

_____

_____

_____

_____

_____

_____

_____

_____

_____

_____

_____

_____

_____

# Vocabulary Exercise

## *Semester 1, Unit 4, Lesson 17*

Name: _____

Date: _____     Class: _____

Define the following terms as completely as you can.

### *EDO memory*

_____

_____

### *EPROM*

_____

_____

### *floppy drive controller*

_____

_____

### *infrared connection*

_____

_____

### *ISA bus card*

_____

_____

**main memory specification**

_____

_____

**mini-DIN connector**

_____

_____

**multi I/O specification**

_____

_____

**PCI bus card**

_____

_____

**slot specification**

_____

_____

**system BIOS specification**

_____

_____

**USB connection**

_____

_____

# Focus Questions

## *Semester 1, Unit 4, Lesson 17*

*Name:* _____

*Date:* _____   *Class:* _____


**1.** Why is the model number on a motherboard important?

_____

_____

_____


**2.** What components are covered in the motherboard manual specifications?

_____

_____

_____


**3.** What is an AGP video card, and what is its function?

_____

_____

_____


**4.** What is a form factor specification?

_____

_____

_____


**5.** How many serial ports are typically located on the back of a PC? Why?

_____

_____

_____

# SEMESTER 1, UNIT 4, LESSON 18
# Motherboard Configuration

In Lesson 17 you learned about the specifications contained in the motherboard manual. In this lesson, you will learn how to configure the motherboard based on those specifications.

## The motherboard location map

The motherboard manual provides a location map of the major components or hardware features that are on the motherboard. You can use this map to orient yourself to the board layout. Everything listed in the specifications section is depicted and labeled on the map. The map is a very important tool because it provides enough information so that you can identify and properly install components according to the instructions listed in later sections of the manual.

The location map also provides additional information that will be useful during installation and assembly. For example, on the map, the main memory may be subdivided into slots, identified and numbered in sequence: DIMM1, DIMM2, DIMM3, DIMM4. This tells you that when you install the DIMMs, you must install them in the sequence indicated on the map.

## Configuring the motherboard

Configuration of the motherboard means the following:

- Installing the CPU in the specified way

- Installing the memory DIMMs or SIMMs in the specified way

- Connecting the power supply cables to the motherboard power connectors and connecting miscellaneous connectors to the correct switches and status lights on the front case bezel

- Setting the system BIOS

The following sections discuss these facets of configuration in detail.

### *Configuring the CPU*

A motherboard can usually support several models of CPUs, so you need to configure it to support the specific model that is to be installed. To complete this configuration you need to set jumpers, which, as you learned earlier are devices that bridge pins on circuits. Closing the circuit allows data to travel on the circuit. An open bridge, on the other hand, cannot permit data to flow on the circuit: The bridge is open, and no data can pass. On newer, or current-technology motherboards, most jumpers relate to the CPU.

## *Configuring memory*

The motherboard manual shows the permissible combinations of DIMM types that can be installed in the system and how they should be installed.

For example, the manual might state that the maximum memory size is 512 MB and that the size of each DIMM can be 8 MB, 16 MB, 32 MB, 64 MB, or 128 MB. Any combination of these sizes can be used. For example, depending on your memory needs, you might have four 128 MB DIMMs installed in the memory banks on the motherboard. Or, you could have two 128 MB DIMMs and two 64 MB DIMMs installed in the memory banks on the motherboard. However, when DIMM sizes are mixed on the motherboard, it is important to remember to put the DIMM with the largest memory size in the first bank. The system automatically reads the size of the first DIMM and records it as the largest. If a smaller DIMM were put in the first bank, the system could read it as the largest and might fail to recognize or use the additional memory capacity in any of the DIMMs placed in the subsequent banks.

## *Configuring connectors*

The motherboard manual also covers the configuration of connectors, which are commonly labeled as JPs in a motherboard manual. Other connectors are also depicted in the manual. By following manual diagrams, you will be able to correctly configure the motherboard for the case controls and monitor lights on the front case bezel. Some connectors are "keyed" by a missing pin or a blocked connector. Care should be used with front panel connects because they often cause problems. The colored wire is positive and the white or black wire is ground or negative. I/O connectors are only briefly discussed in the manual because they follow industry-standard conventions.

## *Configuring the BIOS*

The ROM BIOS and CMOS contain the software that sets and records the master configuration for all components in the system, including those on the motherboard and the logic chipsets. The BIOS typically has an interface that can be accessed at boot-up time after the initial **diagnostic tests** run. This is done by pressing a key listed in the motherboard manual (for example, for the GMB-P6LIAK motherboard, the key is the Delete key). The BIOS also sets up other components such as the type of hard drive and floppy settings.

The BIOS interface can be keyboard driven, or it can be graphical and mouse driven. As components such as drives are replaced, memory is upgraded, or adapter boards are added, the BIOS setup is updated to reflect the configuration changes and saved to the CMOS chip. The BIOS configuration is covered in more depth in the next lesson.

# Concept Questions          *Semester 1, Unit 4, Lesson 18*

Demonstrate your knowledge of the concepts in this lesson by answering the following questions in the space provided.

**1.** What does it mean to configure the motherboard?

**2.** Why must you be careful, when configuring your CPU, to watch the model specifications?

_____

_____

_____

_____

_____

_____

_____

_____

_____

_____

_____

_____

_____

_____

_____

_____

# Vocabulary Exercise  *Semester 1, Unit 4, Lesson 18*

*Name:* _____

*Date:* _____  *Class:* _____

Define the following terms as completely as you can.

**diagnostic tests**

_____

_____

**front case bezel**

_____

_____

# Focus Questions

## *Semester 1, Unit 4, Lesson 18*

*Name:* _____

*Date:* _____  *Class:* _____

**1.** What are the steps involved in configuring the motherboard?

_____

_____

_____

_____

_____

**2.** How is memory configured?

_____

_____

_____

**3.** How are the connectors configured?

_____

_____

_____

**4.** How is the BIOS configured?

_____

_____

_____

**5.** How is the CPU configured?

_____

_____

_____

# SEMESTER 1, UNIT 4, LESSON 19
# Motherboards and the BIOS

You have learned how the BIOS manages the motherboard, connected devices, and peripherals. This lesson examines the central role of the BIOS much more fully and demonstrates a specific computer system BIOS configuration.

The BIOS contains the program code required to control all the basic operating components of the computer system. In other words, the BIOS contains the software required to test hardware at startup, start up the operating system, and support the transfer of data between hardware components. For example, the BIOS is like a computer program at the driver's license office. The official asks specific questions and has spaces on the screen to input the data. The base screen stays the same, but new information is installed as new drivers are tested. The information is stored in the computer's memory, and it can be changed and edited.

The BIOS code is typically embedded in a read-only memory (ROM) chip on the motherboard. The cannot be changed, which protects it from disk or RAM failures that could corrupt it. It also ensures that the BIOS code is always available, since it is required for the system to boot.

The BIOS initially runs basic device test programs and then seeks to configure these devices. The configuration data required by the BIOS is stored on a CMOS chip. The CMOS chip has rewritable memory because the configuration data can be changed or updated as the components or devices are changed.

Although the BIOS cannot be changed while loaded in memory, the basic BIOS program can be updated. Newer BIOS ROM chips are of a type called electrically erasable programmable ROM (EEPROM), also called **flash BIOS**. Flash BIOS allows you to upgrade the BIOS software from a disk provided by the manufacturer, without replacing the chip. BIOS upgrades are used by manufacturers to fix flaws in the BIOS code, called **bugs**, and improve system capabilities.

The basic design standard of the system BIOS was originally developed by IBM for use in its XT and AT computer systems in the early 1980s. Unfortunately, the IBM BIOS only worked with IBM hardware. Therefore, other manufacturers who built clones of these systems had to guarantee compatibility of the computers with the IBM standard.

Cloning was necessary in order to guarantee that the computer software applications developed for IBM systems would run on their systems as well. By the late 1980s, a few companies had successfully developed compatible BIOS that other manufacturers could use. Three companies eventually came to dominate this market:

- Phoenix Technologies

- American Megatrends, Inc. (AMI)

- Award Software (Award)

Of these three, Phoenix now concentrates primarily in the specialized laptop computer market, whereas AMI and Award are the chief suppliers to the modern non-IBM computer market.

## The function of the BIOS

If you system *crashes*, or fails unexpectedly, you can restart it thanks to the BIOS. The read-only BIOS code, which resides in a chip, cannot be corrupted. Built in to the BIOS is a comprehensive self-diagnostic routine called the **power-on self-test (POST)**, which checks the internal system circuits at boot-up and gives error codes. After the initial circuit checks, the BIOS also checks the internal components against the known list of operating devices stored in the CMOS chip. So, if your system does crash, it displays an error message when you restart it if the problem lies in hardware. These error messages help in diagnosing and repairing problems.

The BIOS is capable of checking the basic system hardware at startup because it contains the codes necessary for the hardware to function in system memory. When the system is booted, the BIOS loads all the program code for the internal system devices into memory. After the initial drivers for internal system devices load, the drivers for installed expansion adapters load into their own **memory addresses**.

Many of the major adapter types have their own BIOS codes, called *BIOS extensions*, embedded into chips on their circuit boards. An example is the VESA BIOS found on the SVGA video adapters. This BIOS extension's program code would load into memory immediately after the internal system devices.

A third type of driver, the software driver, is not resident in the BIOS, but loads after the operating system boots. The software driver also has a memory address and functions similarly to BIOS-level drivers, but is distinct because it is not part of the core hardware system.

To summarize, when the BIOS loads at boot time, it runs a diagnostic scan of the internal circuits first, and then checks the components and devices it finds against the known configuration list in CMOS, before finally loading the device program code. So, in order for the BIOS to have meaningful diagnostics and error checking, the internal components and devices need to be configured properly in CMOS.

## The BIOS configuration list

Because the BIOS scans the system at boot time and compares what it finds against settings in CMOS, it must be properly configured in order to avoid errors. Proper operation of the system depends on the BIOS loading the correct program code for its devices and internal components. Without the correct code and **device drivers**, the system either does not boot properly or works inconsistently with frequent errors. Therefore, the correct initial configuration of the BIOS is critical.

Configuration of the BIOS on a computer is called the *system setup*. It is also called the *CMOS setup*, after the chip that stores the BIOS settings. Each manufacturer's BIOS setup routine is slightly different, although the basic items to be configured remain about the same.

# Entering the award BIOS setup

When you turn on the system for the first time, the system runs a series of self-diagnostic tests, the most important of which is the memory test. After this you see the system startup screen. At the top of the screen, you see a title line that gives the general version of this BIOS, as in the following example:

**Award Modular BIOS v4.51PG**

This is the base model of Award BIOS licensed by the manufacturer. The next significant line is the specific BIOS version, as customized by the manufacturer for the motherboard, which might look as follows:

**50-0103-2A59GG39-V1.03**

At this point, the system CPU identifies itself and runs a memory test while identifying how much memory the system has:

**6x86-P166+ at 133MHz Memory Test: 32768k**

The next line lists a BIOS extension from the manufacturer to support the Intel plug-and-play specifications:

**Award Plug and Play BIOS Extension v1.0A**

These lines of identifying information should be written down as part of the system documentation. If the BIOS manufacturer were to find a bug in the basic software, you might need to know this information in order to determine what patch is necessary. Or, if the system crashes and will not come up, the BIOS identification information is your only way to request specific information for technical support.

There is a short pause, when you see this message line at the bottom of the screen:

**Press DEL to enter SETUP**

Pressing the Delete key at this point causes you to enter the main setup screen. Note at the very bottom of the screen this information line:

**10/04/96-i430vx-W877-2A59GG39C-00**

This lists the date of the BIOS (10/04/96); the system chipset (**i430vx**, which means Intel 430VX); and the BIOS version number that basically repeats the core of the third screen line.

## The main setup screen

The first screen you see after pressing the Delete key is the CMOS Setup utility screen. Note the header at the top of the screen:

**ROM PCI/ISA BIOS (2A59GG39)**

**CMOS SETUP UTILITY**

**AWARD SOFTWARE, INC**

The header tells you that it is the main BIOS setup screen. Notice that the number in the parentheses duplicates that found in two places on the system startup screen. This is the actual manufacturer-specific version of the Award BIOS.

This screen is the main control center for the CMOS Setup utility. The individual sections within this screen are where the BIOS is configured for the system. It is called the CMOS Setup utility because the resulting system-specific configurations entered are saved to the CMOS chip on exit unless you explicitly say not to. Note the individual sections:

**STANDARD CMOS SETUP**

**BIOS FEATURES SETUP**

**CHIPSET FEATURES SETUP**

**POWER MANAGEMENT SETUP**

**PNP/PCI CONFIGURATION**

**LOAD SETUP DEFAULTS**

**INTEGRATED PERIPHERALS**

**SUPERVISOR PASSWORD**

**USER PASSWORD**

**IDE HDD AUTO DETECTION**

**HDD LOW LEVEL FORMAT**

**SAVE & EXIT SETUP**

**EXIT WITHOUT SAVING**

Each section has an illustration in the motherboard manual, showing a graphic of the screen as it appears before configuration. Along with the graphic are instructions describing the available choices. From these options, you select the correct configuration for the components and devices you have installed. You should choose the Standard CMOS Setup option and press the Enter key to open the Standard CMOS Setup screen. *Be very careful if you go into the BIOS. You must document everything you change. Write it down—do not try to remember it.*

# Concept Questions         *Semester 1, Unit 4, Lesson 19*

Demonstrate your knowledge of the concepts in this lesson by answering the following questions in the space provided.

*1.* Explain the function of the BIOS.

*2.* Explain why it is important to keep a written record of the information in the BIOS.

_____

_____

_____

_____

_____

_____

_____

_____

_____

_____

_____

_____

_____

_____

_____

_____

_____

_____

_____

# Vocabulary Exercise     *Semester 1, Unit 4, Lesson 19*

*Name:* _____

*Date:* _____    *Class:* _____

Define the following terms as completely as you can.

**BIOS**

_____

_____

**CMOS**

_____

_____

**CMOS setup**

_____

_____

**flash BIOS**

_____

_____

**memory address**

_____

_____

**POST**

_____

_____

*system setup*

_____

_____

# Focus Questions

## *Semester 1, Unit 4, Lesson 19*

*Name:* _____

*Date:* _____     *Class:* _____


**1.** Describe how the configuration list is maintained in the BIOS.

_____

_____

_____

_____


**2.** Describe what you do in the first screen of the CMOS Setup utility.

_____

_____

_____

_____


**3.** What three companies dominate the BIOS market?

_____

_____

_____

_____

# SEMESTER 1, UNIT 4, LESSON 20
# Unit 4 Exam

If you have access to the online Aries A+ curriculum, contact your instructor for the Assessment System URL. If you do not have access to the online curriculum, please continue to Unit 5.

# SEMESTER 1, UNIT 5

- Lesson 21: Motherboard Identification Lab Exercises
- Lesson 22: Microprocessors
- Lesson 23: Microprocessors (continued)
- Lesson 24: Voltage Selection Settings
- Lesson 25: Unit 5 Exam

# SEMESTER 1, UNIT 5, LESSON 21
# Motherboard Identification Lab Exercises

If you have access to the online Aries A+ curriculum, go online to follow along with this lab exercise. If you do not have access to the online curriculum, please continue to the next lesson.

# SEMESTER 1, UNIT 5, LESSON 22
# Microprocessors

You have learned a great deal so far in this book about parts that are attached to the motherboard, as well as the motherboard's core components, such as the central processing unit and the memory. In this lesson you will learn more about the central processing unit and how it connects to the motherboard.

## An introduction to the CPU

The **central processing unit (CPU)** is a **silicon**-based **microprocessor**. Sometimes referred to as the brain of the computer system, the CPU goes into computing action when you turn on your computer. Like your brain, the CPU sets impulses it receives into action. The CPU's embedded instructions can be manipulated by software to achieve a desired action.

The motherboard manual should indicate where the CPU is located on the motherboard.

### *Connecting older-technology CPUs to the motherboard*

Older-technology microprocessors, such as the **Intel** P24T, P24D, 80486DX4, 80486DX2/DX/SX-SL, and 80486DX2/DX/SX; the **Cyrix** CX486DX2/DX/S and 5X86; or the **AMD** AM486DX4/DX2/DX or UMC U5 CPUs attach to the motherboard by means of a specially designed socket, sometimes called **Socket 3**.

To attach the CPU to the motherboard, follow these steps:

*1.* Lift the small lever.

*2.* Slide the small pins on the CPU into the corresponding holes on the socket.

*3.* The chip will fit into the socket only one way, so first match the corresponding beveled, chamfered, socket corners and chip before inserting the chip into the socket, and then set the chip into the socket. (The motherboard manual should indicate which corner of the socket is chamfered.)

*4.* Secure the contact by pushing the lever to the down position.

Some models of motherboards use the older-technology Intel **Pentium** P54C and P55C series CPUs, Cyrix 6x86 and 6x86L, or AMD K6-series 32-bit processors. On these motherboards the CPU attaches to the motherboard by means of a specially designed socket, sometimes called **Socket 7**. To insert the CPU in this type of motherboard, you follow the same procedure as for motherboards that use Socket 3.

## *Connecting newer-technology CPUs to the motherboard*

On newer motherboards using Pentium Pro CPUs (for example, the GMB-P6IPS-VO), the CPU attaches to the motherboard by means of a special socket, sometimes referred to as **Socket 8**. Other features, such as fans and spring clips, distinguish newer CPUs from their older counterparts as well.

To insert the chip in Socket 8, do the following:

1.  Shift the lever slightly to the right, and then put it in the raised position.

2.  Slide the small pins on the CPU into the corresponding holes on the socket. This allows the pins to make the proper connections.

3.  The chip can only be set into the socket one way. You can identify the correct position by noting that the pin pattern is different on each end: One end's pins are arranged in groups of five, and the other end's pins are arranged in groups of four. Make sure the pins on the CPU line up with the pin patterns on the socket. Slide the CPU into the socket so that all the pins make contact with the matching holes.

4.  To secure the contact, push the lever to the down position.

In more recent motherboards that use the Intel **Pentium II** series CPUs, the CPU attaches to the motherboard by means of a specially designed slot, Slot 1, rather than a socket. Rather than the individual pins used with earlier CPUs, the Pentium II uses edge connectors like those found on expansion cards. This is also referred to as a *single-edge cartridge (SEC)* connector.

## *Completing the connection*

Follow these steps to complete the installation of a CPU on the motherboard:

1.  Before inserting the CPU into the slot, make sure the fan is attached to it. There should be a conductive material spread on the back of both the fan and the CPU.

2.  Insert the pins on the back of the fan into the holes on the back of the CPU.

3.  Insert the spring clips on the front of the fan to help secure the connection.

4.  Slide the joined CPU and fan into the slot so that a good connection is established between the edge connector and the slot.

Table 5-1 and Table 5-2 show the evolution of Intel first-, second-, and third-generation microprocessors.

**Table 5-1**     *First-generation Intel microprocessors*

| Model | Series | Clock Speed | Internal Cache | Data Bus | Math Co-processor | Clock Multiplier | Voltage |
|-------|--------|-------------|----------------|----------|-------------------|------------------|---------|
| 8086 | XT/PC | 4.77 MHz–7.16 MHz | None | 8 bit | 8087 | 1X | 5v DC |
| 8088 | XT | 4.77 MHz–12 MHz | None | 16 bit | 8087 | 1X | 5v DC |
| 80286 | AT | 6 MHz–25 MHz | None | 16 bit | 80287 | 1X | 5v DC |
| 80386SX | 386 | 16 MHz–33 MHz | None | 6 bit | 80387SX | 1X | 5v DC |
| 80386DX | 386 | 16 MHz–40 MHz | None | 16 bit | 80387DX | 1X | 5v DC |
| 80486SX | 486 | 25 MHz–33 MHz | 8 KB | 32 bit | 80487SX | 1X | 5v DC |
| 80486DX | 486 | 25 MHz–50 MHz | 8 KB | 32 bit | Built in | 1X | 5v DC/3.3v DC |
| 80486DX2 | 486 | 50 MHz–66 MHz | 8 KB | 32 bit | Built in | 2X | 5v DC |
| 80486DX4 | 486 | 75 MHz–100 MHz | 8 KB | 32 bit | Built in | 2X | 5v DC/3.3v DC |
| Pentium | Pentium | 66 MHz | 16 KB | 64 bit | Built in | Varies | 5v DC/3.3v DC |
| Pentium | Pentium | 75 MHz–200 MHz | 16 KB | 64 bit | Built in | Varies | 3.3v DC/2.8VDC |
| Pentium | Pentium | 166 MHz–233 MHz | 16 KB | 64 bit | Built in | Varies | 3.3v DC/2.8v DC |
| Pentium Pro | Pentium Pro | 166 MHz–200 MHz | 256 KB–512 KB | 64 bit | Built in | Varies | 3.3v DC/2.8v DC |

**Table 5-2**     *Second- and third-generation Intel microprocessors*

| Model | Clock Speed | Internal Cache | Comments |
|---|---|---|---|
| Pentium Celeron processor | 333 MHz–466 MHz processor speed<br><br>2.0v | 128-KB L2 cache | Lower-cost Pentium processor with Pentium II system board |
| Pentium II processor | 300 MHz–450 MHz processor speed<br><br>66-MHz system bus<br><br>100-MHz front side bus, available with 400 MHz–450 MHz<br><br>2.0v | 512-KB L2 cache, with each at 167 MHz | MMX media-enhanced<br><br>SEC, dynamic execution, dual independent bus |
| Pentium III XEON processor | 400 MHz–450 MHz processor speed<br><br>66-MHz system bus<br><br>100-MHz front-side bus, available with 400 MHz–450 MHz<br><br>2.0v | 1-MB to 2-MB L2 cache XEON, with each at 167 MHz | Specifically developed for high-performance applications, graphics, CAD engineering<br><br>MMX media enhanced<br><br>Dynamic execution<br><br>Dual-independent bus |
| Pentium III processor | 450 MHz–550 MHz processor speed<br><br>70 new instructions<br><br>P6 micro architecture<br><br>100-MHz system bus<br><br>2.0v | 512-KB L2 cache at 225 MHz | Improved Internet application<br><br>Streaming SIMD extensions<br><br>MMX media enhancements<br><br>Dynamic execution<br><br>Dual-independent architecture |
|  | 500 MHz –550 MHz processor speed<br><br>70 new instructions<br><br>P6 micro architecture<br><br>100-MHz system bus<br><br>2.0v | 512-KB to 1-MB L2 cache at 225 MHz | Improved Internet and high-end applications<br><br>High-performance scientific applications<br><br>MMX media enhancement technology<br><br>Dynamic execution<br><br>Dual-independent architecture |

# Concept Questions     *Semester 1, Unit 5, Lesson 22*

Demonstrate your knowledge of the concepts in this lesson by answering the following questions in the space provided.

1. Explain the difference between attaching a Pentium II CPU to the motherboard and attaching an earlier-version CPU to the motherboard.

2. Explain how the evolution of the microprocessor led to increased computer capability.

_____

_____

_____

_____

_____

_____

_____

_____

_____

_____

_____

_____

_____

_____

_____

_____

_____

# Vocabulary Exercise     *Semester 1, Unit 5, Lesson 22*

*Name:* _____

*Date:* _____     *Class:* _____

Define the following terms as completely as you can.

**microprocessor**

_____

_____

**Socket 3**

_____

_____

**Socket 7**

_____

_____

**Socket 8**

_____

_____

# Focus Questions     *Semester 1, Unit 5, Lesson 22*

*Name:* _____

*Date:* _____     *Class:* _____

**1.** Describe the steps you take to connect to the motherboard an older-version CPU that uses a Socket 3.

_____

_____

_____

_____

_____

**2.** Describe the steps you take to connect to the motherboard an older-version CPU that uses a Socket 7.

_____

_____

_____

_____

_____

**3.** Describe the steps you take to connect to the motherboard an older-version CPU that uses a Socket 8.

_____

_____

_____

_____

_____

**4.** Describe how you connect a Pentium II CPU to the motherboard.

_____

_____

_____

_____

_____

# SEMESTER 1, UNIT 5, LESSON 23
# Microprocessors (continued)

You have learned how different types of CPUs are connected to the motherboard. In this lesson you will learn more about the CPU and how it works.

## Data transmission to and from the CPU

The CPU chip has many small pins that plug into a special socket or slot on the motherboard. Each pin on the CPU makes contact with a corresponding circuit, which appears as a line on the motherboard. Each of these lines represents a separate data path. All these data paths together form a data highway, called the **processor bus**. The processor bus transfers data between the CPU and the main system bus that supports the other main system components. The logic chips that support the main system bus are commonly called a *chipset*.

All data coming into and going out of the processor is carried along the processor wires in the form of electronic signals that represent 1s and 0s. Because only one signal at a time can be represented on the bus, the more wires or circuits there are, the more individual bits can be transmitted during the same time interval.

The width of the processor bus provides a rough idea of the performance potential of the CPU. As a general rule, the more paths in the bus, the more information can be processed rapidly. Usually, when you see a computer described as a 16-bit or 32-bit system, these numbers refer to the processor bus.

## How much information the CPU can process

Three factors determine how much information can be operated on at any given time and how fast the CPU can process that information:

- The size of the internal bus

- The size of the address bus

- The processor's speed ratings

The following sections discuss each of these factors in more detail.

### *The size of the internal bus*

In addition to the external processor bus described previously, some CPUs have an **internal bus** for data. It is composed of data paths and storage units, called the **internal register** or **I/O bus**. Often the internal data bus is larger than the external processor bus. The CPU therefore requires 2 cycles to fill a register before it can operate on that register.

To see how this works, imagine that you have a 1-cup measuring cup. However, to fill the cup, the container you must use only holds 1/2 cup. In order to fill the measuring cup, you would need to use two of the 1/2-cup containers. Two examples that fit this model are the 8088 CPU and the 386SX. Each of these chips has an internal data bus that is twice the width of the external bus. Internally, for example, the 386SX can pass data around using a register that is 32 bits in size. However, the data that it receives from the outside is restricted to a data bus that is 16 bits wide.

The Pentiums have 32-bit registers, but newer-generation Pentiums can have 64-bit or even wider processor buses. This is because modern processors operate so fast that it is worthwhile to bring data into the processor from memory in big chunks.

## The size of the address bus

Although the width of the processor bus can tell you how much data can be pumped through the CPU to and from the system, it cannot tell you how the data is organized. Because the CPU is the brain of the computer and executes program instructions in RAM, it has to know where these bits of data must be assembled in order to function. More simply, because the working space for the CPU where it executes instructions is in memory, the way in which it organizes data bits is critical.

To organize data bits, the CPU uses the **address bus**. The address bus is another group of wires that carry data. The data they carry contains addresses that identify the memory location to which the data bits are being sent or from which they are being retrieved. To see how this works, think of the memory location as being much like a postal address. Each wire on the address bus carries an individual bit of data. Each data bit is an individual number in the address. Therefore, the more wires that are located in the address bus, and the more pins bearing addresses that are in the CPU, the more memory locations or addresses the CPU can handle.

Let's use an Intel Pentium CPU as an example. It has an address bus of 32 bits, which means it has 32 address pins. The way in which the addresses are defined differs somewhat from the manner in which postal addresses are determined. When a CPU has 32 address pins, it can address, at most, 4 GB of data. To visualize this, think of how many different addresses you can get by changing the signals on a bus. If the bus had one wire, there would be only two addresses (0 and 1), and so the CPU could only address 2 bytes of memory. If there were two wires, then there would be 2 x 2 possible addresses. Each time you add an address wire, you double the number of possible addresses. So for 32 wires, we have 2 x 2 x 2 x 2 x 2 (32 times) = $2^{32}$ = a little over 1 billion x 4.

## The processor's speed rating

You may have heard a CPU described as a Pentium 133, a Pentium 166, or a Pentium 200. These numbers are specifications that indicate the maximum operating speed at which the CPU can perform its instructions.

The CPU chip's speed is something that has been certified by the manufacturer and represents the maximum speed the processor can safely maintain. However, the CPU's speed is not controlled by the CPU itself. Instead, it is controlled by an external clock located on the motherboard. Essentially, this motherboard clock is a quartz crystal. The crystal vibrates as electricity passes through it, and generates a steady pulse for every component that is synchronized with this signal.

This voltage wave form is known as the **clock signal**. The speed is measured in the frequency of the clock signal. Typically the speed is expressed as a certain number of cycles per second. For modern CPUs, the speed is usually measured as millions of cycles per second, or **megahertz (MHz)**.

It is important to realize that the CPU speed and the speed of the clock signal are not always at a one-to-one ratio. This is because the CPU usually can run at much higher MHz internally than other chips on the motherboard clock can operate. Consequently, there is a **variable-frequency synthesizer circuit** built into the motherboard. This synthesizer circuit multiplies the clock signal so that the motherboard can support several speeds of CPUs.

The smallest element of time for the CPU is a cycle. Every CPU action requires at least 1 cycle. However, because the CPU can operate at a much faster rate than the main system memory or RAM, it may require several cycles for each action. To see how this works, let's use the 8086 CPU as an example. An 8086 chip requires 4 cycles, plus what are called **wait states**, for each action it performs. In simple terms, a wait state is a clock tick during which nothing happens. Wait states are used to ensure that the processor does not get ahead of the rest of the computer. Therefore, the faster the cycle, the less time is required for the CPU to perform a given action.

As new CPUs have been developed, the time required to execute instructions has dropped. For example, the original 8086 and 8088 CPUs took an average of 12 cycles to perform a single action or instruction. When the 286 and 386 CPUs were developed, they dropped this rate to about 4.5 cycles per instruction. Then the 486 dropped the rate even further, to 2 cycles per instruction. Because the Pentium includes twin instruction paths and other improvements, the rate has dropped to just 1 cycle per instruction.

# Concept Questions     *Semester 1, Unit 5, Lesson 23*

Demonstrate your knowledge of the concepts in this lesson by answering the
following questions in the space provided.

1. What factors determine how much information the CPU can process at any given
   time?

2. How does the size of the internal register help determine how much data the
   CPU can process at any given time?

_____

_____

_____

_____

_____

_____

_____

_____

_____

_____

_____

_____

_____

_____

_____

_____

_____

# Vocabulary Exercise        *Semester 1, Unit 5, Lesson 23*

*Name:* _____

*Date:* _____        *Class:* _____

Define the following terms as completely as you can.

**address bus**

_____

_____

**clock signal**

_____

_____

**internal register**

_____

_____

**I/O bus**

_____

_____

**MHz**

_____

_____

# Focus Questions

## *Semester 1, Unit 5, Lesson 23*

*Name:* _____

*Date:* _____ *Class:* _____

**1.** How does the processor speed rating affect how the CPU processes data?

_____

_____

_____

_____

**2.** What is a wait state?

_____

_____

_____

_____

**3.** How does the address bus affect how the CPU processes data?

_____

_____

_____

_____

# SEMESTER 1, UNIT 5, LESSON 24
# Voltage Selection Settings

One of the first items to pay very close attention to in the motherboard manual is the voltage specification. This lesson is very simple, very blunt, and very important! Unless you intend to fry your motherboard, you need to match the correct voltage for your CPU via jumper settings. Even if you don't damage your motherboard, your whole system will never operate correctly without the correct voltage settings.

## Determining the correct voltage

To determine the correct voltage for your computer, you must be able to read the settings from the motherboard manual. The information you need for voltage setting should be contained in the "Jumper Settings and Connectors" section.

Motherboards are flexible enough to handle a variety of CPUs, but most CPUs are very particular about the amount of voltage they can handle. Generally, CPU voltage varies between 1.8v and 3.5v. Dual voltage requirements accompany some CPUs: This means that two separate voltages, a core voltage and an I/O voltage, are required for these CPUs to function.

Following are some specific voltage examples from a GMB-P57IPS motherboard manual:

• Intel Pentium CPU—Unless you're fortunate enough to be working with a Pentium II, you will need to examine the bottom markings on the Pentium processor to identify the CPU type.

• Intel Pentium with MMX technology (P55C) CPU—The Intel Pentium with MMX technology (P55C) CPU offers dual voltage supply. The following is an example:

| I/O Voltage | Core Voltage |
|-------------|--------------|
| 3.3v        | 2.8v         |

- Cyrix 6x86, 6x86L, and 6x86 MX CPUs indicate their type on their top side. The following Cyrix CPU has a dual voltage supply identical to that in the Intel Pentium example:

| Function | Jumper Settings |
|----------|-----------------|
| 3.3v (I/O)<br><br>2.8v (core)<br><br>Dual voltage CPU<br><br>For P55C, Cyrix 6x86L | JP1: open<br><br>JP5: open<br><br>JP7: A–B open, 1–2 open, 3–4 open, 5–6 short |

- AMD-K6 CPU—The AMD-K6 CPU family require dual voltage power for operation. Examples are listed:

| Operating Voltage | I/O Voltage | Core Voltage |
|-------------------|-------------|--------------|
| 2.2v | 3.3v | 2.2v |
| 2.9v | 3.3v | 2.9v |
| 3.2v | 3.3v | 3.2v |

Now it's a matter of setting the jumpers. First find the correct table for your CPU:

| Function | Jumper Settings |
|----------|-----------------|
| 3.3v (I/O)<br><br>2.2v (core) dual voltage CPU for AMD-K6233 or 266 | JP1: open<br><br>JP5: open<br><br>JP7: A–B open, 1–2 short, 3–4 open, 5–6 open |

Then simply set your jumpers to match the manual.

- Cyrix 6x86 CPU—The Cyrix 6x86 has different nominal voltage requirements depending on its type, noted on the top of the CPU. It's always advisable to take a look at additional frequency options the motherboard manufacturer has provided. You must examine its CPU marking closely and note its speed:

| Function | Jumper Settings |
|----------|-----------------|
| For 133-MHz Intel Pentium, AMD-K5-PR133 (REV C), and Cyrix 6x86-P166+ CPU | JP9: 2–3 short  JP10: 1–2 short  JP12: 1–2 short, 3–4 open  JP13: 1–2 short |

Once again, set your jumpers to match the manual.

Intel has manufactured a simple solution for the motherboard voltage configuration. Its Pentium II motherboards do not require jumpers to set the correct voltage. Pentium II CPUs adjust automatically to the voltage, so they do not require voltage configuration. Technicians everywhere are likely celebrating this development.

With some hands-on experience, you should be able to set the voltage configuration for any motherboard you come across. Just keep yourself well grounded, check CPU specifications, and examine the motherboard manual, and the voltage component will be all set.

# Concept Questions          *Semester 1, Unit 5, Lesson 24*

Demonstrate your knowledge of the concepts in this lesson by answering the following questions in the space provided.

**1.** Explain why the correct voltage setting is so important and how it is determined.

**2.** After selecting the correct CPU voltage, why must you correctly set the jumpers to match the motherboard's specifications?

_____

_____

_____

_____

_____

_____

_____

_____

_____

_____

_____

_____

_____

_____

_____

_____

_____

_____

# Vocabulary Exercise    *Semester 1, Unit 5, Lesson 24*

*Name:* _____

*Date:* _____    *Class:* _____


Define the following terms as completely as you can.

**AMD**

_____

_____

**Cyrix**

_____

_____

**Pentium**

_____

_____

**Pentium II**

_____

_____

# Focus Questions

## *Semester 1, Unit 5, Lesson 24*

*Name:* _____

*Date:* _____ *Class:* _____

**1.** Where do you find motherboard voltage settings listed?

_____

_____

_____

_____

**2.** What is the advantage of the Pentium II motherboard voltage configuration?

_____

_____

_____

_____

**3.** Describe the differences between the jumper settings for AMD-K6 and Cyrix 6x86 CPUs

_____

_____

_____

_____

_____

_____

**4.** Describe the differences between the voltage settings for AMD-K6 and Cyrix 6x86 CPUs.

_____

_____

_____

_____

_____

_____

# SEMESTER 1, UNIT 5, LESSON 25
# Unit 5 Exam

If you have access to the online Aries A+ curriculum, contact your instructor for the Assessment System URL. If you do not have access to the online curriculum, please continue to Unit 6.

# SEMESTER 1, UNIT 6

- Lesson 26: Memory
- Lesson 27: Memory Types
- Lesson 28: Floppy Disk Drives and Media
- Lesson 29: CD-ROM Drives and Media
- Lesson 30: Unit 6 Exam

# SEMESTER 1, UNIT 6, LESSON 26
# Memory

The memory of a computer is like the top of your desk: It has limited space and must be accessed quickly when you need it. This lesson focuses on the many forms memory takes and how memory functions in combination with permanent storage devices to process and preserve data.

Computer **memory**, such as random access memory (RAM), is temporary memory. RAM is stored only as long as the computer is on, and it is a volatile storage medium, meaning that data stored in it ceases to exist when the system is powered off. To prevent data loss, data must be saved to, or stored in, nonvolatile, permanent, storage, which is unaffected by the computer's shutdown.

Because data is processed in a computer's memory, it is one of the most important components of the system. If a computer does not have enough memory, the number and type of programs that run on the system can be limited. As you have learned, the basic measurement of memory is a byte. Each character, such as the letter D, takes up 8 bits of memory, which is equal to 1 byte. Bigger units of measurement are kilobytes and megabytes. A **kilobyte (KB)** is equal to $2^{10}$, or 1,024, bytes. A **megabyte (MB)** is equal to $2^{20}$, or 1,048,576, bytes. Today, it is not uncommon for computers to be equipped with 64 MB of RAM or more.

There are two classes of RAM:

- **Dynamic RAM (DRAM)** is inexpensive and somewhat slow, and it requires that the computer be on to maintain the data. When the computer is turned off, the data is lost. DRAM is the most commonly used memory for computers.

- **Static RAM (SRAM)** is expensive and fast, and it holds its data when the computer is turn off for a brief period of time (such as in an unexpected loss of power). It is used for cache memory, which is the fast memory that stores frequently used data for rapid retrieval by the processor.

In newer-technology motherboards such as those that use the Pentium II and Pentium Pro CPUs, the cache is incorporated with the CPU, thus shortening the distance for more rapid accessing. Placing additional RAM chips on expansion boards that are inserted into memory sockets on the motherboard can expand memory.

## RAM cache

There are two types of caches in RAM: the memory cache and the disk cache. Each is made up of a different area in memory.

### *Memory cache*

Memory cache contains frequently used data. It is made up of very fast SRAM chips. This type of RAM is expensive. Normally, the CPU checks the memory cache first, because it is quicker to get data from SRAM than from ordinary RAM.

### *Level one and level two cache*

To mediate between the data speeds of the main memory bus and the processor bus, the logic chipset manages a set of very fast memory chips, whose job is to cache or store the incoming and/or outgoing data bits. You usually see this logic chipset called the **level two cache (L2 cache)**. The L2 cache consists of extremely fast SRAM chips. For all intents and purposes, the CPU chip is generally not aware that the L2 cache exists. Anytime the processor needs data that is not in its own internal cache memory (**level one cache**, or **L1 cache**), it generates the address on the bus to the memory controller in the bus controller chipset.

If the memory controller finds the data in the L2 cache, it routes the request to the SRAM chips. If it does not find the data there, it generates a wait state—a pause in the CPU operation—until the memory can respond to the processor's request and route the request to the main memory.

### *Disk cache*

The disk cache is set up in ordinary RAM. It contains the most recently used data from the floppy, hard, and CD-ROM drives. Disk cache speeds up access to files by keeping them in ordinary RAM. While ordinary RAM chips used for the disk cache are not as fast as SRAMs, it is still faster to retrieve data from it than from the disk drives.

## The DRAM connection to the motherboard

As described earlier, on most PCs you find two types of **memory modules** in current use: dual in-line memory module (DIMM) cards and single in-line memory module (SIMM) cards. Although DIMMs and SIMMs are different, they share common metal edge connectors and fit into slots on the motherboard called **RAM sockets**. RAM sockets used for DIMM cards are often called **DIMM sockets**. RAM sockets used for SIMM cards are often called **SIMM sockets**.

When the DIMM or SIMM card is inserted into the slot, each edge connector makes contact with a corresponding gold line on the motherboard. Each gold line represents an individual data "road." Just as the gold lines leading to the CPU make up the processor bus, all these gold lines make up the memory bus. The memory bus data highway is used to transfer data between the RAM and the CPU.

# How RAM works

Inside each RAM chip are small on/off circuits. Each circuit represents data that is currently being processed. An on circuit represents a 1. An off circuit represents a 0. Because a source of external power is needed to keep all the switches set to either the on or off position, RAM is only a temporary holding area for data. Every time power to the system is turned off, any data that is being held in the RAM chips is lost. Any data that you wish to keep must be saved either to the hard disk or to another **nonvolatile** memory storage device, like a floppy or zip disk, before power to the computer is shut off.

As a general rule, the CPU can access RAM much more quickly than it can access data stored on a disk.

## *The CPU and RAM*

The same logic chipset, called the **bus controller chipset**, governs both the CPU's processor bus and RAM's memory bus. The processor bus is much faster in data **throughput** than the memory bus: Main memory RAM is typically much slower than the CPU.

For example, a 500-MHz CPU clock has a cycle time of 2 nanoseconds, but main memory takes a minimum of 10 nanoseconds to respond with new data. Thus the CPU computes very quickly, and waits for the chipset to send it more data to compute. Because of this difference in throughput speed, the bus controller chipset manages the flow of data traffic between the CPU and RAM.

To understand how this works, look at the Intel Pentium. If one instruction in the CPU halts waiting for data from main memory, it not only holds up all the instructions behind it, but it also freezes the instructions executing in the other register. In the time required to get information from main memory, the CPU could have executed several software instructions.

## *The address bus and RAM*

Addresses in the bus system are handled by another bus system, the address bus. The address bus is actually an independent subset of both the memory and processor bus that connects the two directly. It indicates to the RAM or CPU where the information transfer is to take place. That is, it indicates on what pins from the processor to what connectors on the RAM boards or cache memory the transfer is to occur. Both the memory and processor buses feed into the I/O bus.

## *The role of the I/O bus*

All other components attached through the external or internal I/O connectors hook directly into the I/O bus and communicate through it to the CPU and RAM on their respective buses. Optional device cards can be added for additional capabilities by means of the expansion slots. Because of this, they can be integrated in the system as needed.

There are two subtypes of I/O bus. As PCs have evolved, design of the expansion slots has changed. Thus the two subtypes of I/O bus reflect different generations of adapter or expansion slot types. PCI bus slots are for newer, faster types of expansion cards that need high-speed access to the memory and processor bus. ISA bus slots are for the older, slower types of expansion cards that do not necessarily need this privileged access.

PCI and ISA use 33-MHz and 66-MHz bus speeds. New motherboards have a 100-MHz bus speed.

# Concept Questions        *Semester 1, Unit 6, Lesson 26*

Demonstrate your knowledge of the concepts in this lesson by answering the following questions in the space provided.

*1.* Explain how the various levels of cache make up different memory areas.

*2.* Explain how random access works.

_____

_____

_____

_____

_____

_____

_____

_____

_____

_____

_____

_____

_____

_____

_____

_____

_____

_____

# Vocabulary Exercise        *Semester 1, Unit 6, Lesson 26*

*Name:* _____

*Date:* _____        *Class:* _____

Define the following terms as completely as you can.

**cache**

_____

_____

**DRAM**

_____

_____

**nonvolatile**

_____

_____

**RAM**

_____

_____

**SRAM**

_____

_____

**volatile**

_____

_____

# Focus Questions

## *Semester 1, Unit 6, Lesson 26*

*Name:* _____

*Date:* _____  *Class:* _____

**1.** What is the purpose of RAM on the motherboard?

_____

_____

_____

_____

**2.** How is RAM added to the motherboard?

_____

_____

_____

_____

**3.** Why might 32 MB of RAM be better to have than 16 MB of RAM?

_____

_____

_____

_____

**4.** Why is data in RAM lost when power to the computer is turned off?

_____

_____

_____

_____

**5.** What is the purpose of the bus controller chipset?

_____

_____

_____

_____

**6.** How does the bus work with RAM?

_____

_____

_____

_____

**7.** What are ISA slots and PCI slots?

_____

_____

_____

_____

# SEMESTER 1, UNIT 6, LESSON 27
# Memory Types

In this lesson you will continue to learn how memory is organized and configured on a motherboard. RAM is critical to the operation of the computer, which will not function appropriately if RAM specifications are not set. Therefore, this lesson provides you with information on the specifications of RAM chip speed, RAM chip type, and voltage.

## How memory is organized

The physical memory in a computer system is determined by the CPU and motherboard architecture. Processors have a number of pins, called the external data bus. The external data bus pins match the processor and memory bus sizes. For example, if a Pentium has a 64-bit external data bus, it means there is a 64-bit processor bus and a 64-bit memory bus. The bus controller chipset is dedicated to transferring the data from the processor bus to the memory bus.

RAM sockets are connected to the memory bus in much the same way expansion slots are connected to the I/O bus. RAM sockets are grouped into banks on the motherboard. A **bank** is the smallest amount of memory that can be addressed by the CPU at any one time. A bank usually corresponds to the data bus width of the CPU and can vary in size. The number of sockets per bank is determined by the bit size of the RAM boards.

## RAM board form factors

RAM boards are sometimes called *memory modules*. They come in three standard form factors: 30-pin, 72-pin, and 168-pin. Both the 30-pin and the 72-pin RAM boards are SIMMs. The 168-pin form factor is newer in design, and it is a DIMM.

Each form factor has a different bit size. The 30-pin SIMM has 9 bits. The 72-pin SIMM has 36 bits. The 168-pin DIMM has 72 bits. The bit size of each memory bank must correspond to the bit size of the memory bus that connects the CPU to RAM. Newer CPUs such as the Pentium, Pentium Pro, and Pentium II have a 64-bit external data bus. If 30-pin SIMMs were to be used, a bank of 8 sockets would be required. If 72-pin SIMMs were to be used, a bank of two sockets would be required. If the choice were to use the 168-pin DIMM, then a bank consisting of only 1 socket would be required. For efficient use of space on the motherboard, 168-pin DIMMs are standard with newer CPUs.

## Bits in SIMMs and DIMMs

You may have noticed in the preceding section that there are slightly more bits in the SIMMs and DIMMs than the CPU and its external data bus require. The extra bits are used for **parity-checking**. Parity-checking is a method originally developed by IBM for error checking of the data throughput as it comes in. This is done by generating a parity or control bit that is tracked by memory monitoring circuitry on the motherboard.

One control bit is generated for every byte of data that is passed through RAM. Remember that 1 byte is equal to 8 bits. The control, or parity, bit can be either a 1 or a 0. Therefore, on a 30-pin SIMM, 8 bits are used for data, and the ninth bit is used for parity-checking. On a 72-pin SIMM, 32 bits are used for data, and 4 bits are used for parity-checking. On a 168-bit DIMM, 64 bits are used for data, and 8 bits are used for parity-checking.

When parity-checking is used, an extra bit is included with each byte. The byte and extra bit are then checked when later read back into RAM from storage. If the byte has changed, the monitoring circuitry generates a **nonmaskable interrupt (NMI)**, which causes the system to cease processing and display a **parity error** message. This prevents data corruption in the system, and alerts the technician to where the error occurred.

More recent systems often do not use parity-checking memory and may even have the monitoring circuitry disabled on the motherboard. This is done to reduce costs for manufacturers; however, the quality control employed by major manufacturers is able to keep parity errors to a minimum.

## Additional memory module specifications

As you have learned, motherboards support other memory module specifications besides form factor. These specifications are

- RAM chip speed

- RAM chip type

- Voltage

The following sections discuss each of these in more detail.

### *RAM chip speed specifications*

**Refresh timing** refers to how quickly the RAM chip is able to refresh its memory, or how quickly the electrical cells in the chip can shuttle the data bits through. The speed at which this can be accomplished is expressed in **nanoseconds (ns)**.

### *RAM chip type specifications*

**RAM chip** type refers to the memory architecture of the SIMM or DIMM. The two types commonly used are extended data output and synchronous DRAM:

- **Extended data output (EDO)** memory is designed so that the module can simultaneously read new data bits into memory cells and send out the old ones. EDO's ability to do this dramatically shortens the refresh timing rate.

- **Synchronous DRAM (SDRAM)** memory is similar in architecture to EDO. However, SDRAM moves the data bits through in timed, high-speed bursts. A clock on the SDRAM module synchronizes the data flow with the CPU clock on the motherboard. By doing this, SDRAM is able to enhance efficiency and thereby the performance of the board. SDRAM is only found on late-model motherboards.

### *Voltage specifications*

**Voltage** refers to the voltage supplied by the motherboard for RAM operation. RAM modules can run at either 3.3v or 5v. 3.3v is the norm on newer motherboards and usually indicates more efficient, faster components.

## Other important CPU specifications

The other important specifications about CPUs are their internal cache and voltage requirements. Modern CPU chips have a small amount of internal memory, the L1 cache, to hold recently used instructions and data.

# Concept Questions     *Semester 1, Unit 6, Lesson 27*

Demonstrate your knowledge of the concepts in this lesson by answering the following questions in the space provided.

1. How does the motherboard support other memory module specifications besides form factor?

2. How is memory organized?

_____

_____

_____

_____

_____

_____

_____

_____

_____

_____

_____

_____

_____

_____

_____

_____

_____

_____

# Vocabulary Exercise     *Semester 1, Unit 6, Lesson 27*

*Name:* _____

*Date:* _____     *Class:* _____

Define the following terms as completely as you can.

**bank**

_____

_____

**EDO**

_____

_____

**NMI**

_____

_____

**parity-checking**

_____

_____

**parity error**

_____

_____

**SDRAM**

_____

_____

## Focus Questions

## *Semester 1, Unit 6, Lesson 27*

*Name:* _____

*Date:* _____     *Class:* _____

**1.** Describe the difference between a RAM socket and a RAM bank.

_____

_____

_____

**2.** Describe the difference between DIMMs and SIMMs.

_____

_____

_____

**3.** Describe what SDRAM is and how it works.

_____

_____

_____

# SEMESTER 1, UNIT 6, LESSON 28
# Floppy Disk Drives and Media

In this lesson you will learn about floppy disk drives and media, which are distinct from other forms of storage drives and media. For many years, floppy drives performed an important function for the storage of data and data transportation. *Storage* denotes more permanent data retention. Data is stored, kept safe and retrievable, even after the computer is turned off. There are two types of storage devices: those with removable **media** and those with fixed media. Disks are housed within enclosures called disk drives. **Floppy disk drives** have removable disks. Drives with permanently fixed disks are called **hard disk drives**. CD-ROMs are a read-only optical storage medium and reader unit.

Usually, floppy disk drives are called floppy drives, and hard disk drives are called hard drives. The removable floppy drive disks are called floppy disks, or **disks**. The fixed media in hard drives are called **storage platters**.

Storage devices such as floppy drives and hard drives are mounted in the computer's chassis in the drive bays or drive brackets.

Other kinds of large-volume storage devices called **mass storage** are generally **proprietary** or are read-only media. But in most PCs, the hard drive storage media is both readable and writable: Data can be written to and read from the hard drive.

## Floppy drives

A floppy drive is basically a drive enclosure with removable floppy disks. Because floppy disks can be removed, data and software can be stored and removed to be transported between systems. Floppy disks let you take data from one computer and use it in another.

Floppy drives and their media (floppy disks) come in two different forms. One is the 5 1/4-inch floppy disk drive. The other is the 3 1/2-inch floppy disk drive. The legacy 5 1/4-inch drives are rarely used on today's systems. Since the beginning of the 1990s, the smaller 3 1/2-inch form has become the standard for new systems.

### Types of floppy drives

The 3 1/2-inch floppy drive comes in three versions, each with a different capacity. The three capacities of floppy disk are 720 KB, 1.44 MB, and 2.88 MB. Even though the 2.88-MB floppy drive has the largest capacity, the 1.44-MB model is the most widely supported and most frequently used in new systems.

### *How floppy drives function*

A floppy disk is composed of three major parts:

- The **magnetic media disk**—A round plastic disk coated with a magnetic substance that is encoded with data by the floppy disk drive.

- The **plastic jacket**—The hard outer shell that protects the magnetic media disk in a floppy disk.

- The **metal sheath**—A sliding shutter that protects the media-access hole on a floppy disk when it is not in the drive.

A disk is logically organized into **tracks** and **sectors**. Data is encoded onto these logical structures by the drive heads. Tracks, numbered from the outside in, are concentric circles on the disk. The outermost track is track 0. The floppy disk's tracks are organized into pie-shaped slices called sectors. Tracks and sectors are found on both sides of the floppy disk. The track-and-sector structure is commonly referred to as the **drive geometry**.

The different capacities of floppy disks are calculated by the number of tracks per side, the number of sectors per track, and the number of bytes of data per sector. The floppy disk's plastic jacket is a hard outer shell that protects the magnetic media disk. The plastic shell is cut away at the top to expose the disk for read/write operations. A sliding metal sheath or shutter protects this read/write window, or **media-access hole**.

Several floppy drive components work together to read and write to or from the magnetic media disk. These components are **read/write heads**, the head actuator, the stepper motor, the **spindle motor**, the circuit board, the faceplate, and connectors.

A floppy drive has two read/write heads, one for each side of the disk. When the floppy disk is inserted into the drive through the faceplate, the faceplate shutter retracts, exposing the media-access hole to the heads. At the same time, the drive's spindle motor spins the disk so that the data index is under the read/write heads. These heads move in unison in a straight line across the tracks. The heads are supported by a head actuator platform and driven by a stepper motor. This motor is called a stepper because it moves the heads across the media disk in fixed increments called **detents**. Each detent, or **stopping point**, is a track where the heads read data from or write data to the media disk. The heads are in direct contact with the disk because they are spring-loaded and grip the disk lightly between them. The logic chips on the circuit board control the various components.

## Reading to and writing from a media disk

A write operation occurs when the drive head saves data to the disk media. A read operation occurs when the drive's head retrieves data from the disk media.

Before a write operation, the disk's magnetic particles are randomly oriented on the disk media. After a write operation, the magnetized disk particles "polarize" in patterns to store the now-written data. A particle is a 0 or 1, depending on its magnetic polarity.

During a read operation, the disk's 0s and 1s are read as data and sent to the drive controller, which forwards that data to the CPU or another device.

The floppy disk's read/write status can be easily shifted from write protected to write enabled. On every floppy disk there is a small sliding tab that can be slid up or down, so it either covers or uncovers a small rectangular hole in a corner of the plastic jacket. When the sliding tab is positioned to block the hole, the disk is write enabled, meaning the drive can write to the disk. When the sliding tab is positioned so the hole is open, the disk is write-protected, meaning the drive cannot write to it. The open-hole feature prevents disk data from being accidentally overwritten.

## Connecting the floppy drive to the computer system

The floppy drive connects to the computer system so it can draw power and exchange data. A small cable drive connector from the power supply provides the power to the floppy drive. The cable connector has a female 4-pin plug that mates to a male 4-pin connector at the rear of the floppy drive. The pinouts or wire scheme are color-coded to identify the proper voltages of the wires.

The two different voltages reflect the different power requirements of the floppy drive components. The circuit board and the logic chips it hosts are designed for low power and use +5v power. The drive motors, on the other hand, require more power and use +12v power.

The floppy drive exchanges data with the motherboard devices and CPU via a 34-pin flat ribbon cable. The ribbon cable connects from a 34-pin male connector at the rear of the floppy drive to a 34-pin male connector on the motherboard.

The cable plugs, drive connector, and floppy controller are all keyed, beginning at pin 1, for proper alignment. The pin 1 edge of the cable connector can be identified by the red stripe on the edge of the cable. Lining up the red-stripe edge with pin 1 of the drive connector or drive controller **interfaces** assures correct alignment.

The system BIOS can support up to two floppy drives on one controller, via a daisy chain cable arrangement. A daisy chain cable arrangement is actually a type of data bus, much like the hardware buses on the motherboard discussed earlier. This means that attached devices require unique identifiers.

Usually the two drives are identified as Drive A and Drive B. Originally, identification for the two drives was set by means of two jumpers located on the logic board. The jumpers were labeled DS0 and DS1. When Drive Select 0 (DS0) was bridged, it selected the drive as Drive A. When Drive Select 1 (DS1) was bridged, it was selected as Drive B. However, today most drives have the DS jumpers set for DS1 by default. In addition, they use the cable position to identify the drive.

Cable pinouts 10 through 16 are cross-wired between the middle drive connector and end drive connector, producing a twist that reverses the DS configuration of the drive plugged into the end connector. This feature, called cable select, automatically configures the drive on the middle connector as Drive B and the drive on the end connector as Drive A. This greatly simplifies installation and configuration of the floppy drives. In addition, quite a few 34-pin cable have the connectors for either a 3 1/2-inch or 5 1/4-inch floppy.

## How a floppy drive operates

Higher-capacity floppy drives are backward compatible with lower-capacity disks. This is possible because of a **media sensor** that detects an inserted floppy disk's capacity. Then the sensor switches the drive into the proper read/write mode.

Also, the floppy drive needs to know when a different disk has been loaded into the drive. The floppy drive controller and drive data connector share pin 34 to exchange a special signal called the disk changeline. When a disk is inserted or ejected, a disk change signal is sent to the floppy drive controller to advise it of the status change. If the signal is not received again before the next read/write operation, then the system assumes that the disk has not been changed.

# Concept Questions      *Semester 1, Unit 6, Lesson 28*

Demonstrate your knowledge of the concepts in this lesson by answering the following questions in the space provided.

1. Identify the three major components of a floppy disk and explain how they work together.

2. Explain the process for connecting the floppy drive to the computer system.

_____

_____

_____

_____

_____

_____

_____

_____

_____

_____

_____

_____

_____

_____

_____

_____

_____

_____

# Vocabulary Exercise    *Semester 1, Unit 6, Lesson 28*

*Name:* _____

*Date:* _____    *Class:* _____

Define the following terms as completely as you can.

**detent**

_____

_____

**floppy disk**

_____

_____

**floppy drive**

_____

_____

**media sensor**

_____

_____

**sector**

_____

_____

**storage**

_____

_____

***track***

_____

_____

# Focus Questions

## *Semester 1, Unit 6, Lesson 28*

*Name:* _____

*Date:* _____  *Class:* _____

*1.* What is the essential difference between memory and storage?

_____

_____

_____

*2.* How does a floppy drive operate?

_____

_____

_____

*3.* How do floppy disks make the transportation of data between computers convenient?

_____

_____

_____

*4.* What floppy disk size is most likely found in new computers, and why is this size preferred?

_____

_____

_____

**5.** What are the two important parts of the floppy disk's drive geometry?

_____

_____

_____

**6.** Describe how to write protect a floppy disk.

_____

_____

_____

**7.** How is a floppy disk written?

_____

_____

_____

**8.** Describe the connection between the computer's power supply and the floppy drive.

_____

_____

_____

**9.** Describe the connection between the motherboard and the floppy drive.

_____

_____

_____

**10.** How many floppy drives can be supported by one computer, and why?

_____

_____

_____

# SEMESTER 1, UNIT 6, LESSON 29
# CD-ROM Drives and Media

In this lesson you will learn about CD-ROM drives and media. The technology behind the CD-ROM is not new. It dates back to 1978, with the introduction of the audio compact disc (CD) by the Phillips and Sony Corporations. In fact, the size of the medium has not changed, nor has the CD-ROM's basic design. The CD-ROM's impact on modern computing makes it an important technological development.

In a basic sense, a **CD-ROM** is a single-sided, read-only optical storage medium and reader unit. A CD-ROM can hold up to 682 MB of data. The types of data it can hold include text, sound, and graphics. This medium is used to publish and distribute much of the data and software distributed in the computer market today. As such, it is essential to the usage of most systems built today.

## The components of a CD-ROM

The term *CD-ROM* can refer to both the medium and the reader unit, sometimes also called a *CD-ROM drive*. Sometimes you also see the medium referred to as a *CD*. For starters, let's take a look at the CD disc.

The computer CD disc still possesses the same form factor, or physical dimensions, as its music predecessor. It is a layered disc with a polycarbonate body, approximately 4 3/4-inches in diameter, coated with thin film of aluminum alloy. A plastic coating protects the disc from scratches, and data is inlaid on the alloy film. The CD disc you buy at the store looks like a tiny record album, and comes with a label on the top, and the data is read from the bottom of the disc.

The CD is usually produced or mastered at a factory with a laser that etches the data onto a master disc. The recording technique is a physical one rather than a magnetic one, as is the case with floppy and hard disk media. The production laser burns **pits** into the smooth surface of the disc, leaving flat surfaces in between. The patterns of pits and **lands** represent data. After the master is produced, it is used to stamp copies. Up to 682 MB of textual, audio, video, and graphical data can be written to a disc. After the copies have been made, they are sealed for distribution.

### *Internal components of CD-ROM drives*

Just as with hard drives, the major internal components of a CD-ROM drive are the optical head assembly, the head actuator mechanism, the spindle motor, the **loading mechanism**, connectors and jumpers, and the logic board.

### *External components of CD-ROM drives*

In addition to the eject button, there are two other external components of CD-ROM drives: the audio output jack and the volume control. Both are located on the front bezel of the drive. The jack is for headphones. The other control is used to regulate the volume level.

# How a CD-ROM works

As you have learned, data is stored in the form of indentations and bumps on the reflective surface of every CD-ROM. When data is being read, light from the laser is bounced off the pits and lands located on the underside of the disk. Because the pits reflect less light, they are read by the CD-ROM drive as 0s. Because lands reflect more light, they are read as 1s. Together these 1s and 0s make up the binary language understood by computers.

The light bounced off the pits and lands is sent back to a second mirror and lens assembly, the purpose of which is to focus and direct the reflected light to a **photodetector**. From there, the signal generated from the reflected laser light is sent back to the processor on the logic board. The photodetector changes the light signals into electrical signals computers can understand. The data is then sent by means of the interface to the system CPU.

### *Regulating disc speed*

During the entire time of the read operation, the disc media spins. The disc sits on a hub that is driven by a spindle motor. The speed at which the CD-ROM spins is not constant. Instead, it varies over the width of the disc. Because the diameter of the tracks grows progressively smaller toward the center of the disk, the spindle motor adjusts the speed in relation to the where the head assembly is on the disk.

The ability of the disc to spin at different rates ensures that the amount of data that goes past the lens assembly during a fixed increment of time remains constant. Sometimes, you see this referred to as the constant linear velocity (CLV) of the CD-ROM drive. Newer multispeed drives use a different approach, called constant angular velocity. When this approach is used, the speed of the spin is allowed to vary from the edge to the center. This technology moves the track data past the read laser at different speeds, depending on where the track is physically located over the diameter of the CD. Tracks toward the center of the disk play faster than tracks toward the edge, because the rate of spin is kept constant.

### *The CD-ROM's disc-loading mechanism*

Because the CD is a removable medium, it requires some kind of loading mechanism. For CD-ROMs, there are two types of loading mechanisms: the **tray** mechanism and the **caddy** mechanism.

The tray is a gear-driven rack. It slides out whenever the eject button located on the front of the case is activated. A niche with a cut-out in the center holds the loaded CD. When retracted with the disc loaded, the **spindle** raises up, lifts the disc off the tray, and spins it at a predetermined **revolutions per minute (rpm)**.

The caddy mechanism is found on high-end CD-ROM drives. A caddy is a small plastic carrier with a hinged lid. It also has a retractable metal slot in the bottom that allows access when loaded into the drive. CD-ROMs with caddy load mechanisms are more sturdy and last longer than those with tray mechanisms.

# Configuring and installing CD-ROM drives

Because the CD-ROM drive coexists with other devices on the IDE or SCSI bus channels, it is connected and configured by jumpers in much the same fashion as IDE or SCSI drives. When a CD-ROM drive is used with an IDE interface, it is configurable as either a master or a slave. For SCSI, it has a SCSI ID jumper set and termination jumpers. A 40-pin IDE cable can have two components attached to it: One is set as the master, and the other as a slave. A second cable is called IDE 2, and it can also have a master and slave.

The CD-ROM drive interface and the controller circuitry are installed on the logic board much like regular drives. The only connector that is unique to this device is the audio output connector. It is located next to the controller interface at the rear of the drive. It allows an audio cable to be attached that leads to a sound card for multimedia effects.

# CD-ROM drive specifications

Specifications can provide a good idea of how well a CD-ROM will perform. Common specifications include the following:

- Transfer rate

- Access time

- Seek time

- Cache memory

- Interface

- Error correction

The following sections discuss each of these in more detail.

## *The transfer rate specification*

The **transfer rate** states the maximum data rate that the drive can sustain when reading from a CD and transferring to the system. The transfer rate is the same over the entire CD due to the CLV format. This rate is given as kilobytes per second (KBps). The standard rate for original CD-ROM drives was approximately 150 KBps. All performance specifications that read 4x, 6x, 8x, 10x, and so on are multiples of this original standard rate, due to the increase in the CLV.

## *The access time specification*

**Access time** is the time period or delay between the initial read command to the drive and the moment it actually begins to deliver the data. This time is measured in **milliseconds (ms)**. Because the mechanism has to move over the surface of the disc to locate the data, the time is actually an average of the several random accesses performed.

## *The seek time specification*

**Seek time** is the time delay between when a command is given to find a particular sector and when the lens assembly actually pinpoints the spot. Like access times, this is an average of several random seeks performed. And as with access time, a lower seek time interval is better.

## *The cache memory specification*

The cache memory specification refers to the amount of memory installed on the drive's logic board. This memory is used to provide a buffer for data transfer to the system CPU. The amount of memory is typically 256 KB. On startup, the buffer can read the disc's volume index into memory for quicker response time in locating sectors on the disc.

## *The interface specification*

The interface specification refers to the CD-ROM's actual connection to the system. If the interface is the IDE type, then it requires the correct driver for the **AT Attachment Packet Interface (ATAPI)**.

If the interface is of the SCSI type, it is desirable to have the current SCSI-2 standard and not SCSI-1. However, the SCSI controller built in to the CD-ROM drive does not completely implement the SCSI command set. The CD-ROM drive requires special SCSI software drivers to provide emulation. The ASPI Manager and device-specific SCSI driver are parts of the Advanced SCSI Programming Interface (ASPI) developed by Adaptec.

## *The error correction specification*

**Error correction** is the ability of the CD-ROM drive processor to recover from errors due in large part to media defects. To deal with this issue, the CD-ROM typically sets aside approximately 284 bytes per block of data for error correction, along with error detection. As a general rule, the lower the number of errors, the higher the quality of the unit.

# Concept Questions  *Semester 1, Unit 6, Lesson 29*

Demonstrate your knowledge of the concepts in this lesson by answering the following questions in the space provided.

1.  Describe the components of a CD-ROM disc, and explain how they enable the disc to function.

2.  Explain how specifications can provide a gauge of how well a CD-ROM drive will perform.

_____

_____

_____

_____

_____

_____

_____

_____

_____

_____

_____

_____

_____

_____

_____

_____

# Vocabulary Exercise      *Semester 1, Unit 6, Lesson 29*

*Name:* _____

*Date:* _____     *Class:* _____

Define the following terms as completely as you can.

**access time**

_____

_____

**CLV**

_____

_____

**error correction**

_____

_____

**interface**

_____

_____

**land**

_____

_____

**pit**

_____

_____

**seek time**

_____

_____

**transfer rate**

_____

_____

# Focus Questions     *Semester 1, Unit 6, Lesson 29*

*Name:* _____

*Date:* _____     *Class:* _____

**1.** What are the components of the CD-ROM drive, and how do they function?

_____

_____

_____

_____

**2.** Describe how CD-ROM drives are configured with jumpers and installed on the motherboard.

_____

_____

_____

_____

**3.** Describe the two types of loading mechanisms for a CD-ROM drive and how each functions.

_____

_____

_____

_____

**4.** Describe the two other external components of CD-ROM drives and their location on the drive.

_____

_____

_____

_____

**5.** Describe how a CD-ROM drive is configured.

_____

_____

_____

_____

# SEMESTER 1, UNIT 6, LESSON 30
# Unit 6 Exam

If you have access to the online Aries A+ curriculum, contact your instructor for the Assessment System URL. If you do not have access to the online curriculum, please continue to Unit 7.

# SEMESTER 1, UNIT 7

- Lesson 31: Floppy, Tape, and CD-ROM Lab Exercises
- Lesson 32: Magnetic Storage: Hard Drives
- Lesson 33: Drive Interfaces
- Lesson 34: Hard Drive Lab Exercises
- Lesson 35: Unit 7 Exam

# SEMESTER 1, UNIT 7, LESSON 31
# Floppy, Tape, and CD-ROM Lab Exercises

If you have access to the online Aries A+ curriculum, go online to follow along with this lab exercise. If you do not have access to the online curriculum, please continue to the next lesson.

# SEMESTER 1, UNIT 7, LESSON 32
# Magnetic Storage: Hard Drives

In this lesson you will learn about the main storage medium for the computer system: the hard disk drive, commonly called the **hard drive**. You will also learn about the hard drive's components, operations, interfaces, and specifications.

A hard drive shares many physical and operational characteristics with the floppy disk drive. However, it is more complex in design and provides much greater access speed. In addition, the hard drive has a much greater storage capacity.

The hard drive is composed of relatively inflexible aluminum or glass platters or disks. (This inflexibility led to the name *hard disk drive*.) The hard drive is typically not removable. This is why IBM has referred to hard drives as *fixed disk drives*. In short, a hard drive is a high-volume disk storage device with fixed, high-density, rigid media.

## The components in a hard drive

All hard drives share a common set of components. These components are similar to the components in floppy drives and include the following: the **disk platters**, read/write heads, **head actuator assembly**, spindle motor, logic/circuit board, bezel/faceplate, configuration jumpers, and interface connectors.

**Disk platters** are the media disks that store data in the hard drive. A hard drive typically has 2 to 10 platters. They can be either 3 1/2 inches or 5 1/4 inches in diameter and are typically constructed of aluminum or a glass-ceramic composite material. They are coated with a **thin-film media** that is magnetically sensitive. The platters are double-sided, with thin-film media on each side. Platters are stacked with spaces between them on a **hub** that holds them in position, separate from one another. The hub is also called the spindle.

The disk platters require a read/write head for each side. The read/write head is used to access the media. The read/write heads are stacked, or **ganged**, on a carrier called a rack. Because they are mounted together, they move in unison across the platters with the rack. The heads are joined to the rack by arms. The arms extend from the head actuator assembly. The head itself is a U- or V-shaped device of electrically conductive material wrapped with wires. The wires cause sensitivity to the magnetic media of the platters.

Unlike the heads on floppy drives, which directly contact the medium surface, those of hard drives float a short distance above the surface. Because the platters typically spin at very high speeds, such as 4,500 to 10,000 **revolutions per minute (rpm)**, air pressure builds between them and the head; this is what causes the float. The central hub, or spindle, on which the platters are mounted is spun by a spindle motor, which is connected to the spindle by gears.

The head actuator assembly is moved across the surface of the platters and positioned by a **voice coil actuator**. Unlike the stepper motor in floppy drives that can only move in fixed increments, the voice coil actuator moves without a motor, by electromagnetic force alone.

An electromagnetic coil is attached at the rear of the head rack. When power is supplied to this coil, the head rack is moved. This is caused by either attraction to or repulsion against a fixed magnet that is in the rear of the actuator assembly. When it is moved, it is positioned over a specific track.

## Finding the correct track

You have learned that the magnetic medium on the disk platter is logically organized into tracks and sectors, and that these resembled record grooves and pie slices. The voice coil mechanism is able to find the precise track on the hard disk platter because of a **servo mechanism**. The servo mechanism uses feedback to control the velocity and position of the hard disk heads.

The **gray code** provides the positional information that the voice coil actuator reads in order to precisely position itself over the requested track. The position of the carriage assembly is adjusted based on the strength of the received servo signal from the servo head. This is done so that the data heads are precisely positioned over the data.

The hard disk assembly, as described earlier, is housed in a mounting chassis that mounts into the drive brackets of the system chassis. The bottom of the hard disk assembly is attached to the logic board that contains the control circuitry. The power connector and drive controller connector are located at the rear of the logic board

## How the drive connects to the system

The hard drive connects to the computer system to draw power and exchange data. A large drive connector from the power supply provides the power to the hard drive. This drive connector has a female 4-pin plug that mates to a 4-pin male connector at the rear of the hard drive. The pinouts or wire scheme are color-coded to identify the voltages of the wires.

As with the floppy drive, the hard drive uses two different voltages. The different voltages used reflect the different power requirements of the hard drive components. The circuit board that hosts the logic chips is designed for low +5v power. The drive motors require more power and use +12v power.

The hard drive exchanges data signals with the controller on the motherboard by means of a flat-ribbon, 40-pin cable. The pinouts and cable width are dependent on the type of interface.

## How the drive functions

The hard drive functions similarly to a floppy drive. The disk platters spin at high speed, while the drive heads access the media to conduct read or write operations. Understanding how the heads read and write the data structures on the platter media is important in knowing how the drive functions.

On the drive platters is a layer of magnetically sensitive material. Modern hard drives use a thin film of a cobalt metal alloy, laid in several microthin layers. The magnetic particles in this medium are randomly aligned when the disk is empty of data. However, as the read/write head writes to an area, it causes the particles on that track to align in a specific direction. This is done according to the direction of electric current flow in the heads. This local magnetic direction in the media is called a **flux**. The current in the head can be reversed, causing a **flux reversal**, or an opposite magnetic orientation in the media. As the platter spins, the head lays down a **flux pattern** along the length of a track. This pattern of flux transitions on the track represents the recorded data.

The read operation requires that the drive head function as a flux transition detector. During this operation, the head emits an electrical pulse. These pulses occur at every transition from one flux direction to another. The pattern of pulses coupled with the absence of pulses constitute the read/write pattern. The pattern is translated back into bit data by the drive's circuit board, and then passed back to the disk controller on the motherboard.

# The evolution of the hard drive

Older hard disks retained about 5 MB and used platters up to 12 inches in diameter. Today's hard disks can hold several gigabytes, and generally use 3 1/2-inch platters for desktop computers and 2 1/2-inch platters for notebooks. Some of the older hard disk interfaces used a device-level interface. These older hard disks had many problems with compatibility, data integrity, and speed, because the raw data had to travel over a cable between the controller and the drive.

The original hard disk interface used in the IBM PC/XT, developed by Seagate Technologies, was called the Modified Frequency Modulation (MFM). MFM used a magnetic disk encoding method with the ST-506 interface. Run Length Limited (RLL) is a hard disk interface that is similar to MFM, but has a larger number of sectors. RLL is an encoding method commonly used on magnetic disks, including SCSI, IDE, SMD, ESDI, and IPI interfaces.

The Enhanced Small Device Interface (ESDI) is a hard disk interface that transfers data in the range of 1 to 3 MBps. ESDI is a high-speed interface for small computers and was superseded by IDE and SCSI drives.

# Concept Questions     *Semester 1, Unit 7, Lesson 32*

Demonstrate your knowledge of the concepts in this lesson by answering the following questions in the space provided.

1.  Describe the components in a hard drive.

2.  Explain how the hard drive functions.

_____

_____

_____

_____

_____

_____

_____

_____

_____

_____

_____

_____

_____

_____

_____

_____

_____

# Vocabulary Exercise     *Semester 1, Unit 7, Lesson 32*

*Name:* _____

*Date:* _____     *Class:* _____

Define the following terms as completely as you can.

### disk platter

_____

_____

### flux pattern

_____

_____

### flux reversal

_____

_____

### gray code

_____

_____

### servo mechanism

_____

_____

# Focus Questions                 *Semester 1, Unit 7, Lesson 32*

*Name:* _____

*Date:* _____        *Class:* _____

*1.* Explain how the components of the hard drive function.

_____

_____

_____

_____

*2.* Describe the voice coil actuator and how it functions.

_____

_____

_____

_____

*3.* Describe flux and how it functions with the hard drive.

_____

_____

_____

_____

# SEMESTER 1, UNIT 7, LESSON 33
# Drive Interfaces

Now you know the hard drive's basic components. You are familiar with its disk platters, and its tracks and sectors. You have an idea of how the hard drive functions.

This lesson focuses on the particular differences between two hard drive types in common use today: the **integrated drive electronics (IDE)** and the **small computer system interface (SCSI**, pronounced "scuzzy") types. These drive interfaces have most of the controller circuitry directly on the hard drive, which alleviates a lot of the problems that the older hard disks had to deal with. The drive interface is the way the drive communicates with the computer; it defines a sort of language that allows the drive and the computer to talk to each other.

## IDE

IDE improves on earlier hard drives, especially in its compactness. Its controller electronics reside right on the drive itself. A separate adapter card is not needed. IDE provides today's least expensive way to attach peripherals. You often hear IDE drive interfaces called ATAs. The first ATA standard for IDE drives, which was inconsistent from manufacturer to manufacturer, originated in 1989, as an outgrowth of the original Western Digital ST-506 drive interface.

In the original ST-506 design, all the drive logic was on a separate adapter card that plugged into an ISA bus slot. There were limitations to this design, which led to the eventual development of the IDE design, where the drive logic was integrated into the hard drive circuit board, leaving only a pass-through card on the ISA bus.

## EIDE

Enhanced IDE (EIDE) is the new-and-improved IDE drive interface. Not confined to the IDE's 528 MB of data, EIDE can handle up to 8.4 GB. The IDE could support only two drives, and both had to be hard drives. EIDE features four-peripheral potential. And the peripherals can be of varying types, such as CD-ROMs and tape drives, for instance. You often hear EIDE interface called **ATA-2**. This newer ATA-2 standard brought significant upgrades to the drive, drive controller, and BIOS.

The ATA-2 specification was developed in 1994 and subsequently modified to final form in 1995. The EIDE/ATA-2 specification covers the interface signals on the 40-pin connector, the **drive commands** issued by the BIOS, cable specifications, and drive configuration circuitry.

EIDE is a 40-pin interface connector that is keyed by the removal of pin 20 on the male drive connector site. The corresponding female pin socket on the cable connector is plugged as well. This prevents the cable from being plugged in reverse since the pin will not enter the plugged hole. Notches on the drive and cable connectors sometime also key the connector plugs.

Two key interface signals to understand are the **drive active/slave present (DASP)** signal and **cable select (CSEL)** signal. The DASP signals the presence of a slave drive at startup and is used by both drives after startup to indicate whether they are active. Prior to DASP, there was no standardized way to connect two IDE drives. The CSEL signal indicates the status of two connected drives. One is always designated as the master. The other is always designated as the slave. However, this requires a special cable arrangement that's not usually used.

Configuration jumpers are commonly used with EIDE, and their settings control the DASP signaling on each drive. The jumper settings are single-drive or standalone, master, and slave. Usually, the jumper configuration to be used for each of these is indicated on the drive's circuit board.

The BIOS drive commands supported by the ATA-2 standard are based on the original WD1003 commands. However, the BIOS drive commands include significant enhanced commands. The three most important BIOS drive commands are the **identify drive**, **read multiple**, and **write multiple** commands. The **identify drive** command is issued by the BIOS to the drive to send a 512-byte data block. This data block identifies the make, model, and operating parameters of the drive. Since the 1995 ATA-2 standard, the system BIOS of newer PCs is enhanced to use this command for logical block addressing (LBA). When the drive is asked for how many heads, cylinders, and sectors per track it has, the BIOS uses **sector translation** to group these logical parameters into a form usable by the system BIOS. Prior to this BIOS enhancement, IDE drives were limited to 528 MB, due to limits in the number of cylinders and heads the drive could identify. Sector translation allows EIDE drives in sizes up to 8 GB. There can be only so many sectors, so programmers wrote a program to group sectors together and call it a single sector. The other commands enable the controller and drive circuitry to support multiple sector data transfers concurrently.

The drive controllers listed in the ATA-2 specification are also enhanced over the older IDE standard. The ATA-2 standard allows for two disk channels. Each channel supports a master/slave combination. On the motherboard, these controllers are called the primary IDE and secondary IDE controllers. On the ISA bus, these controllers reserve interrupts 14 and 15, respectively. However, on newer motherboards, the primary controller is attached to the PCI local bus, and the secondary controller is attached to the ISA bus, freeing interrupt 14.

The ribbon cable bus arrangement for IDE drives is similar to those described earlier for floppy drives. The ribbon cable has three 40-pin connectors: one on the end for the IDE controller, one in the middle for the slave drive, and one on the other end for the master drive. A red stripe is used to identify pin 1 just as it does for the floppy drive. The ATA cable specification calls for a maximum length of 18 inches.

Two remaining enhancements in EIDE are also important: faster data transfer and the ATA program interface. The ATA-2 standard provides support for two new methods of improving data transfer between drive and controller: **programmed I/O (PIO)** mode and **block mode PIO**. These were improvements to the drive circuitry and system BIOS that supported different levels of peak transfer rates between drive and controller. Transfer rates are expressed as megabits per second (Mbps). PIO Modes 1 and 2 existed with the first 1989 ATA standard, but only for transfer rates supported through the ISA bus. The newer ATA-2 standard defines three newer PIO modes supported by the new PCI local bus IDE controller.

Block mode PIO includes the ability to use the **read multiple** and **write multiple** commands discussed earlier. Reading and writing in multiple sectors concurrently makes the transfer rate more efficient. This is because the number of interrupts to the processor is consequently reduced. The ATA-2 standard also provides specifications for the support of **direct memory access (DMA)** transfers on IDE controllers. However, this feature has never been generally implemented in actual manufactured systems.

The other major enhancement was in the support of non-hard drive peripherals. Until the ATA-2 standard, such devices used the parallel port, floppy drive interface, or proprietary controllers. However, the ATA-2 specifications support a new standard to support such devices. The **ATA packet interface (ATAPI)** provides support to CD-ROMs and tape drives on the IDE interface.

# UDMA

Although the ATA-2 standard provided specifications for DMA channel data transfers, it has seldom been implemented in actual designs. Intel and Quantum Corporation developed an extension to this standard that builds on the earlier DMA specification. Called **ultra DMA (UDMA)**, the extension allows bypassing of the I/O bus bottleneck to take place during peak sequential transfers. The UDMA specification enables read and write data transfers on both the rising and falling edges of the clock signal without direct CPU intervention.

The UDMA specification adds two modes to the ATA standards, called either ATA-3 or ATA-4. The first is **multi-word DMA mode 2**. This mode utilizes the DMA channel for regular burst read/write operation data transfers. The second is **UDMA mode 2**. This mode utilizes bus-mastering for maximal burst transfer rates.

Because of these higher burst transfer rates, a data protection and verification routine has been added to the interface. This **cyclical redundancy check (CRC)**, like the parity-checking found in main system memory operations, ensures the integrity of the transferred data.

# SCSI

SCSIs were the better and preferred drive interface because they are more architecturally complex. However, as the IDE and EIDE evolved, they became faster and obtained good transfer rates and almost matched SCSI. Today, SCSI drives are similar to EIDE drives in that they both share embedded intelligence in the drive circuitry. In fact, most SCSI drives are internally identical to high-performance EIDE drives, but they include a different data connector and have a **SCSI bus interface controller chip (SBIC)**. The IDE controller, however, is not intelligent and is utilized as a simple pass-through. SCSIs are still better in use for servers and where there is a need for a lot of data storage.

A **SCSI host adapter** is not a disk controller, but a system-level interface. It is a bus much like the I/O bus on the system motherboard. It exists as an adapter card, plugged into a system ISA or PCI bus slot. The controller and interface are embedded into the circuit board of the SCSI hard drive. The host adapter possesses its own BIOS, talks to the controllers embedded on the SCSI, and sends the results to the CPU by means of the system bus. Communication from the system CPU follows the reverse route. In simpler terms, the SCSI host adapter acts as the gateway between the SCSI bus and the main system.

The SCSI standard was originated in 1986 to define the operating parameters of the SCSI I/O bus used to connect the host adapter and the peripheral devices in a daisy chain. Known as the **SCSI-1** standard, it established the basic physical and electrical specifications of the bus and basic command set. However, it did not support the full range of devices that the industry wanted.

Therefore, a revised SCSI standard, **SCSI-2**, was introduced in 1994. This revision included an expanded command set to support the extra range of devices such as CD-ROMs, tape drives, optical drives, scanners, plotters, and other devices. The SCSI-2 standard is the most extensible external bus architecture available. In addition, specifications for higher-speed SCSI buses were included in this standard. When computer users refer to SCSI today, they are typically referring to the SCSI-2 standard. SCSI-3 devices are also appearing on the market.

## *The SCSI bus*

There are differences in the particulars of SCSI buses, depending on the specification. However, all SCSI-2 buses function in the same basic fashion.

As you have learned in this lesson, SCSI is really a bus. The SCSI host adapter in the computer system is just another device on the system bus. Each of the devices on the bus is a peer of the other devices. A host adapter can have one or two bus channels of eight devices each. These devices can be daisy-chained both inside and outside the system, using a ribbon cable. Each drive is an independent device on the bus channel and is coordinated by the host adapter. Because each device is independent, it requires a special identifier called a **SCSI ID** to differentiate it on the bus for purposes of communication. These IDs and other configurations are set up in the BIOS on the SCSI host adapter. If you look at an external SCSI hard drive, you will see a dial to set the ID number. You can also set a jumper on an internal device, using binary numbering.

When the system CPU wants to send a read or write request to a SCSI drive on a channel, the request is sent to the SCSI host adapter. The host adapter either sends the request to the device directly, or puts it in a **command queue** until the host adapter processor has time to attend to it. The process is very much like calling someone on the phone: Answer, answer back, and then communicate. Essentially, it is a polite conversation. The host adapter is in continuous communication with the bus devices, either synchronously or asynchronously.

In asynchronous communication the adapter negotiates a data transfer using a handshake mode called **request/acknowledgement (Req/Ack)**. For each data transfer request, the host adapter sends a request to the device, and the device controller responds with an acknowledgement. The device then receives the read/write request. When the read/write operation is completed, the device goes through the Req/Ack routine again.

**Synchronous communication** is similar to the classic Req/Ack method, but it allows the host adapter to issue multiple requests before receiving acknowledgements. The transfers of data are more efficient because the host adapter can handle more data streams at once. In fact, the transfers of data using this method are generally about three times faster.

When the host adapter is receiving multiple requests simultaneously from contending drives on the bus, it must decide in what order to handle them. It does this through a process called **arbitration**. The host adapter uses a set of priorities to decide the order of processing. These priorities are determined by the SCSI ID of the devices. For example, ID 7 is the highest priority, and ID 0 is the lowest priority. The highest-priority SCSI ID number 7 is always used for the host adapter itself so that it can handle its own transfers to the system CPU first.

Because of the volume of data activity over the SCSI bus, some sort of error-checking is required to ensure that data transfers are reliable. In the basic 8-bit SCSI bus, there are 25 signals. Each signal is represented by a pair of wires. Nine of the wires hold the 8 bits plus a parity bit. If you recall, the first 8 bits are equivalent to 1 byte of actual data. The ninth bit is the parity bit, used in parity checking. The remaining wires carry control function.

In essence, the SCSI host adapter handles all the read/write I/O traffic for the system, offloading this from the CPU. The CPU, not being bothered with the overhead of continuous interrupts to handle I/O requests, can devote itself to other processor-intensive tasks. For these reasons, processor-intensive environments that need multiple types of bus devices tend to use SCSI buses.

## *The SCSI-2 specifications*

The two SCSI extensions are **fast SCSI-2** and **wide SCSI-2**. Standard SCSI-2 uses the basic 8-bit bus width. The fast SCSI-2 specification doubles the synchronous communication speed over SCSI-2. The wide SCSI-2 specification uses a 16-bit bus, doubling SCSI-2's 8-bit width.

Ultra SCSI, sometimes called **fast wide SCSI-2**, combines the synchronous communication speed of fast SCSI-2 with up to the 16-bit bus width of wide SCSI-2. It is important to realize that SCSI-2, in any of its versions, can be run with either an 8-bit bus or a 16-bit bus width.

The basic physical and electrical specifications of the SCSI bus refer to the cables, connectors, device identifiers, and bus termination. The particulars may change with reference to the SCSI type.

## *SCSI cable types*

Two types of ribbon cables—Type A and Type B—are used for different bus widths of the interface. Type A ribbon cable is the classic 50-pin cable used by both SCSI and SCSI-2 bus devices and host adapters. For this type of ribbon cable, the maximum cable length is 6 meters, or about 20 feet. This cable utilizes the 8-bit bus width, 50-pin interface. Type B ribbon cable is the newer 68-pin cable. It is used by fast, wide, and fast wide SCSI bus devices and host adapters. This cable utilizes the 16-bit bus width, 68-pin interface.

## SCSI device identifiers

As you have learned, a typical SCSI bus channel can have up to eight devices. When eight devices are used, the host adapter takes the first address, or the number 7. This leaves seven other IDs, numbered 0 through 6.

Each SCSI ID assigned must be unique, for addressing purposes. This ID is set on the drive by a jumper block, with three jumpers that collectively yield a binary number representation of the SCSI ID number. The proper bridging of these jumpers for the different IDs is either labeled on the drive itself or documented in the accompanying manual.

## How the SCSI bus functions electrically

To understand how the SCSI bus functions electrically, let's use the **single-ended SCSI** as an example. For each signal that is to be sent across the bus, there is a single wire to carry it (and a common ground shared by all). A SCSI bus, like all buses, uses an electrical voltage level to convey the data. The voltage must be kept within certain operating parameters in order to carry the signals properly. Termination of the bus is required to accomplish this. The host adapter almost always terminates automatically when it anchors the bus. The last drive in the daisy chain on the bus must also be terminated.

Termination is usually accomplished by setting a jumper on the circuit board of the last drive of the daisy chain. All drives in between should not be terminated. The jumper settings are always documented in the SCSI drive manual. Sometimes, on extremely long SCSI chains, active termination with special external terminators is required. These external models usually have voltage regulators on them to produce the correct termination voltage. This ensures that the SCSI signals are always terminated correctly at the correct voltage from end to end.

The SCSI ID discussed earlier is more properly known in terms of its electrical function: It is usually called the **physical unit number (PUN)**. A device's ID number is its binary signal address on the chain. The drive from which the system boots is always set as PUN 000b in memory addressing. This translates as SCSI ID 0. Because each SCSI device is a composite of drive and drive controller, each of these also has its own binary address. This is sometimes referred to as a **logical unit number (LUN)**. The PUN uses the LUN to address its internal communication.

## SCSI versus EIDE

Each type of interface system has advantages and disadvantages. EIDE, for example, is limited to only two devices per controller channel, or only four drives on the primary and secondary controllers. However, due to the high speed of sequential data transfers, it is good in situations requiring only one computer system task at a time. This is called **single tasking**. This high speed is in part due to less I/O overhead, since the CPU interacts directly with the drives through the controller. The support for logical block addressing in the EIDE BIOS is shared with SCSI.

The SCSI interface, on the other hand, is much more expandable and extensible. It supports not only more devices per channel (a total of eight), but it supports more kinds of devices as well. The ability to manage multiple device data traffic concurrently is a major benefit in situations requiring a computer system to manage multiple computing sessions concurrently. This is called **multitasking**. The down side of this ability is the increased overhead on data communications, because the CPU request must be mediated by the SCSI host adapter, and requests cannot be sent directly to the drives.

# Concept Questions     *Semester 1, Unit 7, Lesson 33*

Demonstrate your knowledge of the concepts in this lesson by answering the following questions in the space provided.

*1.* Explain IDE and EIDE.

*2.* Explain how the SCSI bus works and the importance of the SCSI specification.

_____

_____

_____

_____

_____

_____

_____

_____

_____

_____

_____

_____

_____

_____

_____

_____

_____

_____

_____

# Vocabulary Exercise        *Semester 1, Unit 7, Lesson 33*

*Name:* _____

*Date:* _____        *Class:* _____

Define the following terms as completely as you can.

**arbitration**

_____

_____

**CRC**

_____

_____

**DASP**

_____

_____

**EIDE**

_____

_____

**IDE**

_____

_____

**PIO**

_____

_____

**SCSI ID**

_____

_____

**synchronous communication**

_____

_____

**UDMA**

_____

_____

# Focus Questions     *Semester 1, Unit 7, Lesson 33*

*Name:*   _____

*Date:*   _____     *Class:*   _____

**1.** Identify and describe the three most important BIOS drive commands supported by the ATA-2 standard.

_____

_____

_____

_____

**2.** Describe sector translation and explain its benefits.

_____

_____

_____

_____

**3.** Describe the function of UDMA.

_____

_____

_____

_____

**4.** Which interface is best for single tasking and which is best for multitasking, and why?

_____

_____

_____

_____

# SEMESTER 1, UNIT 7, LESSON 34
# Hard Drive Lab Exercises

If you have access to the online Aries A+ curriculum, go online to follow along with this lab exercise. If you do not have access to the online curriculum, please continue to the next lesson.

# Semester 1, Unit 7, Lesson 35
# Unit 7 Exam

If you have access to the online Aries A+ curriculum, contact your instructor for the Assessment System URL. If you do not have access to the online curriculum, please continue to Unit 8.

# Semester 1, Unit 8

- Lesson 36: Introduction to Video Adapters
- Lesson 37: Video Display Monitors
- Lesson 38: Monitor Display Specifications
- Lesson 39: Monitor Installation Lab Exercises
- Lesson 40: Unit 8 Exam

# SEMESTER 1, UNIT 8, LESSON 36
# Introduction to Video Adapters

When you enter information and commands into a computer system, the system typically displays the output of these operations on a video display monitor. The CPU computes and determines what you see. Because your main interaction with a computer system is primarily visual, understanding how this works is important. In this lesson you will learn about the basic components of the video adapter, how it functions, and how to choose a good video adapter.

The **video adapter**, also called the video card, translates data from the CPU into a format that the **video display monitor** can use. As you have learned, computer system input and output is in a digital form and uses 1s and 0s. However, the display circuitry on the actual system video display monitor is analog rather than digital. The video adapter converts the CPU's digital output into analog signals that the monitor can show.

## Digital versus analog displays

IBM introduced a new line of computer systems in 1987 called the PS/2. Introduced with this new line was the analog display that still forms the basis of modern video displays.

Based on studies showing that **color gradation** was more important to human perception than **resolution**, IBM chose to use the analog display format because analog displays can show more gradations of color than digital displays and are therefore more appealing. This display was called the **video graphics array (VGA)** and soon displaced earlier standards such as **monochrome display adapter (MDA)**, **color graphics array (CGA)**, and **enhanced graphics array (EGA)**. Subsequently, VGA became the basis for all video display technology.

IBM continued to develop the VGA adapter along its proprietary lines. However, competitors soon formed a standard that eventually became **super VGA (SVGA)**.

## Components of the SVGA display adapter

All video cards in use today have four major components that collectively function to generate a video display: the video chipset, video memory, video BIOS, and the RAMDAC chip. The following sections discuss each of these components in detail.

### *The video chipset*

The **video chipset**, or video processor, is the collection of logic chips that perform the main processing functions of the video card.

On newer video cards, the chipset is usually composed of one or two chips, one of which is called an **accelerator**.

Imagine that you are using a graphics application to draw a box on the video monitor. When the system CPU issues a series of commands to draw a box on the video monitor, it sends the request to the video card to draw a window at a certain location. The video chipset handles this function.

## *Video memory*

The video chipset relies on **video memory** to render the image requested. The basic element of every video image is a **dot** (or **pixel**). Many dots comprise what you see displayed on the monitor. Every dot has a location reserved in video memory. The maximum number of dots that can be displayed relates to the resolution.

Resolution is commonly expressed as a pair of numbers. Each pair of numbers represents the maximum possible number of dots on a horizontal axis and the maximum possible number dots on a vertical axis. Therefore, the basic VGA resolution of 640 x 480 means that there are 640 possible dots on the horizontal axis, and 480 possible dots on the vertical axis. Enhanced VGA has a resolution of 800 by 600 dots. Super VGA has a resolution of 1024 by 768 dots. From these examples, it is easy to see that the higher the resolution, the more memory that will be required to draw the image. However, it is also easy to see that the higher the resolution, the sharper and clearer the image.

When an image is displayed in color (or grayscale), a certain number of bits must be assigned per dot (that is, per pixel) to achieve a given color depth or possible number of colors. The more bits assigned, the more colors or shades that can be presented.

To see how video memory impacts the execution of graphics applications, let's return to our previous example. Imagine once again that you are using a graphics application to draw a box on the monitor screen. When the system CPU issues a series of commands to draw a box, it issues commands to the video memory to draw the box.

## *Video BIOS*

Although the CPU issues instructions to the video card about what to draw, the CPU does not tell the video card *how* to draw. How the image is to be displayed is the responsibility of the **video BIOS**. The video BIOS provides the set of video functions that can be used by the software programs to access the video hardware. The video BIOS allows software to interface with the video chipset in much the same way as the system BIOS does for the motherboard chipset.

When SVGA technology became an industry norm, incompatibilities in the different video BIOS implementations led to the development of a standardized BIOS.

## *The RAMDAC chip*

The display information stored and manipulated in the video memory is in the standard binary format of 1s and 0s. These binary patterns control the resolution and color of each pixel on the video display screen. However, monitors are analog, not digital, devices. In order for the monitor to work, the digital information in the video memory must be translated into analog form for export to the monitor screen. This is the role of the **random access memory digital-to-analog converter (RAMDAC)** chip.

The RAMDAC chip reads the video memory contents, converts it to analog, and sends it over a cable to the video monitor. The quality of this chip affects the quality of the image, speed of the **refresh rate**, and maximum resolution capability. Refresh rate refers to the number of times per second that the video display screen can be redrawn.

# Video performance constraints

Most video cards since the mid-1990s can process commands as quickly as the system CPU can send them. The main bottleneck limiting performance is the speed of the I/O bus through which the video card interfaces with the CPU. The original SVGA video adapters were installed on the ISA bus with a slow 8-MHz bus speed. Almost all new video cards since the mid-1990s have been developed on the relatively high-performance 33-MHz PCI local bus. This bus is connected to the CPU processor bus via a bridge chip. The PCI bus supports a 4-byte data transfer with every cycle of the 33-MHz bus clock. The PCI bus's total transfer rate is 133 MHz per second.

This relationship of local bus video card to CPU processor bus has continued to develop. The most recent development has been the **accelerated graphics port (AGP)** on Pentium II CPU motherboards, pioneered by the Intel Corporation. The AGP port is a special local bus slot with direct access to the processor bus feeding the Pentium II CPU. Instead of relying on a slower I/O bus clock, this local bus supports a 4-byte data transfer twice with every cycle of the 66-Mhz processor bus clock. This is approximately four times faster than with the PCI bus.

Another major factor influencing the performance of video adapters is the type of video RAM used. The standard until very recently has been DRAM. This is the same type traditionally used in main system memory. DRAM is the slowest type because it constantly needs to be refreshed and cannot read information at the same time it is outputting it. EDO RAM is more effective because it can be refreshed with incoming data while simultaneously outputting.

The best kind of memory for video is called **video RAM (VRAM)** or **window RAM (WRAM)**. Both VRAM and WRAM are optimized for video cards and are designed to be **dual-ported**. This means that the chipset processor and RAMDAC chip can access the memory at the same time. Simultaneous access greatly increases video throughput. The newest types of video cards also support the newest system RAM types such as SDRAM.

Finally, another issue that potentially limits video performance is the memory bus width that governs access from the chipset to the video memory. Most high-end adapters have a 64-bit or even 128-bit memory bus for the graphics chip to video memory.

# Video card developments

The growth of multimedia applications has seen the increased consolidation of secondary video capabilities in video adapters. Capabilities such as desktop video, capturing and manipulating film sequences, and 2D/3D graphics that once required expensive secondary cards are increasingly being incorporated as extra chips or coprocessors in video adapter board chipsets.

# Choosing a video card

You should think about the following when choosing a video card:

- Look for high **non-interlaced** screen resolution support. This should mean high refresh rates at higher resolutions. This is typically 80 Hz or better at 1024 x 768 resolution.

- The width of the memory interface should be at least 64 bits.

- The **frame buffer**, which is the maximum area of memory that can hold a video image at a time, should be at least 2 MB, and 8 MB or higher is even better.

- Buy an AGP card for a video adapter, if the motherboard has an AGP slot.

- The conversion rate of the RAMDAC dictates the speed at which pixels can be rendered. Current video cards include RAMDACs with conversion rates of greater than 200 MHz.

- Hardware support for the **MPEG codec** is a standard compression. Playback algorithm is recommended. Also look for hardware support for 2D/3D graphics such as 2D scrolling, plane support, and open GL support.

- The video card should include support for the newer types of video memory such as SDRAM.

- Make sure the feature set or specifications include a driver for the desired operating system.

# Concept Questions     *Semester 1, Unit 8, Lesson 36*

Demonstrate your knowledge of the concepts in this lesson by answering the following questions in the space provided.

1. Explain why you should read the documentation that accompanies a video card to determine if it meets your needs.

2. Explain the criteria you should look for when determining whether a video card meets your needs.

_____

_____

_____

_____

_____

_____

_____

_____

_____

_____

_____

_____

_____

_____

_____

_____

_____

# Vocabulary Exercise     *Semester 1, Unit 8, Lesson 36*

*Name:* _____

*Date:* _____     *Class:* _____

Define the following terms as completely as you can.

**CGA**

_____

_____

**color grading**

_____

_____

**EGA**

_____

_____

**MDA**

_____

_____

**RAMDAC**

_____

_____

**SVGA**

_____

_____

*VGA*

_____

_____

**video adapter**

_____

_____

**video BIOS**

_____

_____

**video chipset**

_____

_____

**video memory**

_____

_____

# Focus Questions

## *Semester 1, Unit 8, Lesson 36*

*Name:* _____

*Date:* _____    *Class:* _____

**1.** What does a video adapter do, and why is it needed?

_____

_____

_____

_____

**2.** Describe what is meant by the refresh rate and why this is important to the user.

_____

_____

_____

_____

**3.** What is a video chipset, and what does it do?

_____

_____

_____

_____

**4.** What is the AGP port, and what does it do?

_____

_____

_____

_____

# SEMESTER 1, UNIT 8, LESSON 37
# Video Display Monitors

You have learned about video display adapters and their function, components, and specifications. However, video adapters are only half of the video subsystem on computer systems. The other half is the video display monitor, also called the display monitor, or simply the monitor. The ultimate usability of the computer is based on the quality of the video display. If the monitor display quality is poor, the usability of the computer system is extremely impaired. This lesson covers the basics of monitor design, construction, and function.

Essentially, the display monitor takes the output from the video card and displays it according to the dictates of the card's RAMDAC chip.

Although there are different technologies for video display monitors, the one currently in widespread use is the cathode ray tube (CRT). The other, the liquid crystal display (LCD), is mainly used on laptop computers, although this is beginning to change.

## CRT display monitors

There are five main functional components to the CRT display monitor:

- The monitor case

- The CRT

- Control circuitry

- The power supply

- The interface and cabling

The following sections describe the first three of these in detail.

### *The monitor case*

The case is the outer plastic housing, which protects the CRT and electronic circuitry. The controls are usually displayed along the front bottom, and ventilation slots and holes allow heat to escape from the components inside. The base of the case contains a stand that allows the monitor to be adjusted.

### *The CRT*

Televisions as well as monitors use CRTs to display images onscreen. Basically, a CRT is a large vacuum tube enclosed in glass. It has an **electron gun** at the rear, and a phosphorescent screen at the inside front end. By applying a large voltage to the filament of the CRT, a beam of **electrons** is accelerated to the screen at the other end of the vacuum tube.

These electrons are focused and steered by a **deflection coil**, also referred to as a deflection plate. The electron streams paint a picture on the screen by starting at the top of the screen, and moving from left to right. This action, called **scanning**, is repeated until the entire screen is painted, from top to bottom. This entire operation is directed by output from the video card.

Each position on the screen is a composite of three different dots, consisting of the different phosphor chemicals. When they are excited by the electron stream, they glow with the computer monitor's primary colors: red, green, and blue. The combination of these three dots is called a *pixel*. Sometimes, the electron gun is actually three guns arranged in a triangular arrangement, called a *delta configuration*. Each gun emits an electron stream specifically aimed at one of the three primary color dots in the pixel.

The redrawing of a screen is called a **refresh**, and the speed at which it happens is called the **refresh rate**. During a refresh, electronic beams fill the screen with lines from top to bottom. Refresh rates are differ from monitor to monitor.

The refresh rate is actually comprised of independent **horizontal** and **vertical scan rates**. The horizontal scan rate is expressed in kilohertz (KHz). The horizontal scan rate is the number of lines that can be painted horizontally on the screen each second. The vertical scan rate, on the other hand, tells you how often the screen is repainted from the top to the bottom line each second. This is expressed in hertz (Hz). Higher vertical refresh rate means less flicker and therefore less user eye strain. Higher horizontal and vertical scan rates combine to provide a usable, flicker-free image.

The CRT can have a **fixed refresh rate** or a **multifrequency rate**. The multifrequency type is now the most common because it supports multiple video signals and various resolutions.

## *The control circuitry*

The **control circuitry** is the dedicated electrical component that reads in the output from the video card RAMDAC chip and controls the electron beam scanning on the CRT. The control circuitry can be manually manipulated by external controls mounted on the front lower bezel of the monitor case.

There are usually three groups of monitor controls: basic, geometric, and color controls. Basic controls are used to adjust brightness, contrast, horizontal sizing and centering, and vertical sizing and centering. Geometric controls such as tilt and pincushion help optimize the image at various displayed resolutions. Color controls allow users to optimize their color display for the room lighting and monitor position.

# LCD display monitors

LCD screens are ideal for modern lightweight laptop computers for two reasons. First, they are low glare due to their flat screen. Second, they have very low power requirements. In fact, some require as little as 5 watts. The downside to LCDs over traditional CRTs for mobile computers are more limited resolutions, smaller size, and high cost. There are two types of LCD displays: passive matrix and active matrix.

## *Passive-matrix LCD display monitors*

In passive-matrix LCD displays, the transistors are arranged along the edge of the display screen. They send electrical impulses through the cells in columns and rows, corresponding to their position along the top and sides of the screen.

## *Active-matrix LCD display monitors*

In active-matrix LCD displays, each cell has its own transistor to charge it, giving greater control and contrast capability. Because each cell has its own transistor, there is no pulsing of the electrical current shared by all cells in a column or row, and the individual cell has its own constant charge. More crucially, each color cell of the pixel has a transistor. There is one each for red, green, and blue.

# Concept Questions          *Semester 1, Unit 8, Lesson 37*

Demonstrate your knowledge of the concepts in this lesson by answering the following questions in the space provided.

*1.* Explain how the CRT works.

*2.* Explain the advantages and types of LCD display monitors.

_____

_____

_____

_____

_____

_____

_____

_____

_____

_____

_____

_____

_____

_____

_____

_____

# Vocabulary Exercise     *Semester 1, Unit 8, Lesson 37*

*Name:* _____

*Date:* _____     *Class:* _____

Define the following terms as completely as you can.

**CRT**

_____

_____

**deflection coil**

_____

_____

**display monitor**

_____

_____

**fixed refresh rate**

_____

_____

**horizontal scan rate**

_____

_____

**LCD**

_____

_____

***vertical scan rate***

_____

_____

***video display monitor***

_____

_____

# Focus Questions

## *Semester 1, Unit 8, Lesson 37*

*Name:* _____

*Date:* _____  *Class:* _____

Before trying to answer the exercises in this lesson, follow these instructions: From the Desktop, go to Settings, and click on Control Panel. From the Control Panel menu, select Display. From the Display Properties dialog box, choose the Settings tab. Click on the drop-down arrow in the Color Palette section.

**1.** How many bits are required for High Color, and why?

_____

_____

_____

_____

**2.** How many bits are required for True Color, and why?

_____

_____

_____

_____

**3.** How much memory is required to draw an image if you have set the resolution of your monitor at 1024 x 768 and selected High Color? Explain why.

_____

_____

_____

_____

_____

**4.** Describe the monitor case and its function.

_____

_____

_____

_____

# SEMESTER 1, UNIT 8, LESSON 38
# Monitor Display Specifications

It is important to examine the monitor's specifications to determine the utility of the device for the user. This lesson deals with the various types of monitor specifications, including the following, in more detail:

- Screen size and viewable area specifications

- Dot pitch specifications

- Shadow mask specifications

- Screen treatment specifications

- Input signal specifications

- Video input connector specifications

- Video bandwidth specifications

- Displayable and recommended resolution specifications

- Supported resolutions specifications

- Control specifications

- Power and management specifications

- Power source specifications

- Form factor specifications

Caution: Remember that you should not open a monitor unless you have the appropriate tools and training to avoid the dangerous voltage.

## Screen size and viewable area specifications

The viewable area of the monitor screen is distinct from the screen size. **Screen size** is what the manufacturer measures as the diagonal width of the monitor from one corner of the screen to the opposite corner. The **viewable area** is smaller than the screen size because the screen image always has a non-usable black border around it. For example, in the CRT section of the linked specification list, the manufacturer might list a 17-inch screen size and a 16-inch viewable size.

# Dot pitch specifications

**Dot pitch** is the distance between adjacent sets of red, green, and blue dots. Dot pitch defines how fine the dots are that make up the image. The smaller the distance between the dots, the sharper the image. Dot pitch measurements can be confusing. For example, a 0.26-mm dot pitch is better than a 0.28-mm dot pitch because the distance between the dots is smaller, and therefore better. A high-resolution capable monitor should have a dot pitch of 0.28 mm or better, for fine graphics and text.

# Shadow mask specifications

Another important specification to look at is the quality of the **shadow mask**. Large, bright display screens can produce heat that can distort a cheap metal mask, consequently distorting the displayed image. A manufacturer may indicate that it uses the **Invar** metal alloy shadow mask, which can handle more heat without distortion.

# Screen treatment specifications

The **screen treatments** given for a CRT can affect usability. Quality monitors generally have tinted screens with antistatic and antiglare surface treatments. The antistatic coating lessens the display's vulnerability to disruption from electrostatic discharge, and also keeps dust attraction to a minimum. The antiglare treatment helps keep user eye fatigue to a minimum during long periods in front of the monitor. The screen treatment specifications indicate whether these treatments have been applied to the monitor.

# Input signal specifications

The **input signal** specification simply states what kind of video input the monitor uses. RGB Analog is the standard for monitors today.

# Video input connector specifications

**Scanning frequency** is another important specification that governs the refresh rate. You need to make sure that the minimum frequency for both horizontal and vertical scan rates is well within the range of the monitor for good performance. The manufacturer might list a horizontal scan range of 30 KHz–95 KHz and a vertical scan range of 50 Hz–150 Hz.

The **Video Electronics Standards Association (VESA)** has established minimum scanning frequencies. For extremely sharp displays at higher resolutions, look for capabilities exceeding 75 Hz in vertical frequency and horizontal frequencies of up to 90 KHz or more.

# Video bandwidth specifications

A less important but potentially useful specification is the **video bandwidth** supported by the monitor. Video bandwidth is the range of signal frequencies the monitor can handle. This determines how much data it can process at a time. As you learned earlier, the video memory on the video adapter holds images in areas of memory called frames. The maximum amount of memory that it can hold per frame determines how much it can send to the monitor at once. The minimum standard for SVGA resolution of 1024 x 768 at 24 bits and 85 Hz is 133.7 MHz. So a manufacturer's rating for monitor video bandwidth of over 130 MHz is a good one.

# Displayable and recommended resolution specifications

The resolution specification states the maximum **displayable resolution** and **recommended resolutions** for the monitor screen size. Even though a monitor can display a certain resolution does not mean the resolution is useful for the user.

For example, your new 15-inch monitor might support 1280 x 1024 resolution, but the display might not be readable. This is because as the resolutions become higher, the pixels become smaller, and so too high a resolution for a screen size makes the display difficult to view comfortably.

For instance, a manufacturer might list a displayable resolution of 1600 x 1200 and recommended resolution of 1280 x 1024 at 85 Hz. Therefore, this manufacturer is stating that the recommended maximum for this model's screen size is 1280 x 1024 for optimal viewing. In this case, if the user set the resolution to the maximum 1600 x 1200, the windows might be too small to read comfortably.

# Supported resolutions specifications

Another useful specification is the range of supported resolutions. This is the range of resolutions supported by the monitor, such as up to 1600 x 1200.

# Control specifications

A very important specification for usability is the range of **user controls** available to adjust the operating parameters of the monitor. This not only includes the basics such as power switch, horizontal/vertical size (H/V size), horizontal/vertical position (H/V position), pincushion, contrast, and brightness, but other optional controls as well. In earlier computers, these controls were dials, and they were easy to adjust. Today's monitors are pushbutton and have their own programming. Users must read the directions to figure out how to adjust the user controls.

## Power and management specifications

Power and management specifications can also be indicators that the monitor's control circuitry is compliant with known standards of power conservation and consumption. For example, a monitor may be rated as **Energy Star** on the power section of the specification list. This means it is certified by the Environmental Protection Agency (EPA) as meeting the EPA's reduced power guidelines during inactive periods. It may also be specified as **VESA DPMS** compliant in power management.

## Power source specifications

The **low radiation** specification is an extremely important one for health reasons. All monitors produce electromagnetic emissions when the electron beam paints the image to the screen. As with televisions, the long-term effects of very low-frequency and extremely low-frequency emissions on people have been of concern to the health industry for 20 years. In response to these concerns, the Swedish regulatory agency, SWEDAC, established a monitor-emission standard called MPR. The latest version, **MPRII**, from 1990, is the current standard for emission certification and has become the de facto standard for all internationally marketed quality monitors.

## Form factor specifications

There are two specifications included in the form factor specification: dimension and weight. They are important when considering where to place the monitor and what to use to support the monitor. Too frequently, people do not consider these factors until the placement becomes critical in a cramped space, or the support is too flimsy.

# Concept Questions    *Semester 1, Unit 8, Lesson 38*

Demonstrate your knowledge of the concepts in this lesson by answering the following questions in the space provided.

*1.* Explain what monitor specifications are and how you interpret them.

*2.* How does the screen size differ from the viewable area?

_____

_____

_____

_____

_____

_____

_____

_____

_____

_____

_____

_____

_____

_____

_____

_____

_____

_____

# Vocabulary Exercise    *Semester 1, Unit 8, Lesson 38*

Name: _____

Date: _____    Class: _____

Define the following terms as completely as you can.

**displayable resolution**

_____

_____

**dot pitch**

_____

_____

**input signal**

_____

_____

**Invar**

_____

_____

**screen size**

_____

_____

**screen treatment**

_____

_____

**shadow mask**

_____

_____

**video bandwidth**

_____

_____

**viewable area**

_____

_____

# Focus Questions

## *Semester 1, Unit 8, Lesson 38*

*Name:* _____

*Date:* _____ *Class:* _____

**1.** What is dot pitch, and what is the minimum dot pitch specification?

_____

_____

_____

_____

**2.** What type of video input connector should generally be used?

_____

_____

_____

_____

**3.** What type of material should be used for the shadow mask?

_____

_____

_____

_____

**4.** What types of screen treatments should be used?

_____

_____

_____

_____

**5.** What kind of input signal specification should be listed?

_____

_____

_____

_____

**6.** What should the video bandwidth specification be?

_____

_____

_____

_____

# Semester 1, Unit 8, Lesson 39
# Monitor Installation Lab Exercises

If you have access to the online Aries A+ curriculum, go online to follow along with this lab exercise. If you do not have access to the online curriculum, please continue to the next lesson.

# SEMESTER 1, UNIT 8, LESSON 40
# Unit 8 Exam

If you have access to the online Aries A+ curriculum, contact your instructor for the Assessment System URL. If you do not have access to the online curriculum, please continue to Unit 9.

# SEMESTER 1, UNIT 9

- Lesson 41: Introduction to Data Communication Devices
- Lesson 42: Serial and Parallel Communication
- Lesson 43: Modems
- Lesson 44: How Modems Work
- Lesson 45: Unit 9 Exam

# SEMESTER 1, UNIT 9, LESSON 41
# Introduction to Data Communication Devices

You have learned some basics about video adapters and about monitor design, construction, function, and specifications. In this lesson, you will get an overview of the different communication systems and their devices, such as modems, serial and parallel ports, universal serial buses, and networks.

## Data communications systems

A data communications system transmits electronic data over communication channels from one location to another. You are using data communications whenever you talk to a friend online, send an e-mail or a fax, or go online to check your bank account. Some of the main components of a data communications system are as follows:

- **Modems**—A modem, whether it is internal or external to the computer, sends and receives data from one computer to another by converting the computer's electronic signals from digital to **analog** and transmitting them over a telephone line. At the other end of the line, a computer translates these signals from analog to digital with its modem.

- **Serial ports**—A serial port is a socket used to connect a modem, scanner, mouse, or other device that uses a **serial interface**. In serial data transmission, bits flow in a continuous series, one at a time, like a train on a one-way track. Modems require a serial connection to the telephone system.

- **Parallel ports**—A computer's parallel port is a socket connecting the computer to a printer or another peripheral device such as a portable hard disk, a tape backup, or a CD-ROM. With parallel transmission, bits flow through separate lines simultaneously, in parallel, like two trains moving side-by-side at the same time on different tracks. Parallel transmission is limited to short distances because it uses lower voltage levels (to represent 1s and 0s) than a serial port.

- **Universal serial buses**—Intel developed the **universal serial bus (USB)** for connecting peripherals to a microcomputer. A USB offers a bandwidth of 12 Mbps. The USB port can connect up to 127 plug-and-play peripherals, such as printers, modems, keyboards, and mouse devices. Operating systems that support USBs include Windows 95, Windows 98, and Windows NT.

## Networks

A **network** interconnects all client and server stations, and it supports hardware and software. Some terms associated with networks are **client**, **host**, **node**, **server**, and **network operating system**.

### Network topologies

A network can be arranged in several different ways, called **topologies**. The four typical network topologies are star, bus, ring, and hierarchical. The following sections describe these four network topologies.

### Star networks

A **star network** links several computers or peripheral devices to a central unit, which could be a host computer or a file server.

### Bus networks

A **bus network** allows each device within the network to handle its own communications control. There is no host computer because all the communications travel along a common connecting cable, called a bus.

### Ring networks

On a **ring network**, each device connects with two other devices that form a ring. There is no host computer. This is the least commonly used of the four network topologies.

### Hierarchical networks

A **hierarchical network** contains several computers linked to a central host computer. Although it is similar to a star network, the computers in a hierarchical network are also linked to other smaller computers or peripheral devices, which give it the hierarchical structure. The host could be a mainframe, and the linking computers could be minicomputers that are linked to microcomputers.

## Types of networks: LANs, MANs, and WANs

A **local-area network (LAN)** connects computers or peripheral devices that are in close proximity to one another—sometimes within the same building. Telephone, coaxial, or fiber-optic cables link the computers together within the network. Business benefits of using a LAN include sharing information, printers, and file servers.

A **metropolitan-area network (MAN)** links office buildings together within a city.

A **wide-area network (WAN)** is potentially a wider-reaching network, connecting nodes countrywide or even worldwide. Microwave relays and satellites allow users to be linked to other computers. The Internet, the most common WAN, allows users to connect with other users worldwide.

# Concept Questions        *Semester 1, Unit 9, Lesson 41*

Demonstrate your knowledge of the concepts in this lesson by answering the following questions in the space provided.

1. How do data communication systems function, and what is their contribution to personal and business computer users?

2. Explain how bus, hierarchical, star, and ring networks are organized and when you might want to use each.

_____

_____

_____

_____

_____

_____

_____

_____

_____

_____

_____

_____

_____

_____

# Vocabulary Exercise          *Semester 1, Unit 9, Lesson 41*

*Name:* _____

*Date:* _____    *Class:* _____

Define the following terms as completely as you can.

**bus network**

_____

_____

**hierarchical network**

_____

_____

**LAN**

_____

_____

**MAN**

_____

_____

**parallel port**

_____

_____

**ring network**

_____

_____

**serial port**

_____

_____


**star network**

_____

_____


**USB**

_____

_____


**WAN**

_____

_____

# Focus Questions          *Semester 1, Unit 9, Lesson 41*

*Name:* _____

*Date:* _____     *Class:* _____


**1.** Describe the similarities and differences between a USB, a parallel port, and a serial port.

_____

_____

_____

_____


**2.** What technology enables WAN networks to link computer users worldwide?

_____

_____

_____

_____


**3.** What technology enables LAN networks to link computer users?

_____

_____

_____

_____

# SEMESTER 1, UNIT 9, LESSON 42
# Serial and Parallel Communication

In this section you will learn about the standard I/O ports, such as parallel ports and serial ports, and how they are used in communication. The standard ports on the back of a PC are the following:

- Keyboard connector

- Mouse connector

- Video connector

- Serial port 1 connector

- Serial port 2 connector

- Parallel port connector

- Universal serial bus (USB)

The mouse and keyboard connectors are round, 6-pin connectors that look alike. The video connector uses a 15-pin, high-density port that allows you to connect a VGA or an SVGA monitor to a computer. The serial port typically uses a two-row, 9-pin connector, and the parallel port uses a two-row, 25-pin connector. With a USB, which uses a 4-pin socket, it is safe to plug or unplug peripheral devices while the computer is running.

## Parallel ports

A parallel port is a socket on the computer used to connect a printer or other peripheral device such as a portable hard disk, tape backup, or CD-ROM. The parallel port contains eight lines for transmitting an entire byte (8 bits) across the eight data lines simultaneously.

The parallel port interface offers 8-bit parallel data words and nine I/O control lines at a 25-pin female **DB**-25 socket located on the back of the system unit. Parallel ports can be configured as LPT1, LPT2, or LPT3.

Data is transmitted over a parallel cable that should be shorter than 15 feet long. Cables that are too long can create errors. Therefore, to ensure data validity, parallel cables should never be longer than 15 feet.

Parallel ports were originally used for printers, but today they can be used for both data input and output devices. This type of parallel port is called *bidirectional* and is often used for rapid transmission of data over short distances. Newer, enhanced parallel ports can be converted from unidirectional to bidirectional through the CMOS setup screen.

The parallel printer interface in early PCs was located on the back of the video adapter card, on a multiple I/O card, or on a dedicated parallel printer card. Today, on Pentium system boards, the parallel port is located directly on the back plate of an I/O card, or it is connected through a ribbon cable to a 25-pin connector on the back of the unit.

# Serial ports

A serial port can be used to connect a modem, scanner, mouse, or other device that uses a serial interface. A common usage of a serial port is to connect a modem, which requires a serial connection to the telephone system. A PC can identify up to four serial ports, but the typical computer contains only two: COM1 and COM2. The serial port is sometimes called the RS-232 port because it uses the RS-232C standard of the **Electronics Industry Association (EIA)**.

Unlike parallel ports, a serial port transmits data bits one after the other (serially) over a single line. Additionally, files can be transferred between two PCs by using **File Transfer Protocol (FTP)**.

The serial port uses a DB-9 connector. The mouse is sometimes used in serial port 1, called COM1, which is a 9-pin male connector. The modem is typically used in serial port 2, called COM2, which is a 9-pin male connector. Both serial ports are located in the back of the computer system. Older computers used a 25-pin connector for the serial port interface.

Table 9-1 shows the 9-pin and 25-pin serial port specifications.

**Table 9-1**    *9- and 25-pin specifications*

| Pin Number for 9-pin | Pin Number for 25-pin | Description | LED Light |
|---|---|---|---|
| 1 | 8 | Carrier is detected—a connection with remote is made. | CD |
| 2 | 3 | Receiving data. | RXD or RD |
| 3 | 2 | Transmitting data. | TXD or SD |
| 4 | 20 | Data terminal is ready. | DTR or TR |
| 5 | 7 | Signal ground—not used with PCs. | — |
| 6 | 6 | Data set is ready—modem is able to talk. | MR |
| 7 | 4 | Request to send—computer wants to talk. | RTS |
| 8 | 5 | Clear to send—modem is ready to talk. | CTS |
| 9 | 22 | Ring indicator—someone is calling. | — |

Serial port information is associated with a specific memory address range and **interrupt request lines (IRQs)**. Only one device can reside at a particular address. When you have two serial ports at the same address, at least one serial device won't work. Table 9-2 show the default port assignments on many computers.

**Table 9-2**    *Default port assignments*

| Port | IRQ | I/O Address |
|------|-----|-------------|
| *Serial Ports* | | |
| COM1 | IRQ 4 | 03F8 |
| COM2 | IRQ 3 | 02F8 |
| COM3 | IRQ 4 | 03E8 |
| COM4 | IRQ 3 | 02E8 |
| *Parallel Ports* | | |
| LPT1 | IRQ 7 | 0378 |
| LPT2 | IRQ 5 | 0278 |

In older computers, the serial port circuits are contained on an expansion card that plugs into an expansion slot inside the computer. Usually, one parallel port, two serial ports, and one game port are all included in this one expansion card. In newer computers, these ports are built on to the motherboard.

## Adding more ports

You can upgrade a PC by adding more ports to it through special expansion cards that equip the PC with additional serial or parallel ports. The expansion cards plug into slots on the motherboard and extend additional ports out the back of the PC.

After you add a port, you need to assign it an address, via the operating system. If your computer doesn't have any available IRQs for the new ports, however, upgrading may be useless.

## Serial interface chips

Manufacturers have developed various single-chip devices that perform all the functions necessary for serial transfers to occur. Serial ports are controlled by a chip called the **universal asynchronous receiver/transmitter (UART)**. The UART chip controls all nine serial port pins, establishes the communication protocol, and transforms the parallel data bits to serial bits for transmission (and vice versa for reception).

The 8-bit 8250 was the first UART chip, and a later version was the 16-bit 16450 chip. A newer high-end version of this chip is called a 16550 UART. The 16550 chip contains a **first-in, first-out (FIFO)** buffer that minimizes the problem of data loss that sometimes occurred with the earlier 16450 UART chips. The FIFO buffer permits FIFO processing, which enhances transfer rate by buffering the transmit/receive signal.

# Concept Questions            *Semester 1, Unit 9, Lesson 42*

Demonstrate your knowledge of the concepts in this lesson by answering the following questions in the space provided.

**1.** What are the standard ports on the back of a PC, and what are they used for?

**2.** How can you upgrade a PC by adding more ports?

_____

_____

_____

_____

_____

_____

_____

_____

_____

_____

_____

_____

_____

_____

_____

_____

_____

_____

# Vocabulary Exercise      *Semester 1, Unit 9, Lesson 42*

*Name:* _____

*Date:* _____      *Class:* _____

Define the following terms as completely as you can.

### EIA

_____

_____

### FIFO

_____

_____

### FTP

_____

_____

### IRQ

_____

_____

### UART

_____

_____

# Focus Questions

## *Semester 1, Unit 9, Lesson 42*

*Name:* _____

*Date:* _____    *Class:* _____

**1.** Describe the mouse and keyboard connectors.

_____

_____

_____

_____

**2.** Describe the video connector.

_____

_____

_____

_____

**3.** Describe the serial port connector.

_____

_____

_____

_____

**4.** Describe the USB.

_____

_____

_____

_____

**5.** What happens when you have two serial ports at the same address?

_____

_____

_____

_____

# SEMESTER 1, UNIT 9, LESSON 43
# Modems

Computers today are commonly used for a variety of purposes, including connecting to remote computers in other locations. People dial in to the Internet, telecommute, and regularly exchange data between computers through telephone lines. All this communicating is possible in part because of modems. Although there are many types of specialized modems, this lesson focuses on the only modem commonly used in computer systems—the asynchronous modem—and the processes of modem-based communications.

**Modulating** and **demodulating** describe how a modem, an electronic computer communication device, sends data signals over the telephone line. The basic purpose of a modem is to enable two computers to send and receive data via a telephone line. The modem must convert digital data from its local computer into analog tones and pulses that can be sent over the telephone line; then the modem at the other end converts these signals back into data to be processed by the receiving computer system. The period of communication between these modems is called a *session*. Modem-equipped computers can communicate via the standard **public switched telephone network (PSTN)**.

Modems are available in two basic form factors: external and internal. External modems sit outside the computer system and are linked to it by a cable, typically attached to an RS-232 serial I/O port. An external modem has its own power supply and has a plug-in port for a telephone line, which goes from the I/O port to the wall plug-in and from there to the PSTN. All communications between external modems and the system CPU go through this same I/O port.

An internal modem is plugged into an expansion slot on the ISA bus of the system motherboard. An internal modem communicates directly with the system CPU by means of this bus, without a serial port, relying on the motherboard for its power.

## How modems communicate

Modem communications consist of two processes. One of these processes occurs between the modem and its host computer system at the beginning and the end of a session. The other key process is the communication between the modems over the telephone line. The following sections discuss these two processes in detail.

### *Communication between the modem and the host system*

Before transmitting any messages to a remote computer, the communication session begins internally between the system CPU and its modem, using system software programs. When running, the CPU uses instructions provided by the software to send binary data to the modem via the system I/O bus.

When an external modem is used, the data goes through the I/O bus to the serial port at the back of the motherboard and across the serial cable to the modem. Because an internal modem has its own serial port built in to the circuitry, data arrives via the ISA bus slot where the modem is installed.

Whether internal or external, serial ports, also called COM ports, are asynchronous serial interfaces. This means that, once the data bits leave the I/O bus through this serial port, the bus clock no longer controls them. No longer synchronized, or evenly spaced apart, by the clock governing the data bus, data is sent and received serially over two pins in the serial port. In the standard 9-pin serial interface, pins 2 and 3 are used for receiving and transmitting data. When a 25-pin interface is used, pins 2 and 3 also send and receive data transmission. The remaining pins in these interfaces are used for signaling line status or for controlling the data flow.

Each byte (or **character**, as it's called in asynchronous communications) lines up in a series and is framed by standard **stop** and **start bits**. The start bit is identified by the number 0 that precedes every byte to tell the receiving system that the next 8 bits constitute a byte of data. The **stop bit** is a binary 1 or 0 that follows the byte. It signals the remote system that a byte of data has been sent. The receiving system recognizes the data bits and their sequence by the stop and start signals that substitute for the clock synchronization.

Internally, data travels over the ISA bus in a parallel manner (that is, simultaneously). This is possible because each bit is sent by means of its own wire. When this data needs to be sent over the serial port, it must be converted to a serial format, which allows only 1 bit of data to be sent at a time. Thus, data sent in serial format, as sequential bits.

The component used to convert data from the parallel format to a serial format and then back again is a UART chip. Every I/O bus signal to the CPU requires an IRQ to gain the CPU's attention for data reception. COM ports are no exception to this rule, and each is assigned an IRQ as well as an I/O (memory) address for caching data into the system memory.

For the times when the host system CPU is too busy to accept data from the serial port, in modern PCs the 16550 UART chip has a 16-byte (128-bit) buffer built in for temporary storage until it can send this data to the CPU. In the reverse direction, the modem can use a method called **flow control** to manage the rate at which the host system sends data to it.

When an external modem is used, the rate of host system data is controlled with modem hardware that sends **request-to-send/clear-to-send (RTS/CTS)** signals on dedicated wires in the cable. When an internal slotted modem is used, rate of data flow is controlled with card/edge connectors that govern the data flow rate to the host system.

## Communication between two modems

Because modems communicate with computers, they must be able to understand the same sorts of digital languages computers use. However, modems must also be able to understand and use another type of language as well—the language used by telephone circuits. Because signals carried on the **local loop** of the telephone system are often analog signals rather than digital, modems must be able to understand and use both digital and analog data signals.

The job of the modem is to take digital data signals and convert them into analog signals that can be transmitted over telephone lines, and then change them back again into the original format at the receiving end. Modems can replicate the peaks and valleys of analog signals digitally, just like an **analog-to-digital converter**. When digital signals are converted into analog, and then back to digital, some signal degradation, called **noise**, occurs.

However, because analog circuits do not cross entirely through the telephone network, the communication session is made even more complex. Only the portion of the telephone network from a home or business to the phone company central switch uses analog signals, and the rest of the telephone network uses digital data. Therefore, the modem analog signal must be converted into digital form at the central phone switch, sent across the phone network, and then converted back again into an analog signal.

The difference between the original analog signal and the reconstructed analog signal causes **quantization noise**. If too much of this type of noise is combined with the original conversion noise, the signal can be completely drowned out. Therefore, engineers have determined that the theoretical limit of modem technology is about 35 Kbps. Not surprisingly, modem manufacturers have found ways to minimize the problems of noise and speed limits.

## Transmission limits and line noise

The way modems deal with transmission speed limits on telephone lines is to follow internationally defined standards to allow two modems to talk to each other. Over the years an organization called the **International Telecommunications Union (ITU)**, also formerly called the **Consultative Committee on International Telephone and Telegraph (CCITT)**, has formulated a set of modulation standards that govern the basic rate or speed of modem communications.

The speed of the connection is usually expressed in **bits per second (bps)**. This is commonly mistaken for the **baud rate**, which is the rate at which a signal between two devices changes in 1 second. The bit rate depends upon how many bits are transmitted per modulation change, so bps is the baud rate times the number of bits per second.

Modems deal with the problem of line noise by using parity-checking. The receiving modem uses parity-checking to identify whether the correct data was received. There are two types of parity checking: even and odd. For even parity, an extra bit is added to the 8 bits that comprise a character. The ninth bit causes the total of all bits to be an even number. For odd parity, the ninth bit makes the total come out odd. Upon receiving the ninth bit to finish a character, the modem adds up the bits to determine whether one of the bits was corrupted. If the character was corrupted, it is retransmitted.

How these parity-checking methods are implemented in modem transmission is defined in an **error correction standard** established by the ITU/CCITT called V.42. This error correction standard is also known as the **Link Access Procedure for Modems (LAPM)**.

If the modems have the same modulation and error correction standards in place, they still need to optimize their transmissions for speed. This is done through the application of **data**

**compression standards**. The dominant data compression standard supported in all modern modems is the ITU **V.42bis** standard, which can compress the data down to one quarter its normal size. This effectively quadruples the throughput at any given speed. In practice, this ideal may never be achieved because of additional demands on error correction, but the net improvement is still significant.

# Concept Questions    *Semester 1, Unit 9, Lesson 43*

Demonstrate your knowledge of the concepts in this lesson by answering the following questions in the space provided.

**1.** Explain how a modem talks with the host system and how a modem is able to talk to another modem.

**2.** Explain how a modem deals with transmission speed limits on telephone lines.

_____

_____

_____

_____

_____

_____

_____

_____

_____

_____

_____

_____

_____

_____

_____

_____

_____

_____

# Vocabulary Exercise     *Semester 1, Unit 9, Lesson 43*

*Name:* _____

*Date:* _____     *Class:* _____

Define the following terms as completely as you can.

**analog-to-digital converter**

_____

_____

**demodulator**

_____

_____

**flow control**

_____

_____

**local loop**

_____

_____

**modulator**

_____

_____

**noise**

_____

_____

*PSTN*

_____

_____

*quantization noise*

_____

_____

*start bit*

_____

_____

*stop bit*

_____

_____

# Focus Questions     *Semester 1, Unit 9, Lesson 43*

*Name:* _____

*Date:* _____     *Class:* _____

*1.* What is a modem, and basically what does it do?

_____

_____

_____

_____

*2.* Describe the two processes in modem communications.

_____

_____

_____

_____

*3.* How do modems deal with the problem of line noise?

_____

_____

_____

_____

*4.* Why must modems understand and use both digital and analog data signals?

_____

_____

_____

_____

# SEMESTER 1, UNIT 9, LESSON 44
# How Modems Work

You now know what modems do to talk to each other, but not how they actually carry on a two-way conversation. This lesson continues with modems and communications, discussing the processes involved in modem operations and functions. Most users click on the connect button and expect the modem to make a connection. A technician, however, needs a more basic understanding of the modem to troubleshoot problems.

## How modems converse during a communication session

Modem communication sessions are like conversations in several ways. Like people, modems initiate contact, give a greeting, and agree on a common topic for their talk. When a user accesses the Internet, the calling modem sends out a tone with a modulation selected by the software. If the answering modem supports the same modulation, it completes the connection immediately.

Conversely, if the same modulation is not supported, then the modems fall back to the next lower level of modulation, until they find one in common and make a connection. This modem negotiating is sometimes referred to as a *handshake*.

To see how this works, let's look at an example:

1. If a V.32 modem calls a V.34 modem, the V.32 cannot connect to the receiving V.34 modem because the V.32 uses an older connecting standard.

2. As a result of the modems' handshake, a procedure called **negotiation**, the V.34 modem falls back to the older V.32 standard, accommodating the incoming call. Because both modems are able to use the V.32 standard, the modems communicate at 9600 bps. In other words, when modems are of differing speeds, the slower speed is the speed used in the conversation. Fallbacks also occur when a particular modulation does not work well enough with error correction over a noisy line. Lower speeds mean fewer bps, which means error correction is easier.

3. After the modems have agreed on what modulation to use, they negotiate their error correction standard. For error correction, there is a fallback from the standard V.42 to the less widely used proprietary standards developed by Hayes Microcomputers, called MNP. It ranges from Level 4 down to Level 1. However, it is important to note that not all modems support the proprietary standards, and fallbacks are not always possible. Data compression is negotiated and handled at the same time as error correction because data compression is dependent on error correction.

4. After the fallbacks described above have been negotiated, data transmission begins and the session continues. High-quality modems can accomplish a communications session in **full-duplex mode**. To manage the modems during the session, communications software is required.

# Communication software

Communications software manages data transmission between two host systems. The software controls the data to be sent, sends commands telling the modem to initiate the call, tells the modem what number to call, passes the data from memory to the modem, and controls when to hang up.

Like the program in memory that issues commands to the CPU to execute based on its internal logic, the communication program sends commands to the modem that manipulate its internal logic. This body of commands is called the **AT command set**, or the **Hayes command set**.

When the program first communicates with the modem, it issues a series of commands called a *modem script*. This initialization string contains the beginning operating configuration based on parameters or guidelines set up in the software.

Once the session is started, communications rely on the modems' hardware-based error correction to monitor the data flow.

# New and emerging modem technologies

Alternative technologies to dialup analog telephone modems have emerged since the mid-1990s. These new technologies include **cable modems, Integrated Services Digital Network (ISDN)** modems, and **Asymmetric Digital Subscriber Line (ADSL)** modems. However, these devices are not really modems, because they do not rely on the modulation/demodulation technology of analog modems. Instead, these technologies represent all-digital replacements to the current analog-based communications framework. Despite the emergence of these new technologies, analog modems will be around for at least a few more years before they are replaced by newer technologies.

Two modem manufacturers have developed an improvement on current modems to reach a theoretical limit of 56 Kbps rather than the common 35 Kbps. One manufacturer is U.S. Robotics, with its X2 technology. The other is Rockwell, with its K56 Flex technology.

These newer digital-to-analog converters don't have the same noise problem as older modems, but they only work with other 56 Kbps modems of the same kind. Beyond this, the receiving 56-Kbps modem needs to be attached directly to a digital backbone on the PSTN rather than to another local loop. So when you communicate in this scenario, there are no analog-to-digital conversions at the digitally attached end, and only one relatively noise-free digital-to-analog conversion at your end. The 56-Kbps modems take advantage of this scenario by offering the greater speed one way—from the backbone-attached modem to you. While seemingly a disadvantage, this is becoming an increasingly popular modem for Internet access where the **Internet service provider (ISP)** is directly attached to the backbone, so you can receive the faster speed but may be restricted to sending data to the ISP at 28.8 Kbps.

# Modem specifications

Interpreting the technical specifications is not generally difficult. Most, if not all, major manufacturers provide the following specifications:

- **Compatibility specification**—The manufacturer lists all the ITU modulation standards that the modem is able to use for communication. These details are important because they determine the level of fallbacks the modem can use in communicating with other modems. If the manufacturer only lists the modem as "Hayes compatible," you should probably avoid it because this is a given for almost every modern modem.

- **Fax compatibility specification**—The manufacturer lists all the ITU or CCITT standards and EIA/TIA standards for fax modulation standards. Many modern modems also include circuitry to support faxing from fax-enabled software.

- **Error control standard specification**—The manufacturer lists the standards and proprietary methods of error correction and data compression supported by the modem. In the linked case, the modem supports all the major ITU standards in addition to major proprietary ones such as MNP.

- **Physical dimensions specification**—Physical dimensions specifications describe the form factor for the modem model: internal or external. The manufacturer specifies the type of external serial pin connectors (for example, 25-pin or 9-pin serial). The type of external serial pin connector is important because it determines the type of serial cable for connection to the local computer.

# Concept Questions        *Semester 1, Unit 9, Lesson 44*

Demonstrate your knowledge of the concepts in this lesson by answering the following questions in the space provided.

1. How do modems carry on a conversation during a communication session?

2. What new and emerging technologies are changing the way modems work?

_____

_____

_____

_____

_____

_____

_____

_____

_____

_____

_____

_____

_____

_____

_____

_____

_____

_____

# Vocabulary Exercise    *Semester 1, Unit 9, Lesson 44*

*Name:* _____

*Date:* _____    *Class:* _____

Define the following terms as completely as you can.

**ADSL**

_____

_____

**AT command set**

_____

_____

**cable modem**

_____

_____

**full-duplex mode**

_____

_____

**Hayes command set**

_____

_____

**ISDN**

_____

_____

**ISP**

_____

_____

**negotiation**

_____

_____

**proprietary standards**

_____

_____

# Focus Questions     *Semester 1, Unit 9, Lesson 44*

*Name:* _____

*Date:* _____     *Class:* _____

**1.** Describe how communication software manages the modem session.

_____

_____

_____

_____

**2.** Describe how to interpret the specifications for a modem.

_____

_____

_____

_____

**3.** What is the compatibility modem specification?

_____

_____

_____

_____

**4.** Why is the fax compatibility modem specification important?

_____

_____

_____

_____

**5.** What is the error control standard modem specification?

_____

_____

_____

_____

**6.** What is the physical dimensions modem specification?

_____

_____

_____

_____

# SEMESTER 1, UNIT 9, LESSON 45
# Unit 9 Exam

If you have access to the online Aries A+ curriculum, contact your instructor for the Assessment System URL. If you do not have access to the online curriculum, please continue to Unit 10.

# SEMESTER 1, UNIT 10

- Lesson 46: Networking
- Lesson 47: The Internet
- Lesson 48: Keyboards, Mouse Devices, and Joysticks
- Lesson 49: Sound Cards
- Lesson 50: Unit 10 Exam

# Semester 1, Unit 10, Lesson 46
# Networking

Go to any convention or gathering, and you will either participate in networking or witness others networking. While people socialize, they exchange information, contacts, ideas and resources, business cards, phone numbers, addresses, and so on.

If you use computers in a work setting or school setting, you are likely to encounter an ideal networking situation. Sharing resources such as printers and modems makes economic sense, as opposed to buying separate printers and modems for several computers. Likewise, it makes a lot of sense to share files and folders in collaborative settings. Essentially, networking connects computers together to share data and resources. Networking requires special hardware and software. This lesson introduces you to various types of networks and networking hardware systems.

## Network architectures

As you have learned, the three main types of networks are LANs, WANs, and MANs. LANs are usually located in single buildings. WANs cover a large geographical area, connecting cities and countries. LANs and/or WANs can be tied together to form MANs, often using leased telephone lines operating between 9600 bps and 1.544 Mbps.

The three most popular architectures for networks are Ethernet, Token Ring, and Fiber Distributed Data Interface (FDDI), which are described in the following sections.

### *Ethernet*

Due to its relative low cost and its 10/100-Mbps standard speed, **Ethernet** is the most popular network technology used today. Ethernet can utilize either a bus network or a star network around a hub. The star arrangement is more widely used because it is much easier to wire and to maintain than the bus arrangement. Another benefit of the star arrangement is that failure of one computer does not affect the other computers as in the bus arrangement. Intelligent hubs can monitor a network and report errors and problems in the star arrangement. Hubs do not control all the signals on the Ethernet network.

Any computer in the Ethernet passive hub network system can originate network signals, as long as the lines are not busy. To gain access to the network, Ethernet computers use the carrier sense multiple access collision detect (CSMA/CD) method. Translated, this means that a computer must sense that the network can handle its transmission, many computers can use the same network, and computers must detect and handle collisions.

Signals transmitted over long distances on an Ethernet network can weaken, so two types of **repeaters** are used. An amplifier repeater simply amplifies the incoming signal, noise, and so on, and a signal-regenerating repeater "reads" the signal and creates a duplicate of the original signal before sending it on.

Ethernet can use any of the cable systems listed in Table 10-1.

**Table 10-1**  *Ethernet cable systems*

| Cable System | Type of Cable | Cable Description |
|---|---|---|
| 10Base5 (thicknet) | Thick coaxial cable | Made of two conductors: a center wire and metallic braid surrounding the center wire. Maximum length is 500 meters. |
| 10Base2 (thinnet) | Thin coaxial cable | Cheaper, smaller cable than thicknet with maximum segment length of 185 meters |
| 10BaseT (twisted-pair) | Unshielded twisted pair (UTP) cable | Two insulated wires that are twisted together inside a plastic casing. Lower grades often used for telephone wires are unsuitable for 10BaseT |
| 100BaseT (Fast Ethernet) | Shielded twisted pair (STP) cable | More costly than UTP and thin coaxial, but less costly than thick coaxial and fiber-optic cable. Thick with shielding around the twisted wires. |
| 10BaseFL | Optical fiber | Glass or plastic fiber in the center transmits light signals. |

As the number of nodes in the Ethernet network increases, speed and reliability can decrease for the entire network. You can **segment** the network—that is, split a large network into smaller segments that contain two or more computers connected by a bridge or router—to counter this.

## *Token Ring*

IBM developed **Token Ring** as a robust, highly reliable type of network. It is more expensive and more complex than Ethernet, which means it is also more difficult to maintain.

Token Ring stations are physically connected in a star formation. Each station connects to a centralized hub called a controlled-access unit (CAU), a multistation access unit (MAU), or a smart multistation access unit (SMAU). The main ring includes any patch cables, the cable connecting the last MSAU ring out to the first MSAU ring in, and the cabling to each PC on the Token Ring. Each workstation contains a Token Ring LAN card with a unique assigned address and a 9-pin connector for the Token Ring cable to connect each workstation to an MSAU. A token controls communication and traffic on a Token Ring network. Tokens are passed from one active station to the next, one at a time.

## FDDI

Another ring-based network using a token-passing traffic control method is **Fiber Distributed Data Interface (FDDI)**. FDDI does not require a centralized hub like Token Ring. At 200 Mbps, FDDI transfers data much faster than regular Ethernet or Token Ring and slightly faster than Fast Ethernet. Although it once only used fiber-optic cabling, FDDI can now also run on UTP and often serves as a backbone network. It can even link a number of Token Rings and Ethernets together.

FDDI's token-passing method is much more sophisticated than Token Ring. It can transmit more than one frame of data without waiting for its return. Instead of a single ring, FDDI has two rings linking each device.

## *Selecting a network architecture*

Each of these three systems has advantages, as shown in Table 10-2.

**Table 10-2**   *Attributes of network architectures*

| Attribute | Ethernet | Token Ring | FDDI |
|---|---|---|---|
| Logical landscape | Bus | Single ring | Dual ring |
| Physical landscape | Star or bus | Ring or star | Ring |
| Media | Twisted-pair, coaxial, or fiber-optic cable | Twisted-pair, fiber-optic cable | Mostly fiber-optic cable |
| Standard bandwidth | 10 Mbps, and 100 Mbps for Fast Ethernet | 4 or 16 Mbps | 100 to 200 Mbps |
| How token is released | N/A | After receive | After transmit |
| Maximum number of nodes | 500 | 260 | 1,024 |
| Advantages | Least expensive and simplest | Operates more reliably under heavy traffic | Much faster than Token Ring and Ethernet, and faster than Fast Ethernet |

# Types of networking hardware

Common networking hardware components include network interface cards, routers, bridges, and gateways.

A **network interface card (NIC)** plugs into a motherboard and provides ports for network connection. This card can be designed as an Ethernet card, a Token Ring card, or a FDDI card. Network cards communicate with the network through serial connections, and with the computer through parallel connections. Each network card requires an IRQ, an I/O address, and upper memory addresses for DOS and Windows 95/98. When selecting a NIC, consider the following three factors:

- The type of network (Ethernet, Token Ring, FDDI, or other)

- The type of media (twisted-pair, coaxial, or fiber-optic cable)

- The type of system bus (for example, PCI and ISA; note that you should always use a PCI bus with FDDI cards because an ISA bus could not handle the speed)

To decrease the amount of traffic on a single LAN and/or to extend the geographic area past what a single LAN can support, networks are often combined; this is known as *internetworking*. When these networks are broken into smaller, more easily managed segments, devices are necessary to connect them. Thus bridges, routers, and gateways are used to link segments together:

- **Bridges** connect network segments, and must make intelligent decisions about whether to pass signals on to the next segment. If placed strategically, a network bridge can improve network performance greatly.

- **Routers** connect networks and act a little slower than bridges, but they are more sophisticated. Routers have to decide how to route packets to other networks. They can be computers with special network software, or they can be other dedicated devices built by network manufacturers. Routers contain tables of network addresses, along with optimal destination routes to these addresses.

- A **gateway** connects networks that use different protocols. A gateway acts like a translator, so you can connect an Ethernet to a Token Ring LAN, and can communicate data from an application stored on another network that uses a different protocol. Because of this added responsibility, a gateway costs more than a router and works more slowly.

When you are familiar with these hardware components necessary for networking, you are on your way to understanding the basics of networks.

# Concept Questions       *Semester 1, Unit 10, Lesson 46*

Demonstrate your knowledge of the concepts in this lesson by answering the following questions in the space provided.

*1.* Describe the three most popular network architectures: Ethernet, Token Ring, and FDDI.

*2.* Explain the advantages and disadvantages of Ethernet, Token Ring, and FDDI networks.

_____

_____

_____

_____

_____

_____

_____

_____

_____

_____

_____

_____

_____

_____

_____

_____

_____

_____

# Vocabulary Exercise     *Semester 1, Unit 10, Lesson 46*

*Name:* _____

*Date:* _____     *Class:* _____

Define the following terms as completely as you can.

**bridge**

_____

_____

**Ethernet**

_____

_____

**FDDI**

_____

_____

**gateway**

_____

_____

**NIC**

_____

_____

**router**

_____

_____

**Token Ring**

_____

_____

# Focus Questions                    *Semester 1, Unit 10, Lesson 46*

*Name:* _____

*Date:* _____    *Class:* _____

**1.** Why is Ethernet the most popular network technology used today?

_____

_____

_____

**2.** How does networking connect computers together to share data and resources?

_____

_____

_____

**3.** What is the function of the network interface?

_____

_____

_____

**4.** Describe the function of bridges, routers, and gateways.

_____

_____

_____

**5.** Why can Token Ring networks handle heavier traffic than Ethernet networks?

_____

_____

_____

**6.** Why is FDDI the fastest network architecture?

_____

_____

_____

# SEMESTER 1, UNIT 10, LESSON 47
# The Internet

You have learned about networks and their architecture. In this lesson you will learn about the largest network in the world, the **Internet**, sometimes referred to as the **Information Superhighway**.

Although the Internet today has exploded into a massive web of computer networks on an electronic highway, it began as a relatively small collection of U.S. government networks within the U.S. Department of Defense in the late 1960s. This network was originally called **Advanced Research Project Agency network (ARPANET)**. Eventually other U.S. government agencies, such as the National Science Foundation, connected to this network of networks. Today, the Internet is used by the civilian world as well, so that libraries, schools, businesses, and numerous individuals are connected to the Internet.

The Internet is not owned or governed by any individual or government; it is a collection of computer networks that are connected and managed by mutual consent. A user can send messages (e-mail), join discussion lists, read and send messages to electronic bulletin boards, chat live online, search databases, receive files, and send files.

To get on the Internet, users need the services of an **Internet service provider (ISP)**, a company whose business it is to connect people to the Internet and **World Wide Web**. This ISP may link to a larger, regional ISP, which in turn may connect to one of a number of major computer centers nationwide. The result is that when you sit down at your computer and surf the Internet, you have the benefit of all these computers networking together to allow you access to countless documents, graphics, videos, music, and other computer users around the world.

## IP addresses

The next time you search for an Internet document, look at the bottom of your screen, and you will likely see a message about connecting to a series of numbers. This is a unique numeric address, called the **Internet Protocol (IP)** address.

Every node on the network is required to have an IP address. Even if you are merely testing network-related software on a computer that is not connected to the network, you might need to temporarily assign an IP address in order to use the software. Network Solutions (NSI), working under an agreement with the National Science Foundation, keeps track of all IP address assignments. This work is done at the Internet Network Information Center (InterNIC). When any organization applies for IP addresses, InterNIC assigns a range of addresses, depending on the number of host machines for that organization's network.

The IP address is made up of four sets of numbers, separated by periods. An IP address is 32 bits long, which makes each of the four numbers an octet. Because the largest 8-bit number possible in binary code is 11111111 (which is equivalent to 255 in decimal), the largest possible IP address would be 255.255.255.255. This allows for a total of 4.3 billion IP addresses, although not all of them are ready for use yet.

## *IP address classifications*

IP addresses are divided into three classes: Class A, Class B, and Class C (see Table 10-3).

**Table 10-3**   *IP address classifications*

| Class | Network Octets (Blanks in the IP Address Are Used for Host Octets) | Number of Possible Networks or Licenses | Host Octets (Blanks in the IP Address Are Used for Network Octets) | Number of Possible IP Addresses in Each Network |
|---|---|---|---|---|
| A | 0.___.___.___ to 126.___.___.___ | 127 | ___.0.0.1 to ___.255.255.254 | 16,000,000 |
| B | 128.0.___.___ to 191.255.___.___ | 16,000 | ___.___.0.1 to ___.___.255.254 | 65,000 |
| C | 192.0.0.___ to 254.255.255.___ | 2,000,000 | ___.___.___.1 to ___.___.___.254 | 254 |

Class A licenses assign a single number, between 0 and 126, to be used in the first octet, which becomes the network address. The other three octets on the right can be used for a host address that uniquely identifies each host on this network. So a company that is assigned 63 as its network number will use 63 for the first octet for every host in the network. Examples of possible numbers for hosts on this network are 63.0.0.1, 63.0.0.2, and 63.0.0.3. The last octet cannot use 0 or 255 as a value; thus, one Class A license can have about 256 x 256 x 254 node addresses, or about 16 million, as shown in Table 10-3.

Class B licenses assign numbers for the first two octets, leaving the last two octets for host address.

Class C licenses assign three octets as the network address, leaving 254 host address. Small companies often do not use all 254 IP addresses, so there is usually no shortage of IP addresses. When an organization with a Class C license does grow past its address allotment, the organization can resolve its problem in two different ways: by assigning a number of its own for a private network or assigning a dynamic IP address.

As long as the organization is using **Transmission Control Protocol/Internet Protocol (TCP/IP)**, it can make up its own IP addresses for machines that have no access to the Internet. The **Internet Assigned Numbers Authority (IANA)** recommends the following IP addresses for private networks:

- 10.0.0.0 through 10.255.255.255

- 172.16.0.0 through 172.31.255.255

- 192.168.0.0 through 192.168.255.255

A few IP addresses are reserved by TCP/IP for special use, and you cannot use them (see Table 10-4).

**Table 10-4**    *TCP/IP reserved addresses*

| IP Address | How It Is Used |
|---|---|
| 255.255.255.255 | Broadcast messages |
| 0.0.0.0 | A currently unassigned IP address |
| 127.0.0.1 | Indicates your own workstation, yourself |

As mentioned previously, the other solution for the an organization that is running out of IP addresses organization is to assign **dynamic IP addresses**, so that machines are assigned an IP address to be used for the current session only. When the user is finished and logs off, the IP address returns to the pool of available addresses for another user.

Due to the vast expansion of the Internet, there will be a shortage of IP addresses in the near future. To solve this problem, a new IP version 6 (IPv6) is being developed. Instead of the current 32 bits that are used, the new IP version will use 128 bits and will be able to automatically assign IP addresses to network devices.

# The Domain Name System

Rather than remember a long series of numbers, many hosts have opted to use alphabetic or word-based names to be identified on the Internet. These names act as aliases for the real names, the IP addresses.

No fixed relationship exists between a domain name and an IP address because computers can move around. That leaves it up to a name resolution service to track the relationship between a domain name and the current IP address of the host computer. The main name resolution service that does this is the **Domain Name System (DNS)**. If you're on the

Internet and enter in your browser an incorrect address or try to link to a dead address, you see the computer working feverishly to find the address, and then it tells you "No DNS entry found."

The heart of DNS lies in its shared database, which must initially be updated by hand. Whenever a new domain name is assigned, the name and its IP address are entered into a database on a top-level domain name server. When a remote computer attempts to access your host by using your domain name, or doesn't know the IP address currently assigned to that domain name, the remote computer communicates with the DNS server, which uses all its networking power to find the IP address.

# TCP/IP protocols

TCP/IP was originally developed to create a network of networks. Computers that are on networks need to have common rules for how messages are to be sent, how messages are to be routed from site to site, how to handle errors, and how to make sure that the network is shared in an efficient way. These rules are called **protocols**.

IP defines rules for routing simple packets of information. For data that needs to be split up into more than one packet (for example, a long file that is much larger than the maximum transit size supported by network hardware), we need more sophisticated protocols. TCP includes some error recovery methods, rules for keeping a sender from sending data too fast for a receiver, and rules for making sure that packets can be reassembled in order, even if the network delivers them out of order.

TCP/IP is used to refer to a TCP protocol that is implemented on top of an IP protocol: TCP uses IP messages and adds additional information and rules.

The sudden explosion of larger networks, more companies using internal networks, fiber optics and resulting technologies such as FDDI, and competition between cable TV companies and phone companies have all complicated the Internet, making it difficult to create a standard to govern worldwide communications. These developments have made TCP/IP indispensable because it is designed to link networks together.

The large number of networks and subnets give the Internet its web-like structure. Routing data through this maze requires a system, and that's where TCP/IP comes in. TCP/IP routes data from one network to another over a large geographical area and over a large number of networks. In transferring data packets from network to network, TCP/IP is really a series of protocols that occur simultaneously during transmission. Depending on the data being transferred and the application software being interfaced, a protocol choice is made immediately at the application layer.

Two protocols occur at the transport layer: TCP and **User Datagram Protocol (UDP)**. TCP verifies correct delivery of data from the client to the server and adds support for detecting errors and retransmitting correct information. TCP requires a connection to be effective, like a telephone call. UDP, on the other hand, operates like a radio broadcast and does not require a connection.

At the network layer, **Address Resolution Protocol (ARP)** translates the IP addresses into the physical network addresses, and its counterpart protocol, **Reverse Address Resolution Protocol (RARP)**, translates physical addresses into IP addresses. One protocol you are likely to see at some point as you search the Internet is **Internet Control Message Protocol (ICMP)**, which transmits error messages and other control messages to routers and hosts. This is the protocol that sends error messages.

# Connecting to the Internet

When PCs in a business or school are connected to a LAN or WAN, most network support is handled by a network administrator. (You will have an opportunity to study network administration in the second semester of the Aries curriculum.)

Individual computer users not hooked up to a network are a different story. Be sure that they have an ISP, the phone number of the ISP, and their user name and password. Using Windows 95 for Internet access requires five steps:

*1.* Install and configure the modem.

*2.* Set up Dial-Up Adapter under Control Panel.

*3.* Set up Dial-Up Networking.

*4.* Install Internet Explorer, Netscape, or some other browser software.

*5.* Install e-mail software.

# Concept Questions       *Semester 1, Unit 10, Lesson 47*

Demonstrate your knowledge of the concepts in this lesson by answering the following questions in the space provided.

*1.* Explain the process that allows you to retrieve information from a Web site.

*2.* How does TCP/IP route data from one network to another?

_____

_____

_____

_____

_____

_____

_____

_____

_____

_____

_____

_____

_____

_____

_____

_____

_____

# Vocabulary Exercise     *Semester 1, Unit 10, Lesson 47*

*Name:* _____

*Date:* _____     *Class:* _____

Define the following terms as completely as you can.

**ARP**

_____

_____

**ARPANET**

_____

_____

**DNS**

_____

_____

**IANA**

_____

_____

**ICMP**

_____

_____

**IP**

_____

_____

**ISP**

_____

_____

**RARP**

_____

_____

**TCP**

_____

_____

**TCP/IP**

_____

_____

**UDP**

_____

_____

# Focus Questions

## *Semester 1, Unit 10, Lesson 47*

*Name:* _____

*Date:* _____   *Class:* _____

**1.** What does an IP address look like?

_____

_____

_____

_____

**2.** Describe how and why IP addresses are divided into classes.

_____

_____

_____

_____

**3.** Describe what an organization with a Class C license can do when it grows past its address allotment.

_____

_____

_____

_____

**4.** Why is IPv6 important?

_____

_____

_____

_____

5. Describe how and why DNS tracks the relationship between a domain name and the current IP address of the host computer.

_____

_____

_____

_____

6. What is the relationship between ARP and RARP?

_____

_____

_____

_____

# SEMESTER 1, UNIT 10, LESSON 48
# Keyboards, Mouse Devices, and Joysticks

**Input devices** enable users to interact with the computer system. An input device is a peripheral that connects to a computer through an I/O port to generate data that goes into the computer so that the CPU can use that data. Your keyboard, for example, allows you to type data and commands: Without it, you would have virtually no way to use software. Another peripheral you recognize without any introduction is the mouse. Joysticks make gaming software popular with their real-to-life simulation potential.

This lesson explores the attributes and uses of keyboard, mouse devices, and joysticks.

## Keyboards

The **keyboard** is the primary input interface to the computer system. This is where commands and data are entered into the system. Keyboards consist of various types of keys, including alphanumeric keys (such as a, f, t, p, 1, and 9), punctuation keys (such as comma, semi-colon, colon, and period), and special function keys (such as control keys, the caps lock key, arrow keys, the scroll lock key, the print screen key, and the Enter key).

### *Keyboard types and layouts*

Two types of computer keyboards are used in modern systems:

- The **101-key enhanced keyboard** was originally introduced by IBM in 1986. It has become the standard for computer systems, and has been copied by almost all keyboard manufacturers.

- The **104-key enhanced keyboard** was developed in 1996 because Microsoft wanted a keyboard with new keys to work with Windows 95 and NT 4.0 operating system software. The 104-key keyboard has Windows keys to the left and right of the space bar and an additional Application key to the right of the right Windows key. The Windows keys open the Start menu for navigation by the cursor keys; the Application key simulates the right mouse button.

Two types of keyboard layouts have been developed:

- The **Qwerty layout** is a descendant of the original typewriter keyboard of the 1880s. It takes its name from the six keys at the top left of the keyboard (q, w, e, r, t, and y).

- The **Dvorak layout** is supposed to be a more speed-optimized keyboard layout. It was introduced in the 1930s, but has not had much accepted use.

Of the two, Qwerty has become the dominant keyboard standard. Both the 101-key and 104-key keyboards are based on the Qwerty standard.

## *Keyboard function*

To understand how the keyboard works, think of the keys as a bank of electrical switches. When you depress one switch—a key—with your fingertip, the switch closes a circuit. A pressed key forces a contact switch to momentarily make an electrical contact in a circuit.

The closed circuit causes the keyboard's controller chip to read the appropriate key character and send it to the system CPU via the keyboard connector. The following sections discuss the function of each of the key components: key switches, keyboard controller chip, scan codes, and keyboard connector.

### *Key switch*

The **key switch** is the fundamental unit of keyboard function. The key switch sends characters to the system. Most keyboards use a variety of mechanical key switches. There are three basic types of mechanical switches:

- The **basic mechanical switch**, also referred to as the pure mechanical switch, is the simplest of all the switches. A basic mechanical switch usually has a metal clip and spring arrangement around the plunger. This tactile feedback mechanism provides a springy or clicky feel when the key is pressed. When you press the key, the mechanism's plunger and metal plate are forced into contact with the contacts on the circuit board, closing the circuit. People trained on IBM electric typewriter usually prefer the clicky feel of the tactile feedback mechanism key switch. It is extremely durable and lasts for years.

- Another type of mechanical switch formerly very popular in keyboards is the **foam buffer key switch**, or foam element key switch. This type of switch is similar to the basic mechanical design, but uses foam with foil laminate in place of the tactile mechanism's metal plate. The foam eliminates the mechanical click and prevents bounce. When you press a foam buffer key switch, the laminated foam is pressed against the contacts on the circuit board, where the foil laminate closes the circuit. A return spring on the plunger causes the key to spring back after contact.

  The foam buffer key switch is generally less expensive than the basic mechanical switch, but it tends to wear out sooner. The foam absorbs moisture, too, so the circuit board contact can erode. Moisture retention can also cause intermittent loss of contact and circuit closure. Because of its moisture retention problems, the foam buffer key switch is seldom used today and tends to indicate cheap manufacture.

- The **rubber dome switch** is a variant of the foam buffer design. The spring is eliminated from the plunger, and a rubber dome is used in place of the foam and foil laminate pad. The rubber dome sits atop the circuit board contacts. Inside the top of the rubber dome is a carbon button. When the plunger is pressed, the top of the dome collapses, forcing the carbon button down onto the contacts and closing the circuit. The rubber dome key switch is extremely durable. In addition, because a rubber sheet covers the contacts, the rubber dome switch is not subject to corrosion. It lacks the clicky feel of the basic mechanical switch, but the rubber dome is a significant improvement over the foam buffer design.

A variant of the rubber dome switch design is the **membrane keyboard**. Membrane keyboards sacrifice all user tactile sensation for the benefits of a rugged design. The membrane keyboard switch's key caps are integrated into a continuous sheet that sits directly atop the rubber dome sheet. The membrane switch is seldom found on computer keyboards, except in harsh conditions or industrial environments.

## Keyboard controller chips and key scan codes

A keyboard is composed of key switches. The switches are arrayed in a grid called a **key matrix**. A processor called the **keyboard controller chip** monitors the key matrix.

The key switch has a very short-lived contact with the circuit. When pressed, the switch bounces rapidly on and off the circuit contacts. The keyboard controller is designed to debounce, or neutralize the bouncing side effect. The keyboard controller chip's 16-byte buffer moderates a succession of rapid keystrokes, sending each stroke separately from the buffer to the serial interface.

When a key switch is pressed, the processor immediately identifies the grid location of the closed circuit and converts the pressed switch to the appropriate scan code, a binary code or number sequence. After the processor has converted the pressed key to the appropriate scan code, it transmits the code to the motherboard through a special serial interface.

The keyboard controller chip communicates with the system motherboard through a special serial port or keyboard interface. The keyboard interface sends data in packets of 11 bits: 8 data bits, 2 framing bits, and 1 control bit.

The keyboard controller chip and the motherboard keyboard controller carry on bidirectional data communication . As the motherboard keyboard controller receives the scan codes from the keyboard controller, it translates them into system scan codes, signals through IRQ1, and sends the data to the system CPU, using I/O port address 60. The system returns data to the keyboard by means of the same port through the motherboard keyboard controller. In addition, when the system sends commands to and checks on the status of the motherboard keyboard controller, it does so via I/O port 64.

A second keyboard controller, called the Intel Universal Peripheral Interface slave microcontroller chip, manages the keyboard interface on the motherboard. There are several versions of this chip, each with various amounts of onboard ROM and RAM.

## Keyboard connectors

The keyboard connects to the motherboard by means of a special serial keyboard interface— a round opening in the computer's case back. Two types of cable connectors plug into the interface: some computers need a 5-pin AT or DIN male connector, and others a 6-pin mini-DIN or PS/2 male connector. Each connects to its female motherboard counterpart. The 5-pin

AT/DIN connector has been the standard for many years. The mini-DIN, originally introduced by IBM with its PS/2 line of computers in 1986, has become more of a standard with the newer ATX motherboard style introduced in 1995. In addition to these two types of keyboard connectors, the newer type of I/O bus, the USB, also supports keyboards.

# Mouse devices

A **mouse** is an input device that allows the user to manipulate items in a graphical user interface (GUI) environment such as Microsoft Windows. The most common computer peripheral after the keyboard, the mouse is really a requirement in the modern computer environment. Moving the mouse on a desktop translates to movements of a pointer on the computer's monitor.

## *Mouse components*

A typical mouse has five major components:

- The **plastic body** is the shell that houses the internal parts of the mouse. The body surface includes two selection buttons. The hollow body encompasses the internal roller ball, with attached sensors. The mouse body has a hole in the bottom so the ball can protrude slightly, allowing it to contact and roll over a flat surface.

- The user uses the mouse's buttons to make selections from menus or to click on icons. The left button is most often the one used to make selections; the right button is used for software-specific tasks.

- The **internal roller ball**, also called a tracking ball, rests inside the plastic shell's body cavity. Usually constructed of rubber or plastic, the tracking ball's movement produces signals that drive the pointer on the computer's monitor.

- The **mouse cable** is a 5-foot to 6-foot, 2-wire cord that relays tracking ball movement signals to the motherboard interface.

- The **interface connector** is the pinout plug at the end of the cord that plugs into the motherboard interface.

## *How the mouse works*

When you move the mouse around, the tracking ball rotates. The rotations are translated into electrical signals by the tracking ball's opto-mechanical mechanism. Those electrical signals are then transmitted to the computer across the mouse cable.

The tracking ball moves against two rollers. One roller translates these movements into X-axis coordinates, and the other translates them into Y-axis coordinates. These coordinates are painted to the monitor as mouse pointer movements.

The rollers are attached to small wheels that rotate between an optical sensor and tiny infrared light. As the wheel rotates, it interrupts the light, producing blinking of the light source. The sensor interprets these blinks and then sends them to the system where a software driver interprets them into movement along the X and Y axes.

The user makes selections or choices with a mouse by pointing to the graphical object or menu choice, and then clicking either the left or right button on the front of the mouse shell. A click is a brief, light tap on the button. A tiny switch underneath each mouse button records the click, and the interval between the clicks. These signals are also sent through the cable to the system.

## The mouse interface with the system motherboard

The signals from the mouse button clicks and ball movements are transmitted through the cable to the system motherboard via a serial interface. Connectors can be of the serial, PS/2, or bus type:

- The serial connection is a typical 9-pin or 25-pin female connector.

- The PS/2 connector is exactly the same as that of the PS/2 keyboard connector. In fact, the PS/2 mouse interface usually sits immediately next to the PS/2 style keyboard connector on the motherboard. The PS/2 mouse port is controlled by the same Intel Universal Peripheral Interface slave microcontroller chip that controls the PS/2 keyboard. Because the PS/2 mouse port uses the same controller chip, it uses the same I/O port addresses as the keyboard: 60 and 64. However, it uses IRQ 12 for the interrupt. For this reason, the PS/2 mouse should always be used instead of the serial mouse if possible. The serial mouse generally uses COM1 or COM2, which will likely share an interrupt with other 9- or 25-pin serial devices. As you learned earlier , COM1 and COM2 use the same interrupts as COM3 and COM4, respectively.

  Although the PS/2 and serial mouse connectors have different pinouts, both types of connectors use the same six wires. In the pinout used by the PS/2 interface connector, two of the six wires are used for data signals, and the rest are used for power, control functions, or are unused.

- The bus mouse is a special type of connector interface because it requires a special adapter board installed in the ISA bus. This board relays the same signals as the other connector types, except it uses the card/edge connectors of the board to relay them across the bus to the CPU.

## Common types of mouse devices

One variant of the standard two button mouse, Microsoft's Intellimouse, has a small rubber wheel stationed between the buttons. Pushing or pulling this wheel causes the mouse pointer on the screen to scroll. This scrolling ability is dependent on software application–specific drivers to be enabled to work. To date, only Microsoft applications support this feature.

Another common type of mouse is a different design from the typical two-button mouse. Called a trackball mouse, it is basically a two-button mouse turned upside down. That is, the plastic body or shell has the roller ball face-up, with the buttons off to one side or on both sides of the ball.

You manipulate the ball directly with your thumb or index finger, while tapping the button with another finger. The internal mechanism is still generally an opto-mechanical mechanism.

Two other types of mouse devices are found mainly in laptops. These are IBM's small control stick—a trackpoint—mounted on the keyboard, and Alps Electric's touch-sensitive pad pointing device—a glidepoint.

# Joysticks

A game adapter is a type of specialized input device designed to enter movement data into the system. The **joystick** is the most common type of game adapter. A joystick has a central stick that sits atop a plastic body. This stick has an ergonomic grip with two buttons, usually located on the top and side of the stick. A six-wire cable connects the stick to a special game port connector that is either on the motherboard or on a special adapter card in an ISA bus slot.

## *Joystick function*

The user can move the joystick's stick in any direction by holding the grip and moving it in any lateral direction. The shaft of the stick is tied to two electric sensors called variable resistors. The user moves the stick against these sensors, transmitting vertical positions (X-coordinates) and horizontal positions (Y-coordinates) to the game port. Each button on the stick is also connected to a variable resistor. These sensors detect changes in pressure in the same way as the stick sensors. These buttons are used to perform selected tasks required by the game software, such as firing guns and missiles.

The signals are sent through the six-wire cable to a 15-pin D-shell interface. The game controller chip on the adapter or motherboard converts these changes in sensor resistance into a digital pulse that can be read by the software. The game port and controller do not use an interrupt or DMA channel because the software scans the device directly by sending a command request for the I/O input. All the incoming and outgoing data goes through I/O address 201.

# Concept Questions     *Semester 1, Unit 10, Lesson 48*

Demonstrate your knowledge of the concepts in this lesson by answering the following questions in the space provided.

**1.** How do keyboard controller chips communicate with the system motherboard?

**2.** Explain the function of the key switch, and identify the three basic types of mechanical switches.

_____

_____

_____

_____

_____

_____

_____

_____

_____

_____

_____

_____

_____

_____

_____

_____

# Vocabulary Exercise    *Semester 1, Unit 10, Lesson 48*

*Name:* _____

*Date:* _____    *Class:* _____

Define the following terms as completely as you can.

**Dvorak keyboard**

_____

_____

**foam buffer key switch**

_____

_____

**input device**

_____

_____

**interface connector**

_____

_____

**internal roller ball**

_____

_____

**joystick**

_____

_____

**key switch**

_____

_____


**keyboard**

_____

_____


**membrane keyboard**

_____

_____


**mouse**

_____

_____


**mouse cable**

_____

_____


**plastic body**

_____

_____


**Qwerty keyboard**

_____

_____


**rubber dome switch**

_____

_____

# Focus Questions    *Semester 1, Unit 10, Lesson 48*

*Name:* _____

*Date:* _____    *Class:* _____

**1.** Describe the two types of keyboards used in modern systems.

_____

_____

_____

_____

**2.** Describe the two types of keyboard layouts.

_____

_____

_____

_____

**3.** Why is Qwerty is the standard keyboard layout for computer systems?

_____

_____

_____

_____

**4.** Describe the 104-key enhanced keyboard and its advantages.

_____

_____

_____

_____

# Semester 1, Unit 10, Lesson 49
# Sound Cards

This lesson is all about sound and how your computer produces it, stores it, and makes it possible for you to hear it. A **sound card** is an expansion card that handles all sound functions: input, output, and making modifications. The sound card's quality depends on the number of bits used to hold each sound sample, or the sample size: The more bits, the better the sound. All sound cards connect to microphones and speakers, and most support **musical instrument digital interface (MIDI)**, which is the industry hardware standard for storing electronic sound.

## The evolution of sound cards

Those of you who booted up a computer in the early 1980s heard some beeps to let you know that the computer was turned on, or that it didn't understand your instructions. But that was about all you heard from the computers. The first real sound cards didn't come out until the mid-1980s, when Creative Labs and Ad Lib Inc. designed an 8-bit card to fit into IBM's motherboard. These first sound cards simulated the arcade games that were so popular in those days, and produced a sound that was only slightly superior to AM radio. Early sound cards could reproduce sound in mono (one channel) and operated in half-duplex mode, similar to two-way radios.

Then **Sound Blaster** exploded on the scene in 1989. Creative Labs came out with its 8-bit Sound Blaster card that year, and developed the first stereo output card, the Sound Blaster Pro—two years later. The company's president personally took his sound board to various developers to build support for it, so other sound boards on the market began to conform to Sound Blaster's specifications.

While Creative Labs was rising in preeminence in computer sound development, Turtle Beach Systems developed a 16-bit sound card to fit in a 16-bit ISA slot on the PC motherboard. Even though this 16-bit card eventually reproduced CD-quality sound, Turtle Beach has never overtaken Creative Labs' top standing in the market.

Microsoft enhanced its Windows software to become a multimedia operating system with its 1991 version of Windows 3.0. Additional storage space became necessary with the development of the sound card, so hardware and software manufacturers created standard machines that could handle multimedia file extensions.

New technologies have produced even greater PC audio enhancements. More realistic sound; full-duplex operations; 3D sound; speech recognition features; audio communication via the Internet; recording, mixing, and editing FM sound; and MIDI are among the recent enhancements, and more are sure to occur.

# Sound card function

As humans we can collect information through our eyes, ears, noses, mouths, and skin. Computers are much more limited: They can only see and store data in digital form, recording information in a binary format. Because computers operate digitally and we humans live in an analog world, sound cards use an **analog-to-digital converter** to convert sound to digital signals and values that are stored in the hard drive using the **pulse code modulation method**. This conversion process is also called **sampling**.

By its very nature, sampling introduces some error. How well the sound sample represents the original depends on the sampling rate and the sample size. **Sampling rate** refers to the number of samples made per unit of time, so a high rate creates a more accurate sound. Similarly, a large **sample size** represents a more accurate digital signal because it represents the number of values (expressed in bits) used to represent each sample.

Because digital sound is stored in binary values and can be both positive and negative, the initial 8-bit sound card ranged in value from –128 to +128, or 255 values. A modern 16-bit card is much more accurate because its sample size ranges from –32,768 to +32,768, or 65,536 values. Thus, a 16-bit card produces sound like a CD player, whereas an 8-bit card produces sound like FM radio music. Because the larger 16-bit samples require twice as much storage space as 8-bit samples, most home users can get by with an 8-bit system.

Sound cards are now advertised with the numbers 32 or 64. Don't let this confuse you with the 32-bit or 64-bit values that indicate the rate at which computer data is processed. In this case, the numbers 32 and 64 indicate the number of sounds that the card can play simultaneously.

Sampling rates haven't changed too much over the years. Sound cards generally have sampling rates from about 4,000 to 44,000 samples per second. These samples may contain one channel (mono) or two (stereo).

Two different types of files are stored: MIDI with .mid file extensions, and sample files, which Microsoft calls WAV files. Game music is usually stored in MIDI files, and multimedia sound is mostly stored in WAV files. The best sound cards can handle game music, multimedia sound, and music CDs.

Many sound cards have a Multimedia PC (MPC) Marketing Council rating. These are minimum standards for the Windows multimedia market, developed by the MPC Marketing Council. You see them referred to as MPC1, MPC2, and MPC3. To get the best multimedia quality, users should seek equipment that carries MPC3 compliance (see Table 10-5).

Besides storing sound, the sound card converts digitally stored sound into realistic analog sound. Sound cards use two methods: **frequency modulation (FM)** synthesis and **wavetable** synthesis. Whereas FM synthesis artificially simulates a sound through mathematical calculation, wavetable synthesis relies on stored sample recordings of the real sound, using a **digital signal processor (DSP)**. Wavetable synthesis produces a better sound, but is costlier than FM. State-of-the-art sound cards support wavetable synthesis.

**Table 10-5**    *MPC ratings for various components*

| Component | MPC1 (1991) | MPC2 (1993) | MPC3 (1996) |
|---|---|---|---|
| Processor | 16-MHz 386SX | 25-MHz 486SX or compatible | 75-MHz Pentium or compatible |
| RAM | 2 MB | 4 MB | 8 MB |
| Hard drive | 30 MB | 160 MB | 540 MB |
| Display | VGA | VGA, 64,000 colors | VGA, full-motion video |
| CD-ROM | 1X (150 KBps) | 2X (300 KBps) | 4X (600 KBps) |
| Average seek time | 400 milliseconds | 250 milliseconds | |
| Sound board | 8 bit | 16 bit | 16 bit |
| MIDI | Yes | Yes | Yes |
| Speakers | Yes | Yes | Yes (3 watts per channel) |
| Operating system | Windows 3.0 | Windows 3.0 | Windows 3.11, DOS 6.0 |

Most sound cards also provide mixing capabilities, combining signals from different input sources and controlling different sound levels.

The latest computer audio development involves 3D sound, utilizing Creative Labs's 3D Positional Audio and Orchid Technology's Spatializer 3D technology to give you the sensation of hearing sounds behind you and above your head. 3D sound is very popular in games that strive to create virtual reality scenarios.

# MIDI

Older cards may only capture audio signals, digitize them, and play them back, but nearly all current cards generate synthetic sounds that are apart from the digitizing process. Thus, the MIDI standard was created to allow music synthesizers and other electronic music devices to communicate with computers.

The MIDI protocol lists 16 instrument channels. The General MIDI Standard defines 128 MIDI program codes, which ensure that the sound produced by different MIDI instruments is consistent. A typical MIDI system contains a MIDI-equipped computer, a keyboard controller/synthesizer, an audio mixer/recorder, and other related sound modules (which are hardware components that contain ROM devices to hold the sampled sounds of real instruments). A typical MIDI system also contains a MIDI interface card.

All MIDI devices communicate through round 5-pin DIN serial connectors. A single connection cable can be used for all three connection types that exist in MIDI systems:

- MIDI-In

- MIDI-Out

- MIDI-Thru

The synthesizer/controller requires two MIDI interface connections. The first involves the controller portion of the keyboard. A MIDI cable runs from the MIDI-Out of the controller to the MIDI-In of the interface. Conversely, on the synthesizer side of the keyboard, a MIDI-In from the keyboard must connect to the MIDI-Out of the interface card. Continuing the MIDI system connection, the interface requires an additional MIDI-Out connection. All the other MIDI devices to the system can use the MIDI-Thru connection. Various other devices use audio out/in patch cards connected to the mixer/recorder.

All MIDI data transfers are done serially. Each MIDI device contains a MIDI controller. Any data produced by the MIDI device is sent to the controller, which converts the data into the MIDI format. This data signal goes to the MIDI adapter card in the computer for processing, and is sent back to the MIDI device.

MIDI data includes a huge amount of information about the instrument, including the patch (that is, the instrument), the MIDI channel, the note played, the velocity setting, and the System Exclusive (SYSX) data.

Although most sound cards are able to directly drive low-power headphones, additional amplification is needed when external speakers are used. The necessary amplification hardware is normally included in the external speaker units.

Now that you have been introduced to the sound card and MIDI components, you can use this knowledge later with some hands-on lab experience installing and troubleshooting the computer's sound devices.

# Concept Questions     *Semester 1, Unit 10, Lesson 49*

Demonstrate your knowledge of the concepts in this lesson by answering the following questions in the space provided.

1.  How do sound cards convert digital data into analog sound?

2.  What does the MIDI standard allow, and what does a typical MIDI system contain?

# Vocabulary Exercise    *Semester 1, Unit 10, Lesson 49*

*Name:* _____

*Date:* _____  *Class:* _____

Define the following terms as completely as you can.

**analog-to-digital converter**

_____

_____

**FM**

_____

_____

**MIDI**

_____

_____

**pulse code modulation method**

_____

_____

**Sound Blaster**

_____

_____

**wavetable synthesis**

_____

_____

## Focus Questions

### *Semester 1, Unit 10, Lesson 49*

*Name:* _____

*Date:* _____  *Class:* _____

**1.** What does the MIDI data include?

_____

_____

_____

_____

**2.** Describe the function of a sound card.

_____

_____

_____

_____

**3.** Describe what represents the most accurate sound replication.

_____

_____

_____

_____

**4.** How are MIDI data transfers accomplished?

_____

_____

_____

_____

# SEMESTER 1, UNIT 10, LESSON 50
# Unit 10 Exam

If you have access to the online Aries A+ curriculum, contact your instructor for the Assessment System URL. If you do not have access to the online curriculum, please continue to Unit 11.

# Semester 1, Unit 11

- Lesson 51: Printers
- Lesson 52: BIOS Setup
- Lesson 53: Operating Systems
- Lesson 54: Windows 95 Setup Basics Lab Exercises
- Lesson 55: Unit 11 Exam

# SEMESTER 1, UNIT 11, LESSON 51
# Printers

You have learned about components for processing, storing, manipulating, and inputting data in a computer. This lesson covers the major printer types and how they function. In the simplest terms, a **printer** is an **output device** that produces hard copy, paper printouts that consist of text and graphics.

## Printer output

All printers, regardless of classification, pretty much do the same thing: They output patterns of dots on paper as text or graphics. The smaller and closer together the dots are, the clearer and finer the resolution. **Resolution** is usually expressed in terms of how many dots per inch (dpi). For example, 150 dpi is considered draft resolution, and 300 dpi is considered letter quality.

All output is in the form of character design sets called **fonts**. A font is the combination of typeface and other qualities, such as size, pitch, and spacing. A commonly used font is Times Roman.

## Printer connection to the host system

Printers connect to the host computer via a cable attached to a parallel port (LPT) at the rear of the system. The cable connects using a male DB-25F connector to a female DB-25F port on the system and a Centronics connector to Centronics port on the printer. This attachment is universal except in some older types of printers, which connect via the serial port.

## Types of printers

Two basic types of printers are

- **Impact printers**, which use print heads to physically strike the paper

- **Non-impact printers**, which never physically touch the paper

The following sections describe these two types of printers.

### *Impact printers*

There have been many types of impact printers since the introduction of computer technology after World War II. However, most of them have become obsolete. The last competitor prior to the current standard—the daisywheel printer—became obsolete in the late 1980s and is no longer produced.

## Dot-matrix printers

A widely used printer type is the **dot-matrix printer**. This durable design remains popular today and still has its functional place, despite the introduction of newer, sharper-resolution printer technologies. Some major manufacturers of these printers are Okidata, Epson, and Lexmark.

A dot-matrix printer creates characters and graphics by striking pins against an ink ribbon, similar to the way a typewriter works. These striking pins print closely spaced dots in the appropriate character shape.

The quality of the printing depends on how closely spaced the dots are, which depends on the number of pins in the print head. Less expensive dot-matrix printers have only 9 pins in their print head, and more expensive ones have 24 pins. As a result, these 24-pin models are capable of near-letter-quality printing. Nevertheless, these printers are seldom used for high-quality correspondence or presentation documents, but are used for high-volume production printouts, such as forms, checks, and draft reports.

The most common type of printer paper used in this type of printer is **tractor-feed paper**. Also called **fan-fold paper**, this bulk paper of connected sheets with perforated, tear-away edges, fits into a **tractor-feed device** on the dot-matrix printer. The tractor-feed device is a pair of sprocket wheels on a rotating bar that fits into the perforated edges of the paper. Once loaded, this tractor-feed device continually feeds the paper into the paper channel of the printer, under a large roller called the *platen*, and around to a spring-loaded bar called the *bail*. When powered, these can either push or pull the paper through the paper channel. The paper can be loaded from the rear or bottom of the tractor mechanism by pushing or pulling the paper through the paper path.

The font, print quality, and speed of these printers are usually set by a series of controls on the front panel of the printer. The print head goes across the paper horizontally on a bar, making one or more passes, striking the paper through a ribbon attached to the print head. More passes means more print density and a higher print quality. The three common modes are draft, near-letter-quality, and letter-quality modes.

Speed, expressed in characters per second (cps), is also related to the print quality. Higher print density requires more passes of the print head over the paper, and thus fewer cps, which means slower printing.

The main advantages of dot-matrix printers are speed, impact capabilities, and inexpensive operation. High-end dot-matrix printers can be very fast, exceeding 100 cps, and printing pages far more quickly than either inkjet or laser printers. Their impact design allows them to handle multipart forms, a quality that is critical for organizations requiring multiple copies of material. They are less expensive to operate per page because maintenance is less costly and ribbons are less expensive than the toner or ink of laser or inkjet printers.

The only major disadvantage of dot-matrix printers is the fact that they are unsuitable for highly professional and letter-quality work.

## Non-impact printers

The two main types of non-impact printers are inkjet and laser printers. **Inkjet printers** use liquid ink to spray characters onto the page. **Laser printers** use lasers to draw an image onto an electrically charged drum that is transferred to electrically charged paper. Major manufacturers of non-impact printers are Hewlett Packard, Canon, Okidata, and Epson.

### Inkjet printers

An inkjet printer creates characters and graphics by spraying characters onto the page. An internal print head has a series of small nozzles that are electrically heated. When the print head is sufficiently heated, the ink "bubbles" and bursts through the nozzles to spray dots onto the paper (hence, the nickname "bubblejet"). Magnetic plates in the ink path direct the ink onto the paper to form characters.

Inkjet printers are commonly used as lower-cost alternatives to laser printers for official and presentation-quality documents. Color support is also dramatically cheaper for inkjet printers than in laser printers. These printers use cut-sheet paper in letter or legal size.

Inkjet printers use the following printing process:

1. The cut-sheet paper feeds into the paper channel from a paper tray in the front or rear of the printer.

2. The paper is pulled into the paper path by an arm and is friction-fed between rollers over a platen and under the print head path.

3. The print head moves across the paper on a rail, much like that in the dot-matrix printer, to spray the ink in the desired pattern.

4. The hard copy end products come out at the front into another tray.

The fonts and print quality are set from a series of buttons on the front panel, much like with dot-matrix printers. Like dot-matrix printers, the density of the dots in the characters determines the quality of the print. Most inkjet printers accomplish this by using less ink spray. They commonly have two densities of print mode. Econo-mode uses less ink and thereby less print density and lower resolution. The regular mode produces resolution anywhere from 300 dpi to 600 dpi, depending on the model. The print heads for this type of printer require a special kind of ink, which comes in a cartridge with a metal face on the bottom. The cartridge is set into a special carrier atop the print head and substitutes for the ribbon cartridge used in dot-matrix printers.

Inkjet printers offer most of the ability of laser printers, with far less expense. Color inkjet printers in particular are much cheaper than color laser printers, costing up to $3,000 less. Inkjet font, graphics, and text print quality can approach that of all but the most expensive laser printers. Inkjet printers greatly exceed dot-matrix printers in their print versatility and font selection.

The major disadvantages of inkjet printers are two-fold. They are very slow compared to dot-matrix and laser printers, and the ink tends to smudge on anything other than high-quality paper and takes a long time to dry.

## *Laser printers*

The laser printer is the highest-quality printer for official correspondence and presentation-quality documents. Color laser printers are available with four-color toners, but they are quite expensive and not very commonly used. This printer type also uses cut-sheet paper with a paper path not unlike the better-quality inkjet printers. It is what happens to the paper along this route that is markedly different.

Laser printers are sometimes called *page printers* because they print an entire page at a time, much like a copy machine. When input comes from the computer, the following happens:

1. First it goes to a printer controller, which is the command center for the laser printer.

2. The controller reads the data output from the host computer into memory and then interprets the commands sent to it for the page format, which includes the fonts, spacing, paper size, margins, text layout, and graphics.

3. The controller converts the page into an array of dots ready for the laser and sends it to the print engine. This stage is called **rasterization**.

4. The print engine transcribes the array of dots created by the printer controller into a printed image. The array is created on a photoreceptor drum with a laser scanning assembly that uses a laser beam with a rotating mirror and a lens.

5. The laser shoots a brief pulse of light for each dot to be printed, and leaves a blank for the non-print areas.

6. The mirror redirects the beam back and forth across the drum horizontally, in precise increments of one dot. The rotating drum is coordinated with this from vertical line to line.

7. The drum rolls through a reservoir of toner. Toner is a very fine powder of plastic particles which are attracted to the charged area of the drum.

8. The paper transport mechanism brings the paper from the paper tray and through the paper path. This transport is coordinated with the imaging process so that, when the drum is ready, the paper is moved beneath the drum.

9. A smaller roller near the drum, called the developer unit, feeds toner onto the drum from a storage bin (that is, a toner hopper) above it. The paper is also electrostatically charged along its route just before going under the drum.

10. When the paper meets the drum, the toner pattern is attracted to the paper.

**11.** The paper then goes through a pair of very hot rollers, called the fuser, which fixes the toner into the paper with heat and pressure. The plastic toner particles are fused into the paper to form the final printed page.

**12.** As the sheet of paper leaves the drum area, another light completely bathes the drum to erase the laser image for the next printed page.

The chief advantages of the laser printer are its high speed and fine resolution. Laser printer speeds are measured in **pages per minute (ppm)**. Resolution is routinely 300 dpi to 600 dpi and can be as high as 1200 dpi. Both the speed and resolution of laser printers are higher than those of inkjet printers; only high-end dot-matrix printers are faster than laser printers. Laser printers routinely excel at printing complex graphics and text, and they generally support more fonts than all but high-end inkjet printers.

The flip side to these advantages are resource requirements and expense. Because a laser printer prints whole pages from memory, complex printing requires large amounts of RAM. Unlike computer memory which is relatively cheap, printer memory is usually proprietary and expensive. Toner and other replacement parts such as a developer unit and fuser are also very expensive. Finally, the color capability in laser printers is very expensive.

### *Computer communication with the printer*

Page description languages (PDLs) control laser printer and inkjet printers. These are what the computer application software uses to send commands to the printer for the desired results. There are two de facto standards for these languages: Printer Control Language (PCL) and Postscript.

Hewlett-Packard pioneered PCL with its early laser printers. There have been several versions as the language has evolved. The most current is PCL6. The later versions are backward compatible so that an application that printed with PCL4 or PCL5 will work with PCL6. However, later PCL versions support features not found in earlier versions, so that the compatibility does not work in reverse.

Postscript is a high-end proprietary language developed by Adobe Systems for desktop publishing with extremely complex text and graphics. This language is standard on high-end laser printers.

Because these two languages are not cross-compatible, printers must sense the difference and auto-switch between them. Postscript is usually a relatively expensive add-on option for less expensive laser and inkjet printers. There are some Postscript emulation software packages for printers, but they usually do not offer full compatibility with actual Postscript, which is implemented in ROM modules.

# Concept Questions     *Semester 1, Unit 11, Lesson 51*

Demonstrate your knowledge of the concepts in this lesson by answering the
following questions in the space provided.

**1.** Explain the advantages and disadvantages of the two basic types of printers,
impact and non-impact printers.

**2.** Explain how the two basic types of printers, impact and non-impact, create
characters on a page.

_____

_____

_____

_____

_____

_____

_____

_____

_____

_____

_____

_____

_____

_____

_____

_____

# Vocabulary Exercise     *Semester 1, Unit 11, Lesson 51*

Name: _____

Date: _____     Class: _____

Define the following terms as completely as you can.

***dot-matrix printer***

_____

_____

***impact printer***

_____

_____

***inkjet printer***

_____

_____

***laser printer***

_____

_____

***non-impact printer***

_____

_____

***PDL***

_____

_____

**resolution**

_____

_____

# Focus Questions

## *Semester 1, Unit 11, Lesson 51*

*Name:* _____

*Date:* _____ *Class:* _____

**1.** How is resolution usually expressed?

_____

_____

_____

_____

**2.** How do printers connect to the host computer?

_____

_____

_____

_____

**3.** Describe the two types of non-impact printers.

_____

_____

_____

_____

**4.** Explain the function of PDLs.

_____

_____

_____

_____

# SEMESTER 1, UNIT 11, LESSON 52
# BIOS Setup

Now that you are familiar with various hardware devices, we will take a look at the BIOS setup that allows you to fine-tune the components of the system to function optimally. Each section of this lesson has a counterpart section in the motherboard manual showing a graphic of the screen as it would appear before configuration. There are instructions with each graphic, giving directions on how to navigate using the keyboard.

## The Standard CMOS Setup screen

The instructions regarding choices in this environment are given in Unit 4. The set of features contains the basic operating parameters you need in order to set up the system to work correctly. These BIOS features are typically universal for all computers.

Note the fields available for entering configuration data:

- Date

- Time

- Hard Disk

- Drive A

- Drive B

- Video

- Halt On

The first two fields are for setting the clock that governs the settings in the operating system. The date and time are necessary for many types of software applications to manage data. Note the format required. If this is the initial setup, a default date is usually assigned (for example, Jan 01 1980). The time is given in the 24-hour format.

The Hard Disk section is composed of fields where the devices that are attached to the two IDE controllers integrated on the motherboard are identified. IDE controllers can have two hard drives, one configured a master and the other a slave. The entries for configuration are the following:

- Primary Master

- Primary Slave

- Secondary Master

- Secondary Slave

Because of the sector translation available in modern IDE drives, setting the Drive Type field to Auto will cause the identify drive command to be issued by the BIOS and configured accordingly. The LBA mode identifies the Auto setting as for only those drives that support sector translation. Otherwise, you will be required to enter the drive geometry into the appropriate fields for the BIOS to recognize and work with the drive.

The next section has two fields, labeled Drive A and Drive B for identifying the types of floppy disk drives using the options available. For example, you might set only one drive, a 3 1/2-inch high-density 1.44-MB floppy drive, for Drive A.

The next field is Video, where the type of video adapter is identified. The choices here are very few and the default EGA/VGA, which has been the standard for everything since 1990. Whether VGA, SVGA, or anything more advanced, all the video adapters since 1990 support the basic VGA BIOS instructions built into the system BIOS.

The last user-definable field in this screen is the Halt On field. The choices here are designed to allow you to specify system response to errors, such as halt on all errors, halt on no errors (do not halt), and halt on all errors but the keyboard. This is so you can be notified of error problems before they corrupt data.

Finally, notice the informational box in the lower-right corner of the screen. This has non–user-definable screens that give information on the memory configuration of the system. For example, the system might tell you that it has 32 MB of total memory, subdivided into 640 KB of conventional DOS memory, 31.7 MB of extended memory, and 384 KB of upper memory area.

## The BIOS Features Setup screen

The instructions governing choices in this environment are given in the corresponding section of the motherboard manual.

This BIOS Setup screen contains advanced features that control the behavior of the system. Some older components and peripherals may need special settings for compatibility, special circumstances may require temporarily adjusting the system, and so on. In short, the BIOS Features Setup screen is where you can tune the system hardware for optimal performance, and disable or enable features for advanced troubleshooting. Most features should be left at the manual-recommended defaults, unless you have a good reason to change them. There are 24 features in all for this setup screen.

## The Chipset Features Setup screen

The instructions governing choices in this environment are given in the corresponding section of the motherboard manual.

This screen of the BIOS setup allows you to fine-tune the control parameters for the main system chipset. You have learned that the chipset controls the system cache, memory, processor, and I/O buses. Because of the potentially disabling nature of these settings, the first feature set choice is Automatic Configuration, with the default set to Enabled. This default should be left always at Enabled unless there is a good reason to change it.

The remaining feature sets are not automatically configurable:

- System BIOS Cacheable—This feature enables or disables the ability to copy slow system BIOS ROM code into main RAM at boot-up. This greatly increases the ability of the BIOS to manage resource quickly due to its being cached in system memory. System BIOS Cacheable should always be enabled, except perhaps during troubleshooting.

- Video BIOS Cacheable—This feature is very similar to System BIOS Cacheable. Enabling this feature allows the system to copy the video VESA BIOS extensions from the video adapter into main system RAM during boot-up. This allows significant performance enhancements in the basic video system by allowing the BIOS extension code to be executed and cached in main system memory.

- Memory Hole at 15m–16m—This feature, when enabled, allows older linear VGA video cards to run a larger frame port. Enabling means this area of memory would be used by the system to write larger frame sizes from the video memory to the monitor screen more quickly.

- Peer Concurrency—This feature controls whether the system can allow more than one PCI device at a time to be active on the bus. It is enabled by default. However, the disable setting is sometimes useful to troubleshoot PCI problems on early PCI bus systems.

## The Power Management Setup screen

The instructions governing choices in this environment are given in the corresponding section of the motherboard manual.

This section of the BIOS setup contains the feature settings you can use to control the system's optional power management for devices. When these features are enabled, you can control when and if some devices in the system go into sleep or suspend mode. These devices are usually the biggest power consumers in the system. The feature set Power Down and Resume Events can be set to monitor the system IRQs for activity in order to start or suspend power management functions.

The wisdom of using these power management features is debated among computer technicians. Some software and operating systems do not deal well with components being powered down. They may not power up again properly, or the software might not recognize a device again properly. Many technicians recommend that the first feature choice, Power Management, be disabled.

## The PnP/PCI Configuration screen

The instructions governing choices in this environment are given in the corresponding section of the motherboard manual.

This section of the BIOS setup contains the feature settings used to control the system I/O bus IRQ and DMA allocation for ISA and PCI **plug-and-play** devices. The master feature is the Resource Controlled By setting. When set by default to Automatic configuration, the BIOS automatically manages the interrupts and direct memory access channels on the I/O bus for the plug-and-play devices to avoid conflicts with the legacy (non–plug-and-play) ISA devices. However, sometimes errant or nonconforming plug-and-play adapters or expansion boards require manual intervention to designate IRQs or DMAs for their use. You can then designate for each IRQ and DMA whether you want it to be available for the expansion card, or whether to remove it from BIOS handling for older fixed IRQ ISA cards.

The second panel in this screen is for setting the IRQs for the IDE hard drive controllers on the motherboard. The defaults are PCI IRQ Activated By Level and PCI IDE IRQ Map To PCI-AUTO. The PCI IDE IRQ Map To feature can be alternately set to use the interrupt of a PCI bus slot.

Setting this part of the BIOS manually requires a good knowledge of the bus devices installed in the system. Because they may not work correctly on manual settings, the Reset Configuration Data feature will clear this portion of the BIOS setup and return it to defaults upon rebooting the system.

## The Load Setup Defaults screen

The instructions governing choices in this environment are given in the corresponding section of the motherboard manual.

This section of the BIOS setup provides a choice of whether to reset the BIOS setup screens to default settings. This will not affect those in the Standard CMOS Setup screen because they are the absolute minimums for the system to function. This optional section allows you to return the system to the settings that will put it into a known stable state. If you are configuring a system for a creative computer experimenter, this is a good way to return to a clean state for troubleshooting. However, it is recommended that you document the BIOS settings before doing so.

## The Integrated Peripherals screen

The instructions governing choices in this environment are given in the corresponding section of the motherboard manual.

The features in this section control integrated peripheral support on the motherboard. These devices typically include the onboard floppy and hard drive controllers, USB controller, serial ports, and parallel port. If the motherboard were to include additional devices such as integrated sound card chip or similar devices, these would be here as well.

The first six features in this section govern hard drive controller activity. The first two are for specifying whether the controller is to use these enhanced transfer modes with the hard drive. Most new hard drives support these functions, but you should check with the drive documentation first. The latter four refer to the BIOS management of the Programmed IO mode of the drive controllers. Setting these features to Auto permits the BIOS to issue the appropriate IDE drive commands to determine what mode the hard drives will support. This is always recommended.

The Reset Configuration Data feature is an escape mode for resetting this section to defaults and resetting them to the last known good configuration during reboot. The next two features are for enabling or disabling the onboard PCI IDE hard drive controllers. The USB Controller feature is for enabling or disabling the controller chip for the USB ports on the motherboard.

## The Supervisor Password screen

This screen has one feature: setting up a master password for locking the user out of the system BIOS setup screen. The feature is used in large institutions where BIOS settings are kept standardized by a computer support staff. Once set, these computer BIOS setups are locked with a master password only known to the network administrator or a designee. This prevents users from accidentally or experimentally changing the settings and causing system problems requiring support staff intervention. You are not likely to find this feature outside large institutions such as corporations or large school districts.

This setting, if chosen, will ask you to enter a password, and then enter it again for confirmation. The instructions for this option are found in the motherboard manual. If you accidentally engage this screen, you can bypass it easily by simply pressing the Enter key, without entering a password at the prompt. Another screen will come up, stating "Password Disabled!" Pressing any key will return you to the main setup screen.

## The IDE HDD Auto Detection screen

As you recall there is a Hard Disk section on the Standard CMOS Setup screen that has an Auto setting for automatically detecting the hard drive geometry. However, sometimes this feature will not work with certain IDE hard drives. IDE HDD Auto Detection is for those situations.

It allows you to manually run the IDE autodetection program. Select the autodetection for each drive on the controller channel, and the BIOS will scan and report drive parameters, which can then be accepted or rejected. If accepted, these are then entered into the Standard CMOS Setup, Hard Drive feature entry. Some experienced technicians use this manual autodetection utility anyway when installing new drives because this alerts them to a disk problem immediately if the autodetection does not work.

## The HDD Low Level Format screen

This is an old legacy utility no longer used for modern hard drives. (Note that the copyright on the utility is from 1994, whereas the main BIOS copyright is from 1996.) These were typically used to reset the drive geometry on older MFM and RLL types of hard drives, such as interleave settings, media analysis to identify and mark bad drive tracks, and so on. These are not used on the modern IDE drives. On the rare occasions when this is necessary with IDE drives, the manufacturer can provide special low-level format utilities for the particular model of hard drive.

## The Save & Exit Setup screen

This setup screen includes only one feature setting that is used to exit the BIOS setup program and save your changes to the CMOS chip. Although there are shortcuts, it is always best to use this exit feature in order to not accidentally lose all your setup modification entries.

## The Exit Without Saving screen

This setup screen also includes only one feature setting that is used to exit the BIOS setup program, but discards all modified settings you have made to it.

# Concept Questions     *Semester 1, Unit 11, Lesson 52*

Demonstrate your knowledge of the concepts in this lesson by answering the following questions in the space provided.

1. Explain the use of the BIOS Feature Setup screen for optimal performance and advanced troubleshooting.

2. Explain how the Chipset Features Setup screen allows you to fine-tune the control parameters for the main system chipset.

_____

_____

_____

_____

_____

_____

_____

_____

_____

_____

_____

_____

_____

_____

_____

# Vocabulary Exercise    *Semester 1, Unit 11, Lesson 52*

*Name:* _____

*Date:* _____    *Class:* _____

Define the following terms as completely as you can.

**BIOS Features Setup screen**

_____

_____

**Chipset Features Setup screen**

_____

_____

**Load Setup Defaults screen**

_____

_____

**Memory Hole at 15m–16m**

_____

_____

**peer concurrency**

_____

_____

**PnP/PCI Configuration screen**

_____

_____

**Power Management Setup screen**

_____

_____


**Standard CMOS Setup screen**

_____

_____


**System BIOS Cacheable**

_____

_____


**Video BIOS Cacheable**

_____

_____

# Focus Questions     *Semester 1, Unit 11, Lesson 52*

*Name:* _____

*Date:* _____    *Class:* _____

**1.** Describe how System BIOS Cacheable allows you to enable or disable the ability to copy slow system BIOS ROM code into main RAM at boot-up.

_____

_____

_____

_____

**2.** Describe how Video BIOS Cacheable allows the system to copy the video VESA BIOS extensions from the video adapter into main system RAM during boot-up.

_____

_____

_____

_____

**3.** Describe how enabling Memory Hole at 15m–16m allows older linear VGA video cards to run a larger frame port.

_____

_____

_____

_____

**4.** Describe how the peer concurrency feature controls whether the system allows more than one PCI device at a time to be active on the bus.

_____

_____

_____

_____

**5.** Explain how the Power Management Setup screen contains the feature settings you can use to control the system's optional power management for devices.

_____

_____

_____

_____

**6.** Explain how the Load Setup Default screen provides a choice of whether to reset the BIOS setup screens to default settings.

_____

_____

_____

_____

**7.** Explain how to set the Supervisor Password screen feature to lock the user out of the system BIOS setup screen.

_____

_____

_____

_____

_____

# SEMESTER 1, UNIT 11, LESSON 53
# Operating Systems

Now you're up to date about the computer system's components and devices. You also know about the BIOS that contains the code required to operate computer components and devices. Coordinating and managing the all those devices and components is the computer's **operating system (OS)**.

The operating system is the software that controls hardware and provides higher-level routines for application programs. For example, most operating systems provide functions to read and write data on files. The operating system translates requests for operations on files into primitive operations that the disk controller can carry out (for example, read a block, write a block).

Operating systems perform the following basic tasks:

- Recognizing input from the keyboard or mouse

- Sending output to the video screen or printer

- Keeping track of files on the floppy and hard drives

- Controlling peripherals such as printers and modems

## Operating system components

The operating system is composed of modular components, each of which has a distinct function. The major design components of any operating system are

- The user interface

- The kernel

- The file management system

These components are described in the following sections.

### *The user interface*

The **user interface** is the operating system shell that you use to issue commands, either by typing them at a command prompt or using a graphical user interface (GUI) to point at objects on a screen and click with a mouse. Essentially, the interface is what the user sees and interacts with.

### *The kernel*

The **kernel** is the core of the operating system. It takes responsibility for memory management, program objectives (tasks), program execution (processes), and disk files. Operating systems can either manage one program at a time, called single tasking, or several concurrently, called multitasking.

### *The file management system*

The **file management system** is the system that an operating system uses to organize and manage files. A file is a collection of data that has a single logical name (that is, a filename). Just about all information in a computer's storage is in this form. Files consist of many types of information, including data files, program files, and text files, among others.

Most operating systems use a hierarchical file system in which files are organized into directories under a tree structure. The beginning of this directory system is called the **root directory**.

## Commonly used operating systems

A variety of operating systems, including the following, are available to run on the standard (nonproprietary) computer system today:

- UNIX

- Linux

- IBM OS/2

- Microsoft DOS

- Microsoft Windows 95

- Microsoft Windows NT

- Apple Macintosh

These operating systems are described in the following sections.

### *UNIX*

**UNIX** is the oldest, most stable, and most robust of the operating systems that run on nonproprietary computer systems. Originally developed by Bell Labs at AT&T in the 1970s, it has spawned several variants, and there are several UNIX standards. The most common variants are those following the UNIX System V standard and those following the standard set by the systems developed at the University of California at Berkeley—the BSD standard. The numerous variants are sometimes not cross-compatible.

UNIX has a reputation for being an enormously powerful, multitasking system that supports several robust file systems, but suffers from a difficult, nonstandardized GUI. The numerous variants are also not cross-compatible. These two factors have limited its acceptance among the general computer user population. Major variants are produced by the Santa Cruz Operation (SCO), Sun Microsystems (Solaris), and Digital Equipment Corporation (DEC).

## *Linux*

**Linux** is a fairly recent development from UNIX developed by a Finnish graduate student named Linus Torvalds in 1991. This operating system was developed as a publicly available variant of UNIX initially distributed via the Internet. Due to its nominal cost and freedom of distribution, Linux has grown to have the fourth or fifth largest user base in the world, with millions of users worldwide. Because of this large number of users, many of whom are programmers and computer scientists, this is a phenomenally well-supported and well-developed multitasking operating system.

More recently, small firms have begun packaging Linux distributions commercially. The major Linux distributions are RedHat, Slackware, Debian, and Caldera. It suffers some of the same problems as UNIX with regard to its GUI, but it can support numerous file systems. The market for Linux is growing rapidly as users find it to be stable, robust, and flexible.

## *OS/2*

**OS/2**, or Operating System 2, was originally developed as a joint project by IBM and Microsoft in the late 1980s. However, due to disagreements over the direction of its development, the codevelopers split in the early 1990s, leaving IBM to continue the development. OS/2's popularity among home and small business computer users has slipped since then, but it continues to be popular in large institutions where its integration with IBM mainframe technologies is prized. OS/2 has an excellent file system called HPFS, supports multitasking, and has a good GUI. Unfortunately, very few applications are designed for its interface, but IBM continues to develop and support it, so it will be around for some time.

## *MS-DOS*

**MS-DOS**, developed by Microsoft in the early 1980s, is the most widespread of the operating systems found on computer systems worldwide. Initially licensed by IBM for its newly developed PC, it was adopted as the standard by all PC clone manufacturers by the mid-1980s. In 1992 Microsoft released a graphical shell for MS-DOS called Windows 3.1.

By itself, DOS is only a single-tasking operating system, but it includes limited multitasking with the Windows 3.1 GUI shell. The MS-DOS kernel, called **command.com**, and variants of its file system, called File Allocation Table (FAT), are still core components of newer Windows operating systems.

## *Windows 95*

**Windows 95**, developed and released by the Microsoft in 1995, is the successor to MS-DOS with its Windows 3.1 graphical shell. Although Windows 95's capabilities are far more reaching than those of its predecessors, it still uses a variant of the MS-DOS kernel and variants of the DOS FAT file system.

Windows 95 is currently the most widely distributed operating system with a GUI interface on the market today. It is a very versatile operating system, supporting MS-DOS, Windows 3.1, and native Windows 95 applications in a multitasking environment. Microsoft has recently released an updated and refined version of this operating system, called Windows 98. It provides many improvements, including better multimedia, networking, and Internet support. Both of these operating systems share a similar GUI with their more robust cousin, Windows NT.

## *Windows NT*

**Windows NT** is an extremely robust and powerful multitasking operating system with a GUI interface that's almost identical to that of Windows 95. However, it has a completely different kernel and file system from other Microsoft operating systems. Introduced in 1993, it has since been through several different versions. Windows NT was developed by designers with previous experience in larger, more complex mainframe/minicomputer operating systems and is intended for heavy-duty application environments. Its capabilities and robust nature reflect these design origins, and each new version has introduced enhanced capabilities.

Most importantly, Windows NT's kernel (**cmd.exe**) is extremely flexible, creating operating environments to support older MS-DOS, Windows 3.1, and even OS/2 applications, as well as its native ones. The file system, NTFS, is extremely secure and fault tolerant for demanding use.

## *Apple Macintosh*

The Macintosh is the final operating system commonly found. Developed by Apple Computer and released in 1984, it was the first true GUI operating system, based on earlier technology developed by Xerox Corporation in the late 1970s. It was an extremely popular alternative to the Microsoft-based DOS and Windows operating systems through the early 1990s. However, the Macintosh operating system runs only on Apple's proprietary hardware, and it has not been seriously updated in several years. These factors have led to a serious decline in its popularity since the early 1990s, but recent developments at Apple, including the development of a totally new operating system based on UNIX with the Macintosh GUI may yet bring about a comeback.

# Operating system installation basics

Each hard disk contains partitions to allow the computer system to load and boot the operating system. The master boot record on the hard drive contains the information the BIOS needs to find the boot partition and initiate the operating system's particular bootstrap loader. For this to happen, the hard drive in a new computer system needs to be prepared for both the BIOS and the operating system.

## *Hard disk organization for booting the operating system*

Labs later in this semester explain hard disk organization in regard to the basic MS-DOS operating system. MS-DOS is used because its file system, FAT, is the basis for variants such as VFAT and FAT32, which are all used and supported by several operating systems: MS-DOS, Windows 95, Windows NT, and OS/2.

The FAT in the DOS file system is an index of stored files on the hard drive. The FAT system supports data stored in 512-byte segments of disk tracks called sectors. Because the extra time spent tracking these small data pieces is too great for most operating systems, the hard disk is broken into larger pieces, called clusters, that are each composed of several sectors.

The bootstrap loader for the MS-DOS operating system is composed of two files that are required to load the operating system kernel. The boot partition's volume contains the volume boot code, much as the master boot record of the hard drive has the master boot code. For MS-DOS, the volume boot code is contained in the two bootstrap loader files, called io.sys and msdos.sys. During the boot process, the BIOS examines the master boot record, locates the boot partition, finds the MS-DOS bootstrap loader files, and loads them into memory. Following this, these files load the kernel (**command.com**) into memory from the root directory.

Windows 95 loads in very similar fashion to MS-DOS, and is in fact installed onto disks already prepared for the MS-DOS file system.

## *Hard disk preparation for the operating system installation*

Because disks must be partitioned to prepare for a usable file system, MS-DOS provides a utility for partitioning the hard disk called **fdisk.exe**. The preparation of the resulting partitions is done by a utility called **format.com**.

MS-DOS has an automatic installation routine, but you need to know the basics in order to prepare other hard drives or to troubleshoot a drive with a corrupted operating system. You will learn this in upcoming labs.

You have learned about how to prepare a new system for installation of several types of operating systems; however, the most common one you will encounter is Windows 95. Installation of Windows 95 requires planning and attention to detail. Before installing

Windows 95 or any other operating system, it is a good idea to find a thorough manual on the process and spend some time becoming familiar with the specifics of the operating system.

It is not the intention of this lesson to provide in-depth details of the setup for Windows 95. You will get this during the second semester; however, information about the basic system requirements, the installation routines, and other details are important for planning prior to its installation.

# Concept Questions        *Semester 1, Unit 11, Lesson 53*

Demonstrate your knowledge of the concepts in this lesson by answering the following questions in the space provided.

1. Explain what an operating system is and what its major components are.

2. Explain how you prepare the hard disk before installing an operating system.

_____

_____

_____

_____

_____

_____

_____

_____

_____

_____

_____

_____

_____

_____

_____

_____

_____

_____

_____

# Vocabulary Exercise    *Semester 1, Unit 11, Lesson 53*

Name: _____

Date: _____    Class: _____

Define the following terms as completely as you can.

**command prompt**

_____

_____

**format.com**

_____

_____

**Linux**

_____

_____

**Macintosh**

_____

_____

**multitasking**

_____

_____

**operating system**

_____

_____

***root directory***

_____

_____

***single tasking***

_____

_____

***UNIX***

_____

_____

***Windows 95***

_____

_____

***Windows NT***

_____

_____

# Focus Questions          *Semester 1, Unit 11, Lesson 53*

*Name:* _____

*Date:* _____     *Class:* _____


**1.** How is the hard disk organized for booting the operating system?

_____

_____

_____

_____


**2.** What operating systems are available today?

_____

_____

_____

_____


**3.** Describe the function of the user interface.

_____

_____

_____

_____


**4.** Describe the function of the kernel.

_____

_____

_____

_____

**5.** Describe the function of the file management system.

_____

_____

_____

_____

**6.** Describe the basics of an operating system installation.

_____

_____

_____

_____

# SEMESTER 1, UNIT 11, LESSON 54
# Windows 95 Setup Basics Lab Exercises

If you have access to the online Aries A+ curriculum, go online to follow along with this lab exercise. If you do not have access to the online curriculum, please continue to the next lesson.

# SEMESTER 1, UNIT 11, LESSON 55
# Unit 11 Exam

If you have access to the online Aries A+ curriculum, contact your instructor for the Assessment System URL. If you do not have access to the online curriculum, please continue to Unit 12.

# SEMESTER 1, UNIT 12

- Lesson 56: Preparation for the System Assembly Process Lab Exercises
- Lesson 57: Motherboard Preparation and Assembly Lab Exercises
- Lesson 58: Motherboard Installation to the Chassis Lab Exercises
- Lesson 59: Drive Assembly Lab Exercises
- Lesson 60: Power Supply Installation to the Chassis Lab Exercises

# SEMESTER 1, UNIT 12, LESSON 56

## Preparation for the System Assembly Process Lab Exercises

If you have access to the online Aries A+ curriculum, go online to follow along with this lab exercise. If you do not have access to the online curriculum, please continue to the next lesson.

# SEMESTER 1, UNIT 12, LESSON 57
# Motherboard Preparation and Assembly Lab Exercises

If you have access to the online Aries A+ curriculum, go online to follow along with this lab exercise. If you do not have access to the online curriculum, please continue to the next lesson.

# SEMESTER 1, UNIT 12, LESSON 58
# Motherboard Installation to the Chassis Lab Exercises

If you have access to the online Aries A+ curriculum, go online to follow along with this lab exercise. If you do not have access to the online curriculum, please continue to the next lesson.

# SEMESTER 1, UNIT 12, LESSON 59
# Drive Assembly Lab Exercises

If you have access to the online Aries A+ curriculum, go online to follow along with this lab exercise. If you do not have access to the online curriculum, please continue to the next lesson.

# Semester 1, Unit 12, Lesson 60

## Power Supply Installation to the Chassis Lab Exercises

If you have access to the online Aries A+ curriculum, go online to follow along with this lab exercise. If you do not have access to the online curriculum, please continue to Unit 13.

# Semester 1, Unit 13

- Lesson 61: Installation of Video Card, Monitor, Keyboard, and Mouse Lab Exercises
- Lesson 62: Final System Assembly and Startup Troubleshooting Lab Exercises
- Lesson 63: System BIOS Setup Lab Exercises
- Lesson 64: Preparation for Operating System Installation Lab Exercises
- Lesson 65: Basic Windows 95 Installation Lab Exercises

# SEMESTER 1, UNIT 13, LESSON 61

# Installation of Video Card, Monitor, Keyboard, and Mouse Lab Exercises

If you have access to the online Aries A+ curriculum, go online to follow along with this lab exercise. If you do not have access to the online curriculum, please continue to the next lesson.

# SEMESTER 1, UNIT 13, LESSON 62

# Final System Assembly and Startup Troubleshooting Lab Exercises

If you have access to the online Aries A+ curriculum, go online to follow along with this lab exercise. If you do not have access to the online curriculum, please continue to the next lesson.

# SEMESTER 1, UNIT 13, LESSON 63
# System BIOS Setup Lab Exercises

If you have access to the online Aries A+ curriculum, go online to follow along with this lab exercise. If you do not have access to the online curriculum, please continue to the next lesson.

# Semester 1, Unit 13, Lesson 64

# Preparation for Operating System Installation Lab Exercises

If you have access to the online Aries A+ curriculum, go online to follow along with this lab exercise. If you do not have access to the online curriculum, please continue to the next lesson.

# SEMESTER 1, UNIT 13, LESSON 65
# Basic Windows 95 Installation Lab Exercises

If you have access to the online Aries A+ curriculum, go online to follow along with this lab exercise. If you do not have access to the online curriculum, please continue to Unit 14.

# SEMESTER 1, UNIT 14

- Lesson 66: Sound Card and Speaker Installation Lab Exercises
- Lesson 67: Modem Installation and Internet Configuration Lab Exercises
- Lesson 68: Network Card Installation Lab Exercises
- Lesson 69: Basic Networking Lab Exercises
- Lesson 70: Unit 14 Exam

# SEMESTER 1, UNIT 14, LESSON 66
# Sound Card and Speaker Installation Lab Exercises

If you have access to the online Aries A+ curriculum, go online to follow along with this lab exercise. If you do not have access to the online curriculum, please continue to the next lesson.

# SEMESTER 1, UNIT 14, LESSON 67

# Modem Installation and Internet Configuration Lab Exercises

If you have access to the online Aries A+ curriculum, go online to follow along with this lab exercise. If you do not have access to the online curriculum, please continue to the next lesson.

# SEMESTER 1, UNIT 14, LESSON 68
# Network Card Installation Lab Exercises

If you have access to the online Aries A+ curriculum, go online to follow along with this lab exercise. If you do not have access to the online curriculum, please continue to the next lesson.

# SEMESTER 1, UNIT 14, LESSON 69
# Basic Networking Lab Exercises

If you have access to the online Aries A+ curriculum, go online to follow along with this lab exercise. If you do not have access to the online curriculum, please continue to the next lesson.

# SEMESTER 1, UNIT 14, LESSON 70
# Unit 14 Exam

If you have access to the online Aries A+ curriculum, contact your instructor for the Assessment System URL.

# SEMESTER 1 GLOSSARY

# GLOSSARY

## Numbers and symbols

**101-key enhanced keyboard**   The standard layout for computer system keyboards, originally introduced by the IBM Corporation in 1986, that has since been copied by all PC-clone manufacturers.

**104-key enhanced keyboard**   A modified version of the 101-key enhanced keyboard with extra command keys added to support Microsoft Windows 95 and NT.

**15-pin mini D-sub**   The standard 15-pin connector used for connecting a video monitor to a video card.

**25-pin serial port**   A type of serial port that has 25 pins or contacts.

**3D sound**   Sound that seems to come from above, behind, and in front of you.

**9-pin serial port**   A type of serial port employing nine pins or contacts.

## A

**abacus**   One of the earliest counting instruments, constructed of sliding beads on small wooden rods slated across a wooden frame.

**AC (alternating current)**   A form of electricity in which voltage alternates direction. The frequency of AC voltage is 60 Hz in the United States, and AC is generally the standard for electrical power in both residential and commercial buildings.

**accelerator**   The primary chip in the video chipset; which handles most of the video processing.

**access list**   A database that lists the authorized users and their permissions for a Windows NT network.

**account**   A file that holds records of users and resources.

**acronym**   A word that is made up of the first letters or syllables of the words for which it stands. For example, *RAM* stands for *random access memory*.

**active partition**   A DOS partition that is read at startup. The active partition should have the files required to boot the system.

**adapter bracket**   A brace or prop used to support and attach expansion cards to the chassis. It is a subassembly of the chassis.

**adapter plate**   A metal cover used to seal holes over unused expansion brackets. The plate prevents dust from entering the case and maintains proper airflow inside the computer's case.

**Add New Hardware**  A Windows 95 option that allows the user to install new hardware devices or configure hardware settings.

**Add/Remove Programs**  A Windows 95 option that allows the user to create a start-up disk, and add or remove programs and components.

**address bus**  A data bus used by the CPU to carry data that identifies the memory locations where the data bits are being sent to or retrieved from.

**ADSL (Asymmetric Digital Subscriber Line)**  A relatively new technology that allows more data to be sent over existing copper telephone lines than previously possible.

**AGP (accelerated graphics port)**  An interface specification developed by Intel Corporation, designed especially for the throughput demands of 3D graphics. It uses a dedicated point-to-point channel, and allows the graphics controller to directly access main memory.

**AGP slot**  A high-speed graphics port created by Intel that features a direct connection between the display monitor and memory.

**alphanumeric key**  A keyboard key that represents a letter or a number.

**Alt**  A key used simultaneously with a second key to produce a desired function.

**Altair 8080**  A microcomputer introduced by MITS in 1975. It is considered by many computer experts to be the first successful PC.

**AMD (Advanced Micro Devices)**  An Intel-clone - producing computer manufacturer.

**analog**  Signals that continually changing strengths or qualities, like sound waves or voltage.

**analog-to-digital converter**  A device that converts analog (sound-based) tones and pulses into digital (binary-based) data for computer use.

**Analytical Engine**  A programmable calculator designed by Charles Babbage in the 1830s.

**antistatic bag**  A bag used to prevent static electricity from passing to electronic components inside. They are used to help prevent ESD.

**antistatic mat**  A mat made of an antistatic material designed to provide a grounding source, used to absorbs static electricity and prevent damage to electronic components.

**API (Application Program Interface)**  The specific method an application program can use to make requests of the operating system or of another application.

**Apple Computer**  The manufacturer of the Apple II and the Macintosh. Steve Wozniak and Steve Jobs founded Apple Computers in a garage.

**Apple II**  The Apple Computer Corporation's second PC, introduced in 1977, believed by many to be responsible for popularizing the PC.

**application**   A software program designed to carry out a task or produce a result such as word processing, creating accounts, database management, and/or inventory control.

**application server**   A machine that holds the applications users frequently access.

**apps.inf**   A Windows file that maintains information about popular MS-DOS programs.

**arbitration**   The process the SCSI host adapter uses to set priorities in handling multiple read/write requests, simultaneously, from contending drives on the bus. Priorities are based on the SCSI ID of the devices, from 0 to 7, in order of increasing priority.

**architecture**   A system's hardware, software, data-access protocols, and overall computer communications system designs.

**archive**   A DOS system attribute that checks if a file has changed since the last backup and requires backing up. Also refers to files stored as backup.

**ARCnet**   LAN technology from the Datapoint Corporation that uses a token-bus system.

**ARP (Address Resolution Protocol)**   The protocol TCP/IP uses to get a domain name address when only an IP address is available.

**ASCII (American Standard Code for Information Interchange)**   A standardized code, using binary values, for representing characters.

**asynchronous**   Not occurring at predetermined or regular intervals. Also, communications in which an interchange of data can start at anytime instead of occurring at fixed intervals.

**asynchronous communication**   Bidirectional data transmission between two devices, in which the length of time between transmitted characters is variable.

**AT command set**   A standard body of commands that communication programs send to a modem to manipulate its internal logic. Also known as the Hayes command set.

**AT tower**   A type of form factor associated with older technologies.

**AT/desk**   A type of form factor associated with older technologies.

**ATA-2 (AT Attachment Standard No. 2)**   An update of the IDE/ATA standard, or a disk drive implementation that integrates the controller on the disk drive itself. ATA-2 is also known as EIDE and fast ATA, depending on the manufacturer.

**Atanasoff, John**   The inventor who, along with Clifford Berry, invented the modern computer.

**ATAPI (ATA packet interface)**   The extension specification of the ATA-2 standard that defines the device-side characteristics for non-hard drive devices such as CD-ROMs or tape drives.

**attribute**   A hidden code in a file that determines the file type and what operations are permitted for that file.

**ATX**    A computer form factor considered the forerunner of the Baby AT. The ATX's motherboard is rotated 90 degrees in the chassis, and the CPU and SIMM sockets have been relocated away from the expansion card slots. Therefore, all the slots support full-length cards. Most Pentium Pro boards use this form factor.

**ATX motherboard**    A standard, desktop computer, motherboard specification currently in widespread use.

**autoexec.bat**    A startup file that runs when DOS is loaded and tells the computer what commands or programs to execute automatically after bootup. **autoexec.bat** commands help a user configure the system to individual preferences.

# B

**Baby AT**    A type of form factor associated with older technologies.

**Baby AT motherboard**    A motherboard specification that replaced the original IBM AT motherboard.

**backbone**    A computer network that links several networks. FDDI is a common backbone network. Also, a large transmission path in a network, into which smaller lines feed.

**backup**    A copy of a disk, program, or other data. Backups should be created on a regular basis in order to protect data.

**backward compatible**    An upgraded computer or software that can handle the commands of previous versions.

**bad sector**    A damaged disk area within a cluster, in a disk partition. Bad sectors cannot be used, but data can be routed away from them after they are identified.

**bandwidth**    The difference between the highest and lowest frequency available for transmission in a communications system.

**basic mechanical switch**    A switch that uses metal contacts in a transient contact arrangement. This is regarded as the simplest and most expensive type of keyboard switch, and provides excellent tactile feedback. It is also called a pure mechanical switch.

**basis name**    The first six characters of a filename, regardless of the name's length, that are retained when an MS-DOS program reads a Windows 95 program.

**baud rate**    The number of electrical oscillations that occur each second in digital communications. Each oscillation encodes 1 bit of information.

**binary file**    A file made up of codes, either 8-bit or executable.

**binary number**    A base-2 number that only uses the digits 1 and 0. Computers and digital devices work with binary numbers extensively.

**binary system**   A number system based on only two digits: 0 and 1. All values are expressed as combinations of these two numbers. For example, the letter A is expressed as 1000001.

**BinderyNetWare**   A server database that contains network information about users, groups, passwords, and access rights.

**binding**   A method for communicating between adapters, protocols, and networking services.

**BIOS (basic input/output system)**   Built-in computer software that determines what functions a computer can perform without accessing programs from a disk. The BIOS contains the code required to control the display screen, disk drives, keyboard, serial communications, and a number of miscellaneous functions.

**bit**   A basic unit of information in the binary system—either a 1 or a 0. A bit is the smallest piece of information that a computer can understand. It takes 8 bits to equal 1 byte, which is the amount of disk space to store one character of information.

**bitmap**   Individual data pieces collected together to produce an image.

**bitmap font**   A typeface designed pixel by pixel, intended for computer-monitor display. Also called raster or screen font.

**blackout**   Complete failure of electric power for a region.

**block mode PIO (programmed I/O)**   Two essential interface signals used to indicate the status of two connected drives on an IDE controller channel. This allows the master and slave IDE drives to coordinate their data transmissions on the bus.

**boot**   To load and start the operating system on a computer.

**boot partition**   A primary partition on a hard drive that has been set to active, or bootable, by the partitioning utility. The BIOS searches for the operating system's bootstrap loader on this partition.

**boot sector**   Another term for the master boot record. Cylinder 0, head 0, sector 1 is considered the beginning of the hard drive containing the initial boot program that the system BIOS loads to begin the boot process.

**bootstrap**   An early computer industry term that means to start up and load a computer's operating system.

**bps (bits per second)**   The same as the baud rate when 1 bit is transmitted per modulation change.

**bridge**   A piece of equipment used to connect segments of a single network or to connect similar entire networks to each other.

**brownout**   A type of power event in which the voltage falls below the nominal voltage carried by a power line.

**browse master**    A utility that acts in an administrative capacity in peer-to-peer networks to list all the servers in the network.

**buffer**    A temporary storage area usually located in RAM, which acts as a holding area that allows the CPU to manipulate data before transferring it to a device.

**bug**    An error or defect in software or hardware that causes a program to malfunction.

**bulletin board**    A computer that can be accessed by a modem to share and exchange messages or other files.

**bus**    A pathway between many devices when used in relation with a network. An assortment of wires through which data is transmitted from one part of a computer to another.

**bus enumerator**    A device driver that identifies devices located on a specific bus and assigns a unique code for each device.

**bus network**    A network in which computers are arranged "down a line," without a centralized hub.

**byte**    A grouping of 8 bits that usually contains a single letter, number, or other symbol. The amount of space that it takes to store one character of information.

# C

**cable modem**    A modem designed to function in unison with the coaxial cable lines owned by cable TV companies. It is not a true modem, but uses a network adapter interface to link to the Internet through the high-bandwidth coaxial cable medium.

**cache**    A storage area for frequently accessed information for faster response. Motherboard cache memory is extra-fast RAM that maintains a copy of recently requested bits from regular RAM.

**case**    The plastic housing that encloses and protects the CRT and associated electrical circuitry.

**case sensitive**    When an operation distinguishes between upper- and lowercase letters.

**CAU (controlled-access unit)**    A Token Ring network's central hub

**CCITT (Consultative Committee on International Telephone and Telegraph)**    Older name for the ITU.

**CD-ROM (compact disc—read only memory)**    A round, flat, disc medium designed to store up to 650 MB. CD-ROMs are also called CDs.

**CD-ROM (compact disc—read only memory) drive**    A peripheral device that uses a read-only optical storage medium to access data, including text, audio, video, and graphics. This type of device can have either an IDE or a SCSI interface.

**CGA (color graphics array)**   The first graphics standard, introduced in 1981; it became obsolete when VGA was introduced in 1987.

**character**   In serial communications, a byte of data or 8 data bits preceded by 1 start bit and ended by 1 stop bit.

**chat**   To "talk" on the Internet with another person who is online at the same time.

**circuit board**   A thin, rectangular plate usually made of silicon, on which chips and other electronic components are placed.

**click and drag**   To move a selected image or block of text with a mouse. By clicking on an item and holding down a mouse button, a user can use a mouse to slide text or images to a designated screen position.

**client**   A user's microcomputer on a network.

**Client for NetWare Networks**   A mechanism that allows a machine to be connected to a NetWare Network.

**client software**   A program that exists on a remote computer in a network.

**client/server network**   A number of individual workstations or client computers that are connected to each other and exchange information via a central server.

**clock signal**   Voltage supplied by the motherboard to a quartz crystal in order to make it vibrate at a predetermined speed. The vibrations of the quartz crystal help control the speed of the CPU.

**close program**   A command in the dialog box that allows you to end a program.

**cluster**   A unit of storage on a disk that contains sectors of data. Clusters are the smallest group of sectors within a partition.

**cmd.exe**   The Windows NT command processor.

**CMOS (complementary metal oxide semiconductor) chip**   A battery-powered memory and clock chip that is used to store system clock settings and configuration data. Another term for this is RTC/NVRAM chip. A commonly used term for the stored system configuration settings that are set up in BIOS.

**CMOS setup**   Another term for the BIOS or system setup utility. The term is technically incorrect, but it is used because the system setup configuration is stored in the CMOS chip.

**cold boot**   Starting up a computer by turning on the power button.

**collisions**   When information is sent by two Ethernet-network computers at the some time, the data "collides." The network waits a random amount of time, and then tries to re-send the data.

**color gradation**    The perceptual factor involved in a monitor's color display design, but more specifically regarding the limited range of a digital display, and the near-infinite number of color shades for analog displays.

**COM**    The name used by MS-DOS to designate serial ports.

**COM1, COM2**    Serial communications ports on the motherboard that can be configured in a number of ways. Multi I/O connectors.

**command interpreter**    Another term for command processor.

**command line**    A DOS function that waits for user commands to be typed according to DOS-specific codes.

**command processor**    The central command file for the operating system kernel, which accepts and executes the operating system commands. This file is accessed directly from a command prompt.

**command prompt**    Also called the command line, the command prompt is the text-based screen interface for an operating system.

**command queue**    The memory buffer used to line up read/write requests from SCSI hard drives until the host adapter processor has time to attend to them.

**command.com**    The MS-DOS command processor. It is also one of the three MS-DOS operating system files that the MS-DOS bootstrap loader searches for in the root directory of the boot disk and loads into memory.

**command-line execution parameters**    Parameters that change the function of a batch file. They are passed to the batch file from the command line of the batch file.

**complete trust domain model**    An arrangement of clients and servers that allows reciprocal trust relationships between multiple domains and resources.

**compound document**    An organized collection of user interfaces that form a single, integrated environment containing text files, audio files, video files, and so on.

**computer**    An electronic device that enables users to input, manipulate, store, and output information.

**computing pen**    An input device similar to a mouse that is usually used to enter data on a small portable computer.

**concatenate**    To join in sequence. For example, Disk Defragmenter concatenates data so that all the data for each file is physically located together on the disk.

**conductive**    Having the capability to transmit electricity, heat, sound, and so on.

**conductor**    Material that transmits electricity, heat, sound, and so on.

**config.sys**    A DOS file that configures some computer resources and loads drivers to control computer-specific hardware.

**configuration**   The way in which a computer and peripherals are connected and programmed to operate. The way a computer's operating system is set up, and the variety of components contained within the system and how they are set up.

**connect network registry**   A command in the Registry Editor that permits the user to edit the Registry of a remote computer.

**connectivity**   The capability of files, data, and resources to be shared and exchanged across a network.

**connector**   Another term for electrical leads and plugs.

**container**   A file that contains linked, common-purpose files or other objects.

**container object**   A file that contains linked common-purpose files or other objects. Also called a *container*.

**contiguous**   Sharing a boundary, next to each other.

**control circuitry**   The dedicated electrical component that reads the output from the video card RAMDAC chip and controls the electron beam scanning the CRT. External controls can manipulate the brightness, contrast, screen shape, and color of this output.

**Control Panel**   A utility represented by an icon in the Windows 95 My Computer default window. It allows users to configure a computer's color, fonts, mouse, desktop, sound, date and time, and other system features.

**conventional memory**   A computer's first 640 KB of memory; contains essential programs, data, and operating system areas.

**cooperative multitasking**   A type of multitasking that requires the currently running task to give up control of the processor and allow other tasks to run.

**copy protected**   Software containing a developer-implanted lock to keep users from unauthorized copying.

**CP/M (Control Program for Microcomputer)**   The first PC operating system, written by Gary Kildall in 1973.

**cps (characters per second)**   The measure of speed of dot-matrix printers. How many characters of a certain quality the printer can output each second.

**CPU (central processing unit)**   A microchip is a tiny computer chip that acts as a computer's brain. A CPU carries out commands, performs calculations, and communication with all the hardware components needed to operate a computer. A CPU is sometimes referred to as a microprocessor.

**CPU cache**   A memory bank that bridges the CPU and main memory. It is considerably faster than main memory and allows data and instructions to be read at a higher speed.

**crash**   For a hard drive or a program to suddenly fail to work while it is running.

**CRC (cyclic redundancy check)**   An error-detection technique used by modems on every block of data sent between them. Detected errors force the re-sending of the bad data.

**CRT (cathode ray tube)**   A glass cylinder that hosts an electron gun at the rear, which emits an electron beam to activate the phosphor-coated screen at the front to create an image. Also, any type of monitor that utilizes the component.

**CSA (Canadian Standards Association)**   A Canadian standards development and certification organization.

**CSEL (cable select)**   One of two key interface signals used to indicate the status of two connected drives on an IDE controller channel. This allows the master and slave IDE drives to coordinate their data transmissions on the bus.

**CSMA/CD (carrier sense multiple access collision detect)**   An Ethernet feature that, after listening for silence, sends packets, re-sending them if a collision is found.

**Ctrl + Alt + Del**   A combination of keys to use simultaneously to close down programs that are hung and/or to reboot the machine, depending on the operating system.

**cut-sheet paper**   Individual-page paper fed into the printer engine one sheet at a time from a manual or tray feeder.

**Cyrix**   A computer manufacturer that produces a Pentium-clone computer, the Cyrix 6x86.

# D

**DASP (drive active/slave present)**   One of two key interface signals used by hard drives on the IDE bus. The DASP device signals the presence of a slave drive at startup, and is used by both drives after startup to indicate whether they themselves are active.

**data**   In the world of computers, any information that goes into or is taken from the computer.

**Data Compression Standard**   The ITU standard for data compression that provides a mathematical algorithm to compress the data to one quarter its normal size over a modem connection.

**data integrity**   The accuracy of data after being transmitted or processed.

**DB (data bus)**   The number of pins on the connector.

**dB (decibel)**   The logarithm of a ratio of power, voltages, current, and so on. A 3-db increase in power represents a doubling in power.

**DC (direct current)**   Electrical current that travels in only one direction, as opposed to AC. It is generally used in electronic circuits.

**debounce**   A programming routine used by a keyboard controller to neutralize the side effects of rapid keyboard switch pressing—a condition that causes the switches to bounce rapidly on and off the circuit contacts.

**decimal system**    A common base-10 numbering system using the digits 0–9.

**Decompression**    The process of restoring the contents of a compressed file to its original form.

**defacto**    A standard generally used in the computing industry, although not officially sanctioned by a standard-setting organization.

**default**    Settings or parameters that are used automatically by a system until it receives different instructions.

**default system icon**    An onscreen graphic depicting a group of linked, common-purpose container objects, such as My Computer, Recycle Bin, and Network Neighborhood.

**default.pif**    A Windows file that stores information about MS-DOS programs that are not contained in the apps.inf file.

**deflection coil**    The portion of the CRT that deflects the electron beam. The deflection causes the beam to strike a specific screen area. Also called the *yoke*.

**defragment**    To rewrite files to a disk so they are in contiguous order.

**Delete key**    A computer keyboard key used to remove alphanumeric characters and other onscreen objects.

**demodulation**    The means by which a modem converts analog data signals into digital signals.

**desktop**    The onscreen space that underlies all work done on the computer. Like an actual desktop, the computer's desktop gives a computer user a location to put and organize work. The Windows 95 desktop is the first Windows 95 logon screen.

**despool**    To remove documents from the print spool before sending them to the printer.

**developer unit**    A small roller near the drum that feeds toner onto the drum from a storage bin above it. The storage bin is called the *toner hopper*.

**device contention**    An enhanced panel option that configures how the system should handle resource conflicts.

**device driver**    A program that controls various devices, including the BIOS, BIOS extension, and operating system.

**device font**    A fast type of printer font stored inside the printer. Also called a *hardware font*.

**Device Manager**    A Windows 95 System Properties utility that notifies the user of device conflicts. It also allows the user to change a computer's properties and the devices attached to it.

**DHCP (Dynamic Host Configuration Protocol)**    A protocol that allows network administrators to centrally manage and automatically assign IP addresses in an organization's network.

**diagnostic software disk**    A disk containing software designed to run system diagnostics and display the results on a monitor or by means of printouts. It provides diagnostics for a computer's memory, processor, disk storage, operating system, and peripherals.

**diagnostic test**    Software used to diagnose problems within the system; for example, anti-virus software.

**dialog box**    An onscreen window, displayed in response to a user request, designed to provide options currently available to the user, and/or the progress of the system's execution of a command.

**Dial-Up Networking**    An object in the Windows 95 My Computer default container that permits user access to modem and Internet resources.

**Difference Engine**    An early steam-powered calculation machine designed by Charles Babbage.

**differential backup**    One type of Microsoft Backup command. Differential backup backs up only files changed or created since the last full backup.

**digital**    Data that is kept as a collection of numbers. For example, a digital image is kept as a collection of numbers that determine the color of each point. Digital signals and information consist of electronic pulses of energy designed to represent the bits and bytes of binary code.

**digital computer**    A computer that accepts and processes data that has been converted into binary numbers. All modern-day computers are digital.

**DIMM (dual inline memory module)**    A small circuit board that holds memory chips. A DIMM chip generally has a 64-bit data path. A DIMM has a 64-bit path to the memory chips, in contrast to a SIMM, which has a 32-bit path to the memory chips.

**directory**    An inventory of file names that indexes organized and grouped files for information retrieval.

**Disk Defragmenter**    A Windows 95 program that defragments disks.

**disk platter**    Media disks that store data in the hard drive. The disks are typically constructed of a rigid composite material covered with magnetically sensitive, thin-film medium.

**display monitor**    Another term for video display monitor, monitor, or video monitor.

**displayable resolution**    A manufacturer's resolution specification that states the maximum physical resolution a monitor model can display.

**DLL (dynamic link library) files**    Small files containing codes common to several Windows programs.

**DMA (direct memory access)**   A means by which data moves between a system device such as a disk drive and system memory, without direct control of the CPU. This frees up the CPU for other tasks.

**DMM (digital multimeter)**   A device used to measure and test voltage, resistance, and amperage of electrical components.

**DNS (Domain Name System)**   Internet computer–locating software that allows users to find specific computer users on the Internet by either a domain name or an IP address.

**dock**   To connect a laptop or notebook computer to a docking station, which contains a power connection, expansion slots, and peripheral connections.

**docking station**   A desktop unit into which a laptop computer connects, which allows the user to use a full-size monitor, keyboard, mouse, and expansion slots.

**Documents**   A Start menu option that lists the computer's most recently used or created documents.

**domain**   An arrangement of client and server computers, with a specific reference name, that share a security permissions database.

**domain controller**   A server that authenticates workstation network logon requests by checking the user accounts database for username and password verification.

**DOS (Disk Operating System)**   Another term for *MS-DOS*.

**DOS parameter**   A parameter that changes how a batch file functions, sometimes referred to as an *environment variable*. Set in autoexec.bat, DOS parameters specify both DOS and batch file functions.

**DOS prompt**   An onscreen prompt in the command prompt window which indicates that the system is ready to receive a user's DOS-driven commands.

**dot**   The smallest elements of a CRT. Dots are the small red, green, and blue phosphorus spots on the inside of the monitor.

**dot pitch**   The distance between adjacent sets of red, green, and blue dots in a given pixel. Dot pitch defines how fine the dots are that make the image on a video display. The smaller the distance between the dots, the sharper the image.

**dot-matrix printer**   A type of printer that creates characters and graphics by striking pins against an ink ribbon. The striking pins print closely spaced dots in the appropriate shapes of characters.

**double-click**   To rapidly choose and open a program by pressing and releasing a mouse button twice in close succession.

**downloadable font**   A font downloaded to a printer's memory as needed from a disk. Also called a *soft font*.

**DPMS (display power management system)**    A power management signaling specification developed for monitors by VESA. This system allows a computer to monitor a video display for inactivity, and power it down until used.

**drag**    To position a mouse pointer over an object, hold the mouse button down, and move the pointer to another screen location. Also known as *drag and drop* and *click and drag*.

**drive**    A device used to write to and/or read information from magnetic platters or disks. It is usually located inside the system unit. Types of drives include hard drives, floppy disk drives, CD-ROM, and optical drives.

**drive bracket**    A brace or prop used to attach a drive to the chassis.

**drive command**    A device command in the system BIOS used to manage hard disk drives through the controller interface.

**drive status light**    An indicator light on the front bezel of the system case that denotes whether a drive is active or at rest. Generally, when the light is on, the drive is in use. A light that is off indicates that the drive is not in use.

**driver**    A device or program that controls another device. Individual drivers allow a computer to utilize specific devices, such as printers or disk drives.

**DriveSpace3**    A Windows 95 utility used to compress data.

**drum**    A magnetic media storage device

**DSP (digital signal processor)**    A very fast digital-processing chip used in devices such as sound cards, cellular phones, and high-capacity hard disks.

**dual boot**    A configuration facility that allows a computer to boot up in either Windows or previously installed MS-DOS.

**dual ported**    A memory architecture design for video memory, especially VRAM and WRAM, that has two access paths and can be written to and read from simultaneously.

**dust plate**    A plate that covers each hole on the back of the computer that is not being used by an expansion card. Another term for an *adapter plate*.

**duster**    Compressed air or carbon dioxide in a can that is used to blow dust off electronic components.

**DVD (digital video disc)**    A two-sided optical disc the size of a standard CD, but featuring considerably more storage space. DVDs are considered the next generation of optical disc storage technology.

**Dvorak keyboard**    A keyboard layout designed in the 1930s by August Dvorak and his brother-in-law, William Dealey. It is not widely used.

**dynamic electricity**    Electricity that results from moving charges within conductors.

**dynamic IP address**    A current-session-only IP address.

# E

**econo-mode**    A low-resolution print mode for inkjet printers that prints at a lower density and uses less ink.

**EDO RAM (extended data output RAM)**    A type of RAM that is faster than conventional RAM. Unlike conventional DRAM, which only allows 1 byte to be read at a time, EDO RAM can copy an entire block of memory to its internal cache. While the CPU is accessing this cache, the memory can collect a new block to send. EDO RAM is faster than the usual DRAM, but generally slower than SDRAM.

**efficiency**    In a power supply, the ratio of input power to output power.

**EGA (enhanced graphics array)**    The second graphics standard, introduced in 1984; it became obsolete when VGA was introduced in 1987.

**EIA (Electronics Industry Association)**    An association that has members from various electronics manufacturers and is based in Washington, DC. It sets standards for electronic components.

**EIDE (enhanced integrated drive electronics)**    The same as the ATA-2 standard.

**EIDE interface**    The 40-pin interface connector that is keyed by the removal of pin 20 on the male drive connector site for the IDE drive and the motherboard controller.

**EISA (extended industry standard architecture)**    A standard bus architecture that extends the ISA standard to a 32-bit interface.

**electrode**    A device that emits or controls the flow of electricity.

**electron**    A subatomic particle that has a negative electrical charge.

**electron gun**    A device in a computer monitor that produces an electron beam.

**e-mail (electronic mail)**    General e-mail features and files transmitted electronically by means of a network or phone line.

**EMF (enhanced metafile format) spool**    A method of print spooling used by Windows 95 that returns application control to the user more quickly than the spooling method used in Windows 3.1.

**EMI (electromagnetic interference)**    An electrical disturbance created by electromagnetic signals, resulting in reduced data integrity and increased error rates on transmission channels.

**Energy Star**    An energy conservation standard created by the U.S. Environmental Protection Agency for computer efficiency. Devices that draw no more than 30 watts when inactive can be certified for this standard and display the logo.

**Entire Network**    A file in the Windows 95 Network Neighborhood default container. It holds other workgroups, servers, and shared network resources.

**environmental variable**    A variable that changes how a batch file functions. Set in autoexec.bat, DOS parameters specify both DOS and batch file functions. Usually called *DOS parameters*.

**EPROM (erasable programmable ROM)**    A type of ROM that retains its contents until it is exposed to ultraviolet light. Once exposed to ultraviolet light, its contents are cleared, making it possible to reprogram the memory.

**ergonomic**    Devices designed and arranged with special attention to their safe and efficient human use.

**error correction standard**    The ITU V.42 standard for error correction in modem communications.

**ESD (electrostatic discharge)**    The flow or spark of electricity that originates from a static source such as a carpet and arcs across a gap to another object.

**Ethernet**    Currently the most popular technology for computer networking. An Ethernet can take either a bus or star configuration.

**expansion adapter**    A device that serves as an interface between the system unit and the devices attached to it. Also called a *circuit board* or *circuit card*.

**expansion card**    A printed circuit board designed to be inserted into a computer's expansion sockets to provide a computer with added capabilities. Examples include video adapters, graphics accelerators, sound cards, and internal modems. Expansion cards are sometimes referred to as *adapters*, *cards*, *add-ins*, and *add-ons*.

**extended memory**    A computer's memory above 1 MB. 386-enhanced mode requires at least 1024 KB extended memory; standard mode requires 256 KB extended memory.

**extended partition**    A partition on a hard disk that is used to hold files. It cannot contain operating system software, and can be subdivided into multiple partitions.

**extension**    A three-character designation added to the end of a filename and preceded by a period that identifies the file as belonging to a particular type or category.

**external drive unit**    A peripheral device such as a floppy disk drive that attaches to the system unit and is used for input and output, such as storage of data.

**external lever switch**    One of two kinds of power on/off switches. It is connected to the older AT form factor power supply.

# F

**fan-fold paper**    Another term for *tractor-feed paper*.

**FAQ (frequently asked questions)**    Information posted in an attempt to answer questions that are common to many users of a newsgroup or Web site.

**fast SCSI-2**    A variant of the SCSI-2 standard that supports data rates of 10 MBps over an 8-bit bus, and uses the 50-pin interface connector.

**fast wide SCSI-2**    An extension of the SCSI-2 standard, sometimes called SCSI-3, that features a 16-bit bus and supports data rates of 20 MBps over the wide SCSI-2 68-pin interface connector.

**FAT (File Allocation Table)**    A catalog of the locations and sizes of all the hard drive files. An operating system, looking for a file, checks the FAT. The FAT file system is the only formatting DOS can use.

**FAT32**    A 32-bit FAT system that allows partitions larger than 2 GB and supports long filenames.

**fax (facsimile)**    A transmission of text or graphics over telephone lines in a digitized form. Also, the equipment used for these transmissions.

**FCC (Federal Communications Commission)**    An independent government agency responsible for the licensing and regulatory authority of television, radio, wire, satellite, and cable in the United States.

**FDC (floppy drive connector)**    A multi I/O parallel connector on a motherboard.

**FDDI (Fiber Distributed Data Interface)**    A technology for computer networking, typically used to link several networks. Based on a ring configuration without a central hub, it is a token-passing network architecture that uses fiber-optic lines to transmit data at 100 Mbps. It can support many users and is a very fast networking architecture.

**fdisk**    A Windows 95 utility that allows the user to create partitions.

**fdisk.exe**    A DOS program file used to partition and activate hard drives for installing an operating system.

**FIFO (first in, first out)**    A method in which items are removed in the same order in which they were added; for example, the first in would be the first out.

**file**    A compilation of saved data with a designated name.

**file handle**    An open file; sometimes, a device.

**file management system**    A portion of an operating system that translates an application's requests into specific tasks. Also refers to the complete structure that names, stores, and organizes files. It includes directories, files, and the information for locating and accessing them.

**File Manager**    A Windows 3.1 utility for simplifying file organization.

**file set**    A set of files that have been backed up and stored in sets by the Microsoft Backup utility for later retrieval.

**file system**    Also known as a *file management system*, it is the portion of the operating system that translates an application's requests into specific tasks, and acts as the file tree structure that names, stores, and organizes files.

**Find**    A Start menu option that offers users options for locating various computer features, files, and folders.

**fixed disk drive**    An alternate term for a hard drive, used by IBM.

**fixed drive**    A disk, like a hard drive, that is a fixed, permanent part of the computer.

**fixed refresh rate**    A design specification for a display monitor that has only one scanning frequency. This limits the monitor's ability to display higher resolutions without image flicker due to the fixed vertical and horizontal scan rates.

**flash BIOS**    A type of memory chip called an EPROM that allows the BIOS to be updated by files from the manufacturer.

**floppy disk**    A removable, reusable magnetic storage media used by floppy disk drives to read and write data. Also called *disks* or *diskettes*.

**floppy disk drive**    A type of disk drive that uses floppy disks. Commonly called a *floppy drive*.

**floppy drive controller**    Electronics that control the floppy disk drive and negotiate the passage of data between the floppy disk drive and the computer.

**flow control**    A method of managing the rate at which the host system sends data to the modem.

**flux**    The magnetic polarity of the particles in the thin-film media of hard drive platters.

**flux pattern**    The pattern of flux reversals or transitions encoded into the thin-film media of the hard drive platters. The timing of these transitions represents the stored data bits.

**flux reversal**    A switch in the magnetic polarity of the particles in the thin-film media of hard drive platters.

**FM (frequency modulation) synthesis**    Synthesizing sound by creating a wave close to the original sound's wave.

**foam buffer key switch**    A mechanical switch similar to the tactile feedback mechanism. It uses foam with a foil laminate in place of a metal plate to strike the contacts. It is also called a *foam element key switch*.

**folder**    A computer's storage place for programs and files. Indicated onscreen by a graphic file folder.

**font**    A character set with a common typeface, style, and weight.

**form factor**    The physical dimensions of a system unit. Two computers with the same form factor are physically interchangeable.

**format.com**   A DOS program file used to create a FAT file system on a hard drive or floppy disk.

**Formatting**   An external DOS command that uses the **format.com** file to prepare a disk to store information and create a FAT.

**frame buffer**   The storage area inside video memory where information is stored about the video image itself.

**front bezel**   A faceplate that covers the front of the chassis and provides attachment points for standardized components.

**front case bezel**   The portion of the computer's case through which the CD-ROM drive and floppy drives are accessed. It may also contain various LED indicators, the reset button, and the on/off switch.

**FTP (File Transfer Protocol)**   A protocol used to transfer files over a TCP/IP network, to download files from or upload files to remote computer systems. It includes functions to log on to the network, list directories, and copy files. It can also convert ASCII and EBCDIC character codes.

**full backup**   An option of the Microsoft Backup command that backs up all hard drive files.

**full duplex**   An updated sound card characteristic, wherein, as in a telephone line, sound can travel in both directions, and do so simultaneously via two channels.

**full tower**   The largest of the tower form factors.

**full-duplex mode**   A mode in which high-performance modems send and receive data at the same time. This is accomplished by sending data bits out of one wire and receiving data in the other wire in a two-wire phone line.

**fuse**   A device used as part of the power supply's internal overload protection circuitry. When the maximum allowable current is exceeded, the fuse intercepts the overload of current and intentionally fails. This interrupts the circuit and protects a power supply's circuitry.

**fuser**   In a laser printer, a pair of hot rollers that affixes the toner into the paper via heat and pressure.

# G

**ganged**   A term for the stacked way that read/write heads are attached to the end of the head actuator assembly of a hard drive. They move in unison as a gang.

**Gates, Bill**   The multibillionaire and Harvard-dropout CEO of Microsoft Corporation.

**gateway**   A device used to connect networks whose protocols differ. Also, a network point (often a proxy server) that acts as an entrance to another network.

**GB (gigabyte)**   A measurement equal to 1,024 MB or 1,073,741,824 bytes.

**GDI (graphics device interface)**     A system that provides graphics support in Windows 95. As it relates to printing, the GDI assists in EMF spooling, to return application control to the user more rapidly.

**GDI Manager**     A core file whose job is to draw images and TrueType fonts, mainly for icons and other windows features, such as dialog boxes and buttons.

**GPF (general protection fault)**     An error a user receives when an application attempts to access an area not designated for its use. Also called a *general protection error*.

**grabber**     File picture-taking software that transfers a single video onscreen image to a disk file.

**graphics tablet**     An input device that has a touch-sensitive surface. When the user draws on the tablet's surface using a special pen, it relays the image that is drawn to the computer, where it can be manipulated in a graphics application.

**gray code**     A binary number system in which the code for a specific number and a number that is one greater differs by exactly 1 bit. It is used to avoid errors that may result from ambiguous readings from a disk platter.

**ground**     Any contact point that is electrically neutral.

**grounding strap**     A device, usually worn on the wrist, that prevents the buildup of ESD.

**group**     Files organized by their file extensions that help organize program icons and menus that run and start programs.

**GUI (graphical user interface)**     A user interface that utilizes a mouse and graphics such as icons and pull-down menus. It is currently the industry standard for interacting with computers.

# H

**HAA (head actuator assembly)**     The hard drive mechanism composed of the read/write heads, the arms that hold them, and the voice coil actuator, which moves these accurately across the hard drive platters.

**half duplex**     An early sound card characteristic, in which, as in a two-way radio, sound travels in both directions, but only in one direction at a time.

**handshake**     An electronic exchange of signals that takes place initially when one modem contacts another over telephone lines.

**handshake mode**     A request/acknowledgement method that a SCSI host adapter uses to negotiate an asynchronous data transfer with a SCSI device on the bus.

**hard disk**     A device comprised of several rotating, nonremovable magnetic disks used for storing computer data.

**hard disk drive**   A high volume, non-removable, internal disk drive with fixed media. Often called a *hard drive*.

**hard disk drive LED**   An electronic device that lights up when electricity is passed through it to indicate that the hard drive is in use.

**hard drive**   A high volume, non-removable, internal disk drive with fixed media.

**hard drive controller**   Electronics that control the hard disk drive and negotiate the passage of data between the hard disk drive and the computer.

**hardware**   The physical components of a computer, including monitors, keyboards, motherboards, and peripherals, such as printers and modems.

**hardware font**   A fast type of printer font stored inside the printer. Also called a *device font*.

**hardware profile**   Data that is used to configure computers for use with peripheral devices.

**harmonic distortion**   A change in an electrical signal that occurs periodically.

**Hayes command set**   Another term for the AT command set.

**HDA (head disk assembly)**   The sealed chamber of a hard drive, containing the disk platters, spindle motor, heads, and head actuator mechanism. It is a single logical component only serviceable by the manufacturer.

**heat sink**   Heat-absorbing material used for chip-generated heat absorption on computer motherboards.

**Help**   A Start menu option that provides a Windows information resource.

**hex (hexadecimal) system**   A base-16 numbering system using the digits 0–9 and A–F. It is often used to represent the binary numbers that computers use.

**hidden**   A DOS system attribute that prevents a file's appearance in the directory. This attribute is usually assigned to system files or other files that require protection against accidental deletion.

**hierarchical network**   A network where one host computer controls a number of smaller computers, and these smaller computers may be a host to a group of PC workstations.

**HKEY_CLASSES_ROOT**   A subdirectory in the Registry structure that contains configuration information about OLE, shortcuts and the GUI.

**HKEY_CURRENT_CONFIG**   A subdirectory in the Registry structure that contains hardware configuration information.

**HKEY_CURRENT_USER**   A subdirectory in the Registry structure that points to another subdirectory, **HKEY_USERS**, for the currently logged-on user.

**HKEY_DYN_DATA**   A subdirectory in the Registry structure that contains plug-and-play configuration information and points to **HKEY_LOCAL_MACHINE**.

**HKEY_LOCAL_MACHINE**    A subdirectory in the Registry structure that contains specific information about installed hardware, software settings, and other information.

**HKEY_USERS**    A handle key containing user configuration information.

**hold time**    The time during which a power supply's output voltage remains within specification following the loss of input power.

**horizontal scan rate**    The rated speed at which the scanning electron beam can write the image across the screen horizontally.

**host computer**    The main computer within a system of computers that are connected by communication links.

**host drive**    A file created by DriveSpace to hold compressed data on the hard drive.

**hot wire**    An ungrounded lead wire used to connect the transformer and electrical devices or appliances by means of an electrical outlet and power plug.

**HTML (Hypertext Markup Language)**    A document format used on the Web, primarily to construct Web pages. HTML defines the page layout, fonts, graphic elements, and hypertext links to many documents on the Web.

**HTTP (Hypertext Transfer Protocol)**    A protocol used for connecting servers on the Internet.

**hub**    Another name for the spindle to which the disk platters are mounted. The term *hub* is also used in networking to refer to a connection that joins network communication lines in a star configuration.

**hung**    Wedged or locked up, not responding.

# I

**I/O (input/output)**    An assortment of wires connecting the CPU with external devices, including all I/O connectors such as drive controllers, serial ports, parallel ports, and keyboard connectors connected to the ISA and PCI buses or adapter cards installed in the ISA and PCI bus slots.

**I/O bus**    A bus for data that is composed of data paths and storage units. It can either be internal or external.

**IANA (Internet Assigned Numbers Authority)**    The IP address registry.

**IBM (International Business Machines)**    The world's largest computer company, which dates back to Herman Hollerith's adding machine.

**IBM compatible**    A computer with a microprocessor that is compatible with the original IBM PC 8088. Not manufactured by IBM, they are often referred to as *IBM clones*, and are usually compatible with IBM software.

**ICMP (Internet Control Message Protocol)** TCP/IP's protocol that sends error and control messages.

**icon** A small onscreen graphic image used to access the computer's applications or devices.

**IDE (integrated drive electronics)** A type of drive interface ratified in 1989, called the ATA standard. The standard gave specifications for the integration of the old ST-506 disk controller circuitry onto the hard drive; it was superceded by the ATA-2 standard in 1995.

**identify drive** An ATA-2 standard drive command issued by the system BIOS to the EIDE hard drive, requesting it send a 512-byte data block identifying its make, model, and drive geometry. A command sent by the BIOS to the IDE hard drive to query the drive for its operating parameters and drive geometry.

**IEEE (Institute of Electrical and Electronic Engineers)** The world's largest technical professional society, it promotes the development and application of electrotechnology and allied sciences.

**impact printer** A printer in which the print heads physically strike the paper.

**Import/Export** A command in the Registry Editor that allows the user to save data in a text file and restore it, either to the same or another computer.

**incremental backup** A backup that backs up only files changed or created since the last full or incremental backup.

**INF file** A Windows 95 or 98 file that contains device installation and configuration information.

**Information Superhighway** Another name for the Internet, the world's largest computer network, made up of smaller computer networks.

**infrared connection** A port on a motherboard that enables an infrared signal to transmit data from one device to another, without the use of cables.

**INI file** A text-based initialization file used by Windows to store system-specific or application-specific information.

**initialization** The process of assigning values to variables and data structures in a program when it first starts up.

**inkjet printer** A type of non-impact printer that uses liquid ink to spray characters onto the page.

**input** Data that is sent to the CPU for processing from an outside source such as a keyboard, CD-ROM, or modem.

**input connector** The 15-pin mini D-sub video cable connector on the back of the monitor.

**input device** A device used for entering data into a computer, such as a keyboard, mouse, or joystick.

**input signal** Manufacturer specification for the type of video input the monitor uses. The standard for modern analog monitors is RGB Analog. This is opposed to the old TTL digital standard.

**insulator** A nonconductor of electricity.

**integrated circuit** An electronic circuit in which more than one transistor is placed on a single piece of semiconductor material.

**intelligent hub** A hub in a star-based network that monitors the network for problems and removes network access from a problem-causing computer.

**interlaced** A scanning mode in which the scanning beam goes across the screen from top to bottom but alternates every other line, requiring two passes across the screen. The first scan is for even lines, and the second is for odd. This allows monitors to support higher resolutions at lower frequencies, but leaves the undesirable flicker.

**internal register** High-speed memory bits inside a microprocessor.

**Internet** The world's largest computer network, made up of smaller computer networks. The Internet began in the early 1970s as a network connecting government agencies, called the Advanced Research Projects Agency Network. Also called the *Information Superhighway* and the *World Wide Web*.

**internetwork** To communicate between two separate computer networks via PCs.

**InterNIC (Internet Network Information Center)** A joint endeavor to provide information services, directory and database services, and registration services for the Information Superhighway. InterNIC is made up of AT&T, General Atomics, and Networks Solutions.

**interoperate** To function between two systems.

**interrupt** A communication to the system from the processor that signals a problem or service request.

**intuitive interface** An easy-to-use user interface in which an object's purpose it denounced by its appearance. For example, the files and folders in Windows look like physical files and folders.

**Invar** Shadow mask metal manufactured by Hitachi that can bear high temperatures without distortion.

**io.sys** One of the three MS-DOS operating system files that the bootstrap loader searches for in the root directory of the boot disk and loads into memory.

**ion** An atom or a molecule that has gained or lost electrons and has a positive or negative charge. In general, negative ions have an excess of electrons, and positive ions lack electrons.

**ionizer** An electrical device used to generate ions into the air. It helps prevent static buildup and ESD.

**IOS (input/output system)**    Built-in software that determines what a computer can do without accessing programs from a disk. The I/O system contains all the code required to control the display screen, disk drives, keyboards, serial communications, and a number of miscellaneous functions.

**IPv6 (IP version 6)**    An update of Internet Protocol version 4.

**IPX/SPX (Internetwork Packet Exchange/Sequence Packet Exchange)**    A networking protocol that interconnects Novell networking clients. SPX is a transport-layer protocol built on top of IPX.

**IrDA (Infrared Data Association)**    A group of device manufacturers that developed a standard for sending data by means of infrared light waves.

**IRQ (interrupt request)**    A signal generated by a hardware device to tell the CPU that a request needs to be executed.

**ISA (industry standard architecture)**    A bus standard for IBM compatibles that extends the XT bus architecture.

**ISA bus**    The bus used in the original IBM PC and still in widespread use.

**ISA card**    A card that attaches to a computer's motherboard to expand the computer's functions. A sound card, for example, allows a computer to produce sound effects, music, and voices.

**ISA expansion slot**    An industry-standard architecture expansion slot on the motherboard that connects to the I/O bus.

**ISDN (Integrated Services Digital Network)**    An international communications standard for sending voice, video, and data over digital telephone lines.

**ISO (International Organization for Standardization)**    A worldwide organization founded in 1946 that representing more than 100 countries and promotes standards for communications protocols.

**isopropyl alcohol**    A type of alcohol used as a solvent.

**ISP (Internet service provider)**    A company that provides access to the Internet for computer users for a monthly fee. It provides an access telephone number, a username, and a password for a modem-equipped user to log on to the Internet and use the Web, transfer files, and access news and email services.

**ITU (International Telecommunications Union)**    Formerly called the CCITT, an organization which sets the modulation standards that govern the basic rate of speed for modem communications.

# J

**Joule**   A unit used for measuring energy. 1 watt of power lasting for 1 second supplies 1 Joule of energy.

**joystick**   An input device that is used to control onscreen movement. It is usually used in game applications to control the movement of some object such as an animated character.

# K

**kernel**   The heart of the operating system, it launches applications, allocates system resources, and manages memory, files, peripheral devices, and a the date and time.

**key matrix**   A grid array of key switches that collectively form the keyboard.

**keyboard**   An input device that allows the user to type in text or enter commands into the computer. Although based on the typewriter keyboard, a typical PC keyboard also contains special keys that are used with computer programs.

**keyboard interface**   A serial port, unlike standard COM ports, that handles serial communications between the keyboard and motherboard.

**keylock**   A security device that when locked with a key, locks all access to system input devices.

**KHz (kilohertz)**   A measure of transmission speeds of electronic devices: 1 KHz = 1,000 cycles per second or 1,000 Hz.

# L

**LAN (local-area network)**   A data network designed to connect workstations, peripheral devices, terminals, and other devices in a single building or other geographically limited area.

**LAPM (Link Access Procedure for Modems)**   An error-correction standard established by the ITU called V.42 that defines how parity-checking methods are to be used in modem transmissions.

**large drive connector**   A large 4-pin power supply connectors that connect to the hard disk or floppy disk drives, and uses a 12-volt motor.

**laser printer**   A type of non-impact printer that uses a laser to draw an image on an electrically charged drum, which is transferred to electrically charged paper using toner.

**laser scanning assembly**   The part of the print engine in a laser printer that transcribes the array of dots into a printable image on the photoreceptor drum.

**LBA (logical block addressing)**   A method used to support IDE hard disks larger than 504 MB on PCs, to provide the necessary address conversion in the BIOS.

**LCD (liquid crystal display)**    A monitor type that uses a polarized, molecular structure liquid, held between two see-through electrodes, as its display medium.

**LED (light-emitting diode)**    A device that illuminates when electrical current passes through it. Depending on the material used, the color can be visible or infrared. Used as indicator lights on many types of electronic devices.

**legacy application**    An older application that is still in use after the system has been upgraded.

**line conditioner**    Equipment that provides some type of filtering and/or regulation from an AC power source.

**line interactive UPS**    Another term for *online UPS*.

**line noise**    Undesirable communications channel signals that occur on an electrical circuit.

**Linux**    A UNIX-like operating system that was designed to provide PC users with a low-cost or free operating system.

**load**    To copy a program from some source into memory for execution.

**load resistor**    A device that maintains and regulates the electrical power flow at a predetermined, minimum operating limit.

**load runtime**    The amount of time a UPS can supply the system with electricity by using battery power only.

**loader**    Another name for the **win.com** file that starts Windows and contains the **win.cnf**, log, and run length encoded files.

**local loop**    The local analog telephone line segment of the telephone network from the nearest PSTN switch. These are the telephone lines between homes or businesses and the telephone company's central switches.

**local printer**    A printer that is connected to one computer, as opposed to a network.

**lockup**    A computer condition in which applications and hardware become temporarily inoperable or incapable of proceeding without intervention. A lockup is different from a crash. If the system crashes, it becomes unable to function; if the system locks up, it is incapable of making progress with a specific computing task.

**logic board**    A circuit board with soldered-on or socketed silicon chips.

**logical drive**    A drive that has been named as such by the system, whether or not that is its actual form.

**logout**    The action of closing an operating system that has been running on a network. Also called *logoff*.

**loopback connector**    A device that enables testing of the circuit or leads. It does this by sending signals out and recognizing whether the correct input is received back.

**low profile**    Another term used for a Slimline form factor.

**low radiation**    A manufacturer specification that indicates a monitor's compliance with international standards for very low frequency and extremely low frequency magnetic emissions. Because these are potentially harmful types of long-term radiation, this standard is designed to minimize exposure.

**LPT (line print terminal)**    Used by MS-DOS for designating printer ports.

**LPT1, LPT2, LPT3**    The names reserved by MS-DOS for the parallel printer ports.

**LUN (logical unit number)**    The physical number of each device connected in a daisy chain of drives.

# M

**make directory**    A command that creates a directory on a drive or disk. Also called the **md** or **mkdir** command.

**MAN (metropolitan-area network)**    A high-speed network that can include one or more LANs. A MAN is smaller than a WAN, but usually operates at a higher speed.

**mandatory user profile**    An administrator-created profile with a **.man** filename extension that prevents the user from modifying the profile.

**master boot code**    The initial boot program, located in the master boot record, that the BIOS loads and executes to start the boot process. This program seeks the boot partition with the bootstrap loader and transfers control to the loader for starting the operating system.

**master boot record**    Another term for *boot sector*.

**master domain model**    An arrangement of client and server computers that allows resources to have separate domains.

**master partition table**    A table located in the master boot record that contains the descriptions of the partitions contained on the hard disk.

**MB (megabyte)**    A unit of measurement used to gauge amounts of storage and data transfers. When used to describe data storage, 1 MB is equal to 1,048,576 bytes. When used to describe data transfer rates, 1 MB is equal to 1,000,000 bytes.

**Mbps (megabits per second)**    A measurement of data transmission speed: 1 Mbps = 1,000,000 bits per second.

**MBR (master boot record)**    The information on the first sector of any disk or hard disk that provides information about the operating system so it can be loaded into the computer's main storage or RAM. Also called the *partition sector* or the *master partition table*.

**MCA (microchannel architecture)**    A computer-expansion slot interface developed by IBM for its PS/2 line.

**MDA (monochrome display adapter)** The first display standard, introduced in 1981 by IBM Corporation as a character-only video display with no graphics capability.

**media** Plural of *medium*. The physical material on which computer data is stored, such as floppy disk or CD-ROM.

**membrane keyboard** A variant of the rubber-dome keyboard design in which the keys are integrated into a continuous sheet that sits directly atop the rubber dome sheet.

**memory address** The numeric identity of a particular memory or peripheral storage location.

**menu** An options list from which users select desired actions, commands, or formats.

**MHz (megahertz)** A measure of transmission speeds of electronic devices: 1 MHz = 1,000,000 cycles per second.

**microphone** A device that changes sound energy into electrical signals and that is used to input sounds into a computer.

**microprocessor** The computer's CPU, which can be thought of as the computer's brain. Intel created the first microprocessor in 1974.

**Microsoft Backup** A Windows 95 utility used to create backup copies of data.

**Microsoft Plus** A Windows 95 utility that enhances the capabilities of DriveSpace, Compression Agent, and System Agent.

**Microsoft Windows 95 Resource Kit** Microsoft's definitive guide to Windows 95.

**.mid** The file extension for MIDI files.

**MIDI (musical instrument digital interface)** A hardware specification that makes it possible to connect synthesizers and other electronic musical equipment to a computer. MIDI data is stored in files with **.mid** extensions.

**MIDI-In** Delivers the data to an instrument.

**MIDI-Out** Sends the data out from an instrument that it originally came from.

**MIDI-Thru** Sends an exact copy of the data coming into the MIDI-In and passes it on to another instrument or device.

**mid-tower** The medium size of the tower form factor.

**mini-DIN (Deutsche Industries Norm) connector** A connector for a motherboard, mouse, or keyboard. On PS/2 systems, this type of connector is a 6-pin connector.

**mini-tower** The smallest of the tower form factor.

**MMX (Multimedia Extensions)** An enhancement to the architecture of Intel Pentium processors that improves the performance of multimedia and communications applications.

**modem (modulator/demodulator)**    An electronic modulator/demodulator device used for computer communications via telephone lines. It allows data transfer between one computer and another. Typically, it converts digital data to analog signals, and then back to digital data.

**modulation**    The process a modem uses to convert a digital computer signal to analog form, for transmission over phone lines.

**monitor**    Another term for a video display monitor, display monitor, or video monitor.

**motherboard**    A computer's main circuit board that holds the microprocessor, main memory chips, and other essential computer elements.

**motherboard connector**    A power supply lead that connects to a motherboard inside a system unit. The number of them varies, depending on the type of motherboard and power supply used.

**motherboard ground screw**    A special hexagonal screw used to ground the motherboard to the mounting plate at specific points.

**motherboard manual**    A booklet or CD containing specifications, instructions, and diagrams for the motherboards, the devices attached to them, and their configuration. Each motherboard model and form factor has a corresponding manual.

**motherboard mounting pan**    Another term for a *motherboard mounting plate*.

**motherboard mounting plate**    Part of the case that provides the attachment surface for the motherboard.

**mounting bay**    A recess or an indentation in the front bezel or face plate of the case for inserting a drive into an drive bracket.

**mounting chassis**    The outer bracket of the hard drive that contains the head disk assembly and includes the mounting screw holes to secure the drive into the drive brackets.

**mounting points**    Holes in the motherboard that are used to secure it to the motherboard mounting plate by means of ground screws and stand-offs.

**mouse**    An input device that allows the user to point to and select items onscreen. It is used primarily with GUI programs to select icons and menu commands. It is also used with most drawing and paint programs.

**mouse pointer**    The mouse's onscreen representation. The pointer usually takes the form of an arrow.

**MOV (metal oxide varistor)**    The active component in a surge suppressor that limits pass-through voltages due to a line surge in voltage. It is capable of absorbing large currents without damage.

**MPC (Multimedia PC)**    Shorthand for the Multimedia PC Working Group, of the Software Publishers Association. It sets industry standards for multimedia PCs.

**MPC1**    The original multimedia PC standard set by the MPC.

**MPC2**   The MPC's second standard level of performance specifications.

**MPC3**   The MPC's third standard level of performance specifications.

**MPEG (Moving Picture Experts Group) codec**   Standards for digital video and digital audio compression.

**MPRII**   An international standard for low-radiation emissions developed for monitors by the Swedish regulatory agency, SWEDAC. It is now the compliance standard for many worldwide manufacturers for their monitors.

**MSAU (multistation access unit)**   The central hub for IBM-computer-station Token Ring networks.

**mscdex.exe**   A file loaded in MS-DOS mode. **mscdex.exe** loads installed CD-ROM drives and Windows 95–installed mouse drivers.

**MS-DOS (Microsoft Disk Operating System)**   The first operating system developed and licensed for the IBM compatible computer system.

**MS-DOS prompt**   A Start menu option that lets the user access MS-DOS commands.

**ms-dos.sys**   One of the three MS-DOS operating system files that the MS-DOS bootstrap loader searches for in the root directory of the boot disk and loads into memory.

**MSN (Microsoft Network)**   An online information service created and maintained by Microsoft.

**MTBF (mean time between failure)**   The average failure rate of a power supply established by the actual operation or calculation from known standards. It is expressed in hours.

**multifrequency rate**   The ability of a monitor to support many different horizontal and vertical scan frequencies, and therefore many resolutions.

**multiple master domain model**   An arrangement of client and server computers in which more than one domain has access to various resource domains.

**multiprogram**   To run two or more programs on a single computer at one time. Another term for *multitask*.

**multitask**   A technique used in operating systems for sharing a single processor to accomplish several independent tasks.

**multithreaded**   More than one thread working simultaneously to accomplish a task.

**multi-word DMA mode 2**   A direct memory access mode drive transfer operation used by some advanced ATA-2 hard drives and incorporated into UDMA hard drives.

**My Computer**   A default Windows 95 desktop icon, a container object, that holds all the computer's resources.

# N

**navigate**    To move around in the Windows environment in order to access and use programs, utilities, and hardware.

**NDIS (Network Device Interface Specification)**    A programming interface for different protocols sharing the same network hardware.

**near letter quality**    A print-quality mode for dot-matrix printers that is between draft and letter quality.

**negotiation**    A process modems use to arrive at a common modulation standard.

**NetBEUI (NetBIOS Extended User Interface)**    A new version of NetBIOS that allows computers to communicate within a LAN, using a frame format.

**NetWare**    Novell's network operating system, developed in the early 1980s, that is a cooperative, multitasking, dedicated server, network operating system with wide client support.

**Netwatcher**    A peer-to-peer networking tool that shows the system's sharing status, and allows users to create or disable shared resources.

**network**    To link computers and their peripherals by means of wires, cables, or telephone lines.

**network adapter**    A network card.

**Network Backups**    Software used to safeguard the data and configurations stored on a peer-to-peer network.

**Network Monitor**    A BackOffice product included with Microsoft System Management Server that servers as a protocol analyzer.

**Network Neighborhood**    A default Windows 95 desktop icon, a container object, that holds all the computer's network-accessible devices.

**neutral wire**    In a circuit, the wire that is connected to an earth ground at the power plant and at the transformer.

**NFS (Network File System)**    A client/server application that lets a user view, store, and update files on a remote computer, as if it were local. It also allows local file systems to be exported across the network.

**NIC (network interface card)**    A card that fits into a computer's motherboard to provide a port for the computer's network access.

**node**    A device connected to the network that can communicate with other network devices.

**noise**    The signal degradation that occurs when stray electrical signals, such as signals caused by fluorescent lights, interfere with data movement.

**nonconductor**  Material that does not transmit electricity, heat, sound, and so on.

**non-impact printer**  The class of printers in which nothing in the printer actually impacts the paper to form characters. This class includes laser printers and inkjet printers.

**noninterlaced**  A scanning mode in which the scanning beam moves across the screen from top to bottom, continuously, over each line. This is currently the standard scanning mode in quality monitors.

**nonpreemptive multitasking**  A type of multitasking in which a task does its job until finished before relinquishing control to the processor.

**non-user definable**  Box screens that provide information about a system's BIOS configuration. Box screens are activated when a system's BIOS does not offer configurable choices for the user. Examples include the autodetect video fields and keyboard fields of the main BIOS setup screen.

**NOS (network operating system)**  An operating system on the server in a LAN that coordinates the activities of computers and other devices attached to the network.

**notification area**  A portion of the Taskbar just left of the system clock. It displays icons relating to status information about system functions.

**NT Server**  The Windows NT server version.

**NT Workstation**  The Windows NT client version.

**NTFS (New Technology File System)**  A file system introduced by Microsoft with the Windows NT operating system in 1993.

**numeric tail**  An abbreviation, denoted by its file extension, at the end of a filename that has been converted by a DOS-based program.

# O

**object**  A folder, file, program, printer, modem, or process represented by an icon in Windows 95.

**Object menu**  The list of options offered when the mouse is right-clicked on a desktop object's icon.

**octal system**  A base-8 numbering system that uses the digits 0–7.

**octet**  An piece of data that is exactly 8 bits.

**offline UPS**  A type of UPS that operates offline. Also called a *standby UPS*.

**OLE (Object Linking and Embedding)**  A protocol for transferring information among applications that either links or embeds the information into the file it has been transferred to. Embedding differs from linking in that, for example, when a graphic is linked to a word processing file, changes made to the original graphics file automatically appear in the linked version. On the other hand, when one file is embedded in another, the embedded file is a copy of the original, and changes made in the original do not automatically appear in the embedded copy.

**online UPS**     A type of UPS that always runs off the battery. This is the more desirable type of UPS.

**Open Program Title Box**     The Taskbar button for every open program in Windows 95.

**operating system boot disk**     A disk used to initialize or start the operating system software.

**optimize**     To improve the performance of a hard drive by rearranging data. Also called *defragment*.

**OS (operating system)**     The software that runs a computer, receives command requests through the user interface, analyzes commands, and then sends out instructions to the various computer components.

**OS Executive**     Another name for the kernel, which is regarded as the heart of the operating system. It launches applications, allocates system functions, and manages a computer's memory, files, and peripheral devices, and maintains the date and time.

**OS/2 (Operating System 2)**     An operating system jointly developed and introduced by Microsoft and IBM in 1987 that was intended as a replacement for DOS.

**oscillation**     A change in the electrical signal that occurs periodically.

**OSI (Open System Interconnect) model**     An international seven-layer model of functions in a telecommunications system.

**outlet tester**     A device that tests for proper conductor connections of electrical outlets. Lights on the tester indicate proper or improper wiring of the outlet.

**output**     The processed data from the CPU that is displayed on the monitor. Other forms of output include information sent to a printer or fax/modem.

**output device**     An internal or peripheral device attached to the system unit that allows the user to view results.

**overload protection**     Protection provided on all outputs against short-circuits.

**overvoltage protection**     A feature of the power supply that shuts down the supply or clamps down on the output when its voltage exceeds a preset limit.

# P

**page description language**     A language designed to transcribe the layout and contents of a printed page and send commands to the printer for the desired results.

**page format** The layout of a page, including the fonts, spacing, paper size, margins, text layout, and graphics.

**page printer** Another term for *laser printer*.

**paging file** Another term for *swap file*.

**paper path** The channel through which the paper feeds and is transported through a printer.

**paper transport mechanism** The electromechanical means by which the paper is moved through the paper path in a printer.

**paradigm** An established way of thinking or a widely accepted belief system. For example, the Windows paradigm is based on its intuitive interface's array of objects that suggest their functions to a user.

**parallel port** A parallel interface for connecting an external device, capable of transmitting more than 1 bit of data at a time. Printers are usually connected to computers using parallel ports.

**parallel processor** An architecture in a PC that can perform multiple operations simultaneously.

**parity checking** A method of ensuring that data that was transmitted via a modem from one computer to another is error free. Parity is achieved by adding a 1 or a 0 bit to each byte as the byte is transmitted. At the other end of the transmission, the receiving modem verifies the parity and the accuracy of the transmission.

**partition** An area of space on a hard drive that is allocated for system use. Also, to configure a free area of disk space for system use.

**Pascal, Blaise** A French mathematician who invented the first recorded calculation machine, called the pascaline.

**pascaline** A calculating machine developed in 1642 by French mathematician Blaise Pascal.

**passive hub network** A network that joins wires from several stations in a star configuration. There is no dedicated device on a passive network to support networking.

**pass-through** To go on to the next phase without stopping.

**patch** A temporary solution to a technical problem. Also, a sample of an instrumental sound sometimes found on a music synthesizer.

**PC (personal computer)** A computer that meets the IBM standard.

**PCI (peripheral component interconnect)** A bus created by Intel to provide superior performance to an ISA, and to allow peripheral devices to automatically configure themselves through the plug-and-play process.

**PCI IDE (peripheral component interconnect and integrated drive electronics)**   A bus used for communication between peripherals and PCs. IDE is the hardware that connects peripherals to a PC.

**PCL (Printer Control Language)**   A proprietary page description language developed by Hewlett Packard for its inkjet and laser printers.

**PCMCIA (Personal Computer Memory Card International Association)**   An organization that creates devices that conform to its standards and plug into specially configured slots in PCs. A PCMCIA modem is about the size of a credit card.

**PDC (primary domain controller)**   A domain server that can authenticate workstations and usually contains master copies of security, computer, and user account databases.

**peer-to-peer network**   A network of two or more computers that use the same program to share data and resources, and in which computers share equal responsibility in acting as a server to other computers in the same network.

**Pentium**   Intel's fifth-generation 80x86 CPU. It followed the 486 processor and began Intel's "fast" CPU line.

**Pentium II**   Intel's follow-up to its initial Pentium chips series. Built-in multimedia extensions and easier upgrading capabilities characterize the Pentium II processor.

**Performance**   A tab in the Control Panel's System utility that offers options to set virtual memory values.

**peripheral**   A computer's hardware device that is separate from the CPU or working memory. Some examples of peripherals are disks, keyboards, monitors, mice, printers, scanners, tape drives, microphones, speakers, and cameras.

**PIF (program information file)**   A Windows file that provides information on how a DOS application should be run.

**PIF Editor**   A configuration utility that produces PIFs, which give Windows instructions on how to handle DOS applications.

**pixel**   Short for picture element, it is the smallest element of a video image and is composed of three primary phosphor color dots.

**pixel rate**   The speed at which the RAMDAC chip can draw the pixels, commonly expressed in MHz.

**plug-and-play**   A feature designed to simplify installing hardware allowing the operating system and the BIOS to automatically configure new hardware devices, thus eliminating system resources conflicts.

**PM (Presentation Manager)**   An ineffective graphical interface to the initial OS/2 system.

**popup**   A type of menu called for and displayed on top of the existing text or image. When the item is selected, the menu disappears and the screen is restored.

**port**   A parallel or serial interface where data is transferred. Generally, a port is located on the back of a computer system.

**portable computer**   A compact version of a desktop computer. Also referred to as *laptops*, portable computers retain most standard, desktop computer features and can operate on either battery or household current.

**POST (power-on self-test)**   A self-check the BIOS performs in the preboot stage to ensure that the machine is working properly

**Postscript**   Adobe's page description language used in all computer platforms. It is the commercial typesetting and printing standard.

**power button**   A button located on the front of the computer that controls electrical current to the power supply.

**power cord socket**   A receptacle or cavity used to connect the power supply to an external power source such as a wall outlet, generally via an electrical cord or lead.

**power cycle**   A reboot.

**power on/off switch**   A lever that allows electrical current to the power supply to be turned on and off.

**power supply**   A device inside a computer's system unit that converts AC electricity from a power outlet to DC electricity used by the computer.

**power supply lead**   A wire capable of conducting an electrical current that connects the power supply to the computer's internal components and drives.

**power supply mount point**   The shelf or ledge on which the power supply rests when it is attached to the chassis.

**Power_Good delay**   The period during which the **Power_Good** signal is delayed until all voltages have stabilized after the system has been turned on.

**Power_Good signal**   A +5v signal sent by the power supply after it has passed a series of internal self-tests. It is sent to the motherboard, where it is received by the processor timer chip controlling the reset line to the processor.

**ppm (pages per minute)**   A measure of laser printer printing speed that tells how many pages per minutes the printer can output at a given resolution.

**PPP (Point-to-Point Protocol)**   A protocol for communication between computers using a serial interface, most often a PC connected by a phone line to a server.

**PPTP (Point-to-Point Tunneling Protocol)**   A VPN protocol built in to Windows NT that ensures secure data transmission.

**preemptive multitasking**   A type of multitasking in which a controller interrupts and suspends a running task in order to run a new task, thus facilitating smoother computer operations.

**primary partition**    The portion of a hard disk that contains the operating system. The system boots from the primary partition. A disk can have up to three primary partitions, but only one of them can be designated active, or in use, at any given time.

**print engine**    The mechanism that transcribes the array of dots created by the printer controller into a printed image.

**print head**    The part of the printer that either physically impacts the paper surface through a ribbon, directs ink to the paper, or burns toner onto the paper.

**Print Manager**    A Windows 3.1 system for managing printer operations and configuring settings.

**print spooler**    Software that manages files sent to a printer.

**printable screen font**    A font used onscreen that has a printer font equivalent.

**printer**    An output device that produces paper printouts from computer software applications such as word processors and spreadsheets.

**printer controller**    The command center in a laser printer that reads the data output from the host computer and then interprets the commands for the page format and then sends them to the print engine.

**printer font**    A font stored in the printer.

**Printers folder**    An object in the Windows 95 My Computer default container that provides a means to configure printers to be used with the operating system and icons for currently installed printers.

**program**    A software application designed to perform some work or achieve some function on a computer.

**program icon**    A small onscreen image that provides the user access to a specific computer program.

**Program Manager**    The main control shell used to perform operations, such as starting programs and organizing files, in Windows 3.1 and Windows NT. It is the onscreen interface for **progman.exe** and is called Windows Explorer in Windows 95/98.

**programming language**    One of many computer languages designed to write computer instructions and programs in which programmers express data with symbols. Some examples of programming languages include BASIC, C++, and COBOL.

**projector**    A peripheral device that enables computer data to be displayed on a large remote screen for presentation purposes.

**prompt**    A text symbol in the DOS command prompt window which indicates that the system is ready to receive commands.

**properties**    The characteristics of a file, an application, or a device, such as size, creation date, and type.

**proprietary**   A product or design that is owned by and unique to a specific company.

**proprietary standard**   A specification set for a specific company's product.

**protected mode**   An Intel-based operational state that allows the computer to address all its memory, while preventing an errant program from entering the memory boundary of another.

**protected-mode driver**   A driver that supports protected mode, which has more advanced features than real mode.

**protocol**   A special set of rules for communicating that components use when sending signals. Often described in an industry or a national standard.

**protocol stack**   Layers of specialized sets of rules for computer communication that occur during a session.

**PS/2 connector**   Another term for *mini-DIN connector*.

**PSTN (public switched telephone network)**   The international telephone system made up of digital and analog telephone lines.

**pulse code modulation method**   A way to sample and digitize sound digitally by recording successive digital sample differences.

**PUN (physical unit number)**   A device connected directly to the SCSI bus. It is the same as the SCSI ID.

**punch card**   An early storage medium made of thin cardboard cards that read data as a series of punched holes.

# Q

**QIC (quarter-inch cartridge)**   A type of tape used for data backup.

**quantization noise**   Signal degradation that occurs during analog-to-digital conversion across the PSTN backbones. It limits traditional modem communications to 33.6 Kbps.

**queue**   A storage area designed to hold temporary data.

**Qwerty keyboard**   The standard English-language typewriter keyboard. The letters Q, W, E, R, T, and Y are the letters on the top-left, alphabetic row of the keyboard. It was designed in 1868 by typewriter inventor Christopher Shoals.

# R

**RAM (random access memory)**   Computer memory that is both readable and writable. When the computer shuts down, RAM data is no longer retrievable.

**RAMDAC (RAM digital-to-analog converter)**   A device that converts the digital images in video memory to analog signals and sends them to the video monitor.

**RARP (Reverse Address Resolution Protocol)**   The protocol TCP/IP uses to get an IP address when only a domain name address is available.

**RAS (Remote Access Server)**   Windows software that permits remote access to a server using a modem.

**raster font**   A typeface designed pixel by pixel, intended for computer monitor display screens. Scaling raster fonts lessens image quality. Also called *bitmap* or *screen fonts*.

**rasterization**   The last preprinting stage in a laser printer, where the printer controller converts the page format to a dot array before burning it to the drum.

**raw**   The print spooling used in Windows 3.1; it is a slower method of printing than the EMF method used in Windows 95.

**raw spool files**   Files created in Windows 3.1 when the **print** command is given.

**read multiple**   An ATA-2 enhanced BIOS drive command that enables the controller and drive circuitry to support multiple-sector disk writes concurrently.

**Read/Write Head Req/Ack (Request/Acknowledgement)**   The method a SCSI host adapter uses to negotiate an asynchronous data transfer with a SCSI device on the bus. For each data transfer request, the host adapter sends a request to the device, and the device controller responds with an acknowledgement.

**read-only**   An attribute that, when enabled, prevents a user from deleting or altering a file. As the name implies, the user is only allowed to open and read the file, but not alter it in any way.

**real mode**   An Intel-based mode of program operation in which the processor can execute only one program at a time and access no more than 1 MB of memory. Such programs are usually part of the operating system or the special application subsystem and can be trusted to know how to update system data.

**real-mode driver**   A driver that supports real mode, an older operating mode that enables the processor to execute only one program at a time. They were often the source of system crashes as they did not include memory boundary protection.

**reboot**   To shut down the computer and immediately restart it.

**recommended resolutions**   Part of the manufacturer's resolution specification, the list of display resolutions that the manufacturer recommends for a monitor model.

**Recycle Bin**   A default Windows 95 desktop icon that holds all deleted hard drive files. It retains deleted files until they are either retrieved or deleted permanently.

**refresh**   To redraw a screen at intervals to keep its phosphors irradiated.

**refresh rate**   The number of times per second that the video screen display is redrawn.

**Registry**   A Windows 95 internal database that contains data on the hardware and characteristics of the computer. Windows programs continually reference the Registry during normal operation.

**Registry Editor**   Software that lets a user edit the Registry's entries.

**rema**   The DOS **remove** command.

**remote button switch**   The remote, power on/off switch found on Slimline and ATX computer models.

**repeater**   A communications device used to extend the distance of data transmission. It amplifies or regenerates a data signal.

**reset button**   A button that you press to activate the reset line that sends the message to the CPU to reboot the system.

**reset switch connector**   A switch located on the front case bezel that is used when the computer locks up so that the system can be rebooted.

**resolution**   An onscreen image's degree of sharpness, expressed as a matrix of horizontal and vertical dots. A reference to the size of the pixels in a display at a given screen size. The higher the resolution, the smaller the pixels.

**resource**   A utility, file, or peripheral that is useful to a client.

**restart**   A command that causes the computer to reload its operating software.

**RFI (radio-frequency interference)**   A form of EMI that creates noise on an electronic circuit. It can be created by an appliance in the computer's vicinity.

**ring in**   A point in a Token Ring network where the data flows into the MSAU.

**ring network**   A LAN where all the nodes are connected in a closed loop, or ring.

**ring out**   A point in a Token Ring network where the data flows out from the MSAU.

**ripple**   Another term for *noise*.

**roaming user profile**   A profile that is stored and configured to be downloaded from a server. It allows a user to access his or her profile from any network location.

**ROM (read only memory)**   A type of nonvolatile storage that can only be read from. It is a nonvolatile storage system, and contains important data that must be saved even when the power is shut off. It is used to hold critical data such as the CMOS setup and other boot-up data for the computer.

**root directory**   The base of any file system directory structure.

**router**   A piece of equipment used to connect networks to each other. It makes more sophisticated data routing decisions than do bridges.

**RPC (remote-procedure call)**   A protocol that allows a program running on one host to cause code to be executed on another host, without the programmer needing understand network details.

**rpm (revolutions per minute)**   The number of times the drive platter spins completely in 1 minute.

**RTS/CTS (request-to-send/clear-to-send)**   Signals sent between the modem and host system to manage the rate of data flow. *See* flow control.

**rubber dome switches**   A variant of the foam buffer design, in which the spring is eliminated from the plunger and a rubber dome is used in place of the foam and foil laminate pad. The rubber dome sits atop the contacts on the circuit board.

**Run**   A Start menu option that provides one method of opening programs.

**run length**   An encoded bitmap file data compression technique used to minimize file sizes by encoding multiple consecutive occurrences of a given symbol.

# S

**safety ground wire**   A safety ground wire that connects the earth ground to the chassis of an electrical appliance or device via an electrical outlet and plug. It is used to ensure that no electrical hazards exist between the chassis of the electrical device and the earth ground.

**sag**   A type of power event in which a decrease occurs that equals 80% below the normal voltage carried by a power line. It is sometimes referred to as a *brownout*.

**SAM (Security Accounts Manager)**   The module of the Windows NT executive that authenticates a username and password in the account database.

**sample**   In computers, to change analog signals to digital format by measuring samples at regular intervals.

**sample size**   The amount of storage designated to a single sound sample when converting analog signals to digital signals.

**sampling rate**   In computerized sound, the frequency at which sound samples are taken. The more sound samples taken per time unit, the closer the digitized sound will match the original analog sound.

**SBIC (SCSI bus interface controller) chip**   A logic chip that governs the SCSI controller circuitry on a SCSI drive.

**scan code**   A unique binary code sent to the motherboard by the onboard keyboard processor, based on the key switch position in the key matrix. When the key is pressed, the processor reads the position and sends the appropriate scan code to the motherboard.

**ScanDisk**   A Windows 95 utility that can repair certain kinds of disk errors.

**scanner**   An input device that reads printed information such as pictures or text and translates them into digital data the computer can understand.

**scanning**   The movement the electron beam makes across the video screen as it writes the image. The scanning movement can be interlaced or noninterlaced.

**scanning frequency**   A manufacturer specification listing the horizontal and vertical scan range of a monitor model.

**scheduling**   Pertaining to Windows 3.1, this refers to an enhanced panel option that specifies how much of the system's resources are reserved for the foreground application.

**screen font**   A typeface designed pixel by pixel, intended for computer monitor display. Also called *raster* or *bitmap font*.

**screen size**   The actual physical size of the monitor screen as measured in inches, from one corner diagonally to the other.

**screen treatment**   A manufacturer specification for CRT monitor screens that details the monitor's type of screen coating. Quality monitors generally have tinted screens featuring antistatic and antiglare surface treatments.

**script**   A program that contains a set of instructions for an application or a utility.

**SCSI (small computer systems interface)**   A bus interface standard initially ratified in 1986 that uses a 50-pin connector and allows up to eight devices to be connected in a daisy chain. Also called SCSI-1 to differentiate it from the SCSI-2 and SCSI-3 revisions.

**SCSI bus interface controller**   A logic chip that governs the SCSI controller circuitry on a SCSI drive.

**SCSI host adapter**   The electronic gateway between the SCSI bus and the host system's I/O bus.

**SCSI ID**   A number set with jumper pins on the SCSI device; it can range from 0 to 7. The order of service priority by the SCSI host adapter is determined in increasing order of number. Also called a *PUN*.

**SCSI-1**   The first SCSI bus standard, ratified in 1986.

**SCSI-2**   The second SCSI bus made standard, ratified in 1994. The enhancements included increased device support and a common set of BIOS commands.

**SDRAM (synchronous DRAM)**   A type of RAM that incorporates features that allow it to keep pace with bus speeds as high as 100 MHz. By allowing two sets of memory addresses to be opened simultaneously, data can be retrieved alternately from each set, eliminating the delays that normally occur.

**sector**   The smallest unit of space on the hard disk that any software can access; it is 512 bytes in size.

**sector translation**    A method used by the enhanced BIOS of computer systems since the mid-1990s to overcome the drive geometry limitations in the BIOS. This allows the BIOS to acknowledge drive sizes beyond 504 MB.

**security provider**    A Windows NT domain or workgroup computer that delegates user group resources and permissions.

**segment**    To split a large Ethernet network into more manageably sized segments connected by bridges and routers.

**serial interface**    An interface used for the serial transmission of data. In this type of transmission, only 1 bit is transmitted at a time.

**serial port**    A general-purpose 9- or 25-pin interface that can be used for serial communications with peripheral devices including modems, mouse devices, and some printers.

**server**    A network computer or program that is accessible to many network users and fulfills users' requests for information access and transfer.

**server-on-a-LAN**    A computer that runs administrative software that controls the workstations of the network. On the Internet, it's a server that responds to commands from the clients.

**servo mechanism**    A control system where the final output is mechanical movement. It uses gray code to control the position and the acceleration of the hard drive.

**session**    An active connection between a client and a peer (often a server) during which data and files are exchanged.

**settings**    A Start menu option that allows users access to Control Panel, Taskbar, and printer features.

**setup**    The process of preparing an application or a program so that it will run on a computer.

**shadow**    Similar to a shortcut, it creates a connection to an actual object on another computer.

**shadow mask**    A masking design composed of fine metal mesh on the inside of the monitor screen that helps to focus the electron beam on the correct pixels.

**share-level security**    A form of network security used on Windows 95 systems in which a network administrator holds passwords for folders and disk drives on the network.

**shell**    A program that provides access to the operating system.

**shortcut**    A user-created desktop icon that gives quick access to a Windows 95 object, such as a program or file.

**shut down**    A Start menu command for closing the operating system.

**SideKick**   A popup program that first appeared as a multitasking shell accompanying DOS programs in the mid-1980s.

**signal**   An electrical impulse used to transmit data over a physical medium for the purpose of communication.

**signal-to-noise ratio**   The number of bits of correct data divided by the number of bits of noise.

**silicon**   Material used as the base for most microprocessor chips.

**SIMM (single, inline memory module)**   A small circuit board that holds a group of memory chips. On Macintosh computers, SIMMs can hold up to eight chips. On PCs, they can hold up to nine chips; the ninth chip is used for parity error checking.

**sine wave**   A waveform whose amplitude varies, proportionally to the sine of the time elapsed. Visually, it appears like the letter *S*, rotated 90 degrees.

**single tasking**   The limitation of an operating system to perform only one operating task at a time.

**single-domain model**   The simplest arrangement of client and server computers, which operates in one unit.

**single-ended SCSI**   The normal SCSI signal standard, in which one cable wire is used to carry the signal from end to end.

**sinusoidal**   Of, relating to, or shaped like a sine curve or sine wave.

**Slimline**   A type of form factor in current use.

**small drive connector**   A small 4-pin power supply connector found on current 3 1/2-inch floppy drives.

**SMTP (Simple Mail Transfer Protocol)**   A protocol that governs e-mail transmission and reception.

**Socket 3**   A motherboard socket where older-technology CPUs connect to the motherboard.

**Socket 7**   A motherboard socket where older-technology CPUs such as the Intel Pentium P54C and P55C series CPUs connect to the motherboard.

**Socket 8**   A motherboard socket where more recent technology Pentium Pro CPUs connect to the motherboard.

**software**   Computer instructions that fall into two categories: systems software and applications software. Systems software includes the operating system and all the utilities that make the computer function. Applications software includes individual programs designed to perform specific functions for a user.

**sound card**    A multimedia card added to the motherboard that allows a computer to record and play WAV or MIDI files.

**speaker**    A device that enables users to hear sound.

**spike**    A sudden burst of power lasting between .5 and 100 microseconds.

**spindle**    The central post or hub on which a disk drive's platters are mounted.

**spindle motor**    The motor in the head disk assembly that powers the spindle to rotate the drive platters.

**spool file**    A file created by the spooler when the **print** command is given.

**spray contact cleaner**    A liquid solvent used to clean electronic connections that has a rapid drying time and does not leave a residue.

**SRAM (static RAM)**    A type of memory that is faster and more reliable than RAM. It needs to be refreshed less often than RAM.

**standby UPS**    A type of UPS that runs off its battery only when the AC mains exhibit problems.

**stand-off**    A small piece of hardware that is used to attach the motherboard to the motherboard mounting plate on the chassis.

**star network**    A network configured like a star, with a centralized hub to which each computer on the network has access.

**start bit**    In a serial communications session, the binary number 0 that precedes every byte to tell the receiving system that the next 8 bits constitute a byte of data.

**Start menu**    Located at the left end of the Taskbar, a menu offers access to almost every program on the computer.

**startup disk**    A floppy disk that contains copies of the computer's operating system files and can be used to start up the computer in case of a crash. Also called a *system disk*.

**static electricity**    Stationary electricity that happens when electrons build up on conductive material.

**stop bit**    In a serial communications session, a data bit that follows the byte (or character) to signal to the remote system that it was sent.

**support resolutions**    The range of resolutions supported by the monitor model, as specified by the manufacturer.

**surge**    A type of power event in which a voltage increase above 110 % of the normal voltage occurs.

**surge suppressor**    A device used to protect equipment from transient power surges that travel from AC power lines and telephone circuits.

**SVGA (super video graphics array)**   Enhancements to the VGA standard that increased resolution to 1024 x 728. (The VGA's resolution is only 640 x 480.)

**swap file**   A hard drive file that holds parts of program and data files that do not fit in memory.

**synchronous**   A form of data communication in which exchanges of data bits are strictly timed by a clocking signal.

**sysedit.exe**   A configuration utility for simultaneous configuration of some DOS and Windows configuration files.

**system**   A group of related components that interact to perform a specific task. Also, the controlling program or operating software on a computer.

**system board**   Another name for the *motherboard*.

**System Monitor**   A peer-to-peer networking device that allows observation of a number of system behaviors that can point to potential and actual problems.

**system policy**   A policy that controls what a user can do and controls the user's environment. It can be applied to a specific user, a group, a computer, or all users.

**System Policy Editor**   A utility located in the Administrative Tools group that is used to create system policies.

**System Resources**   A Program Manager feature that lists the system's available resources.

**system unit**   A computer's case and internal components that allow the computer to process information, store data, and communicate with other parts of the computer. It can include the power supply, motherboard, CPU, RAM, ROM, and one or more disk drives.

**system.dat**   A Registry file that contains information about hardware and software.

**system.ini**   A Windows 3.1 file that stores system-specific information on the hardware and device driver system configurations.

**SYSX (system exclusive) data**   Data that a manufacturer uses to transmit private information about its products.

# T

**Tab**   A key used simultaneously with the Alt key to cycle through each active program.

**tactile feedback mechanism**   The metal clip-and-spring mechanism located beneath the plunger of a key switch, designed to provide a slight spring-fed feel of resistance when the key is pressed.

**Tandy**   A manufacturer of PCs and electronics.

**TAPI (Telephony Application Programming Interface)**    An interface that facilitates communication between computers and telephone equipment.

**Taskbar**    A Windows 95 graphic bar that displays all active programs and allows users to switch between programs.

**TCP/IP (Transmission Control Protocol/Internet Protocol)**    A routable protocol in which messages transmitted contain the address of a destination network and a destination station. This allows TCP/IP messages to be sent to multiple networks within an organization or around the world, hence its use in the Internet.

**TechNet**    A worldwide information service designed for information specialists who support or educate users, administer networks or databases, create automated solutions, and evaluate information technology solutions.

**Telnet**    A program used to access another computer, with the correct permissions.

**terminate**    To seal the ends of an electrical bus to maintain the correct impedance for signal propagation, and to prevent signal echoes that degrade the quality of data exchange.

**text file**    A text character file, such as a word processing or ASCII file.

**thin-film media**    The extremely fine layer of magnetically sensitive cobalt alloy deposited on hard drive platters for data encoding and decoding.

**thread**    A data structure used to prioritize multiple demands for a computer resource. Task requests are placed in order—either a first in, first out or a last in, first out.

**token**    A small token ring frame that makes one-way trips around the ring to be seized by a network computer waiting to send a message.

**token passing**    A type of networking system where bits of information are inserted into an empty frame that is examined by successive workstations and passed on.

**token ring**    A type of computer network based on a star configuration in which a token ring's computers are connected to either a central controlled-access unit, a multistation access unit, or a smart multistation access unit.

**toner**    In laser printers, a very fine powder of plastic particles that is attached to the paper via a charged drum and then fused into the paper by a fuser.

**toner hopper**    In laser printers, a toner storage bin that sits atop a developer unit and feeds toner to the drum for transference onto the paper.

**topology**    A configuration formed by the connection between devices on a LAN.

**touch screen**    An input device that allows users to interact with a computer by touching the display screen.

**trackball**    A type of mouse that the user manipulates by rotating the ball with the thumb, fingertips, or palm of the hand. Its buttons are used to perform basic clicking actions such as selecting commands from a menu.

**tractor-feed device**  The sprocket mechanism in dot-matrix printers that pulls or pushes the paper through the paper path and past the print head.

**tractor-feed paper**  Also called fan-fold paper, tractor-feed paper has perforated edges that can be torn away after the paper has been printed. It is commonly used with dot-matrix printers.

**transfer time**  Pertaining to an offline UPS, the elapsed time between AC main failure time and resumption of power from the battery source.

**transient**  A momentary variation in power, which ultimately disappears. Surges, spikes, sags, blackouts, and noise are examples of transients.

**transistor**  A small, solid-state component with three leads, in which the voltage or current controls the flow of another current.

**TrueType font**  A font that possesses a printed copy appearance identical to its onscreen appearance.

**trust**  Short *for trust relationship*, which is an administrative link that joins two or more domains.

**TSR (terminate and stay resident)**  A type of DOS utility that stays in memory and can be reactivated by pressing a certain combination of keys.

**tunnel**  To transmit data structured in one protocol format within the format of another protocol.

**tunneling protocol**  A data transmission protocol that is designed to serve as a carrier for other data stream protocols.

**TUV**  A German-based service organization that tests and certifies product safety to meet standards and specifications of the European Union.

**typeface**  The name given to a specific print characters design. Aria, for example, is the typeface for an Arial, italicized, 10-point font.

# U

**UART (universal asynchronous receiver/transmitter)**  A buffered computer chip that handles asynchronous communications through a computer's serial ports and contains both the receiving and transmitting circuits required for asynchronous serial communication.

**UDMA (ultra direct memory access, or ultra DMA)**  A protocol developed jointly by Intel and Quantum that promotes bypassing the I/O bus bottleneck during peak sequential operations on EIDE hard drives. It also enables read-and-write data transfers through DMA channels with and without bus mastering.

**UDMA mode 2**  The highest transfer rate mode supported by the new Ultra DMA protocol through DMA channels on ATA-3 hard drives, using bus mastering.

**UL (Underwriters Laboratories)**    An independent not-for-profit agency in the United States that tests and certifies products for safety.

**Underwriters Laboratories of Canada**    The Canadian division of Underwriters Laboratories.

**uninstall**    To remove a software program. Windows 95 provides the efficient Add/Remove Programs feature for eliminating unwanted software programs.

**UNIX**    A powerful, multitasking operating system that is widely used as the master control program in workstations and servers. It is less popular in PCs.

**Update Information tool**    A tool in Windows 95 that allows you to find exactly which files you have installed and which version of Windows 95 you have.

**UPS (uninterruptible power supply)**    A backup device designed to provide an uninterrupted power source in the event of a power failure.

**USART (universal synchronous/asynchronous receiver/transmitter)**    A module that contains both the receiving and transmitting circuits required for synchronous and asynchronous serial communication.

**USB (universal serial bus)**    An external bus standard that supports data transfer rates of 12 million bits per second. It allows peripheral devices, such as mouse devices, modems, and keyboards, to be plugged in and unplugged without resetting the system. It is expected to eventually replace serial and parallel ports.

**user control**    A manufacturer specification that refers to the range of controls in adjusting the operating parameters of the monitor. User controls typically include the power switch, horizontal/vertical size, horizontal/vertical position, pincushion, contrast, and brightness controls.

**user friendly**    A system that is easy to learn and easy to use.

**user interface**    The command-line or graphical representation of software that controls the allocation and use of the computer's hardware. The user interface, the file management system, and the kernel form the operating system.

**user profile**    A device that is used to save each user's desktop configuration.

**user.dat**    A Registry file that contains information that is reflected in user profiles.

**user's manual**    A booklet that accompanies a new computer and generally contains information such as how to set up and use a computer.

**user-level security**    A form of security used on network systems in which a user or an administrator can use passwords to secure a network. Only authorized users have access to system-shared files and resources.

**utility**    A software program that takes care of the internal maintenance of the computer system such as editing files, compressing files, and undeleting files.

# V

**V.42bis**  The ITU data compression standard supported in all modern modems.

**vacuum tube**  An electronic device used as a switch.

**variable frequency synthesizer circuit**  A motherboard circuit that multiplies the clock signal so that the motherboard can support several speeds of CPUs.

**vector font**  Another name for TrueType font; it has a printed appearance identical to its onscreen appearance.

**vertical scan rate**  The number of times an image is refreshed or redrawn in 1 second. It is measured in Hz and is also called the *vertical scan frequency*.

**VESA (video electronics standards association)**  An organization founded in 1989 by the nine leading video board manufacturers to standardize the technical issues surrounding the SVGA video display. This organization has also been involved in other issues since then.

**VESA BIOS extension**  A BIOS extension to the VGA standard introduced by member companies of VESA in 1989 to resolve incompatibilities in the implementations of the SVGA display technology. This provided a standard interface for programmers to write the drivers for their SVGA video adapters.

**VESA DPMS**  A power-management signaling specification that VESA developed for monitors.

**VFAT (Virtual File Allocation Table)**  A virtualized 32-bit FAT, which makes it possible for Windows 95 to support long filenames.

**VGA (video graphics array)**  The first analog video graphics standard, introduced by IBM Corporation in 1987. The hardware that determines a monitor's screen resolution and color range capability. A VGA-supported monitor displays at least 256 separate colors, and 640 x 480-dpi resolution.

**video adapter**  An expansion board that plugs into a computer system to give it display capabilities. In conjunction with the display monitor, it forms the video system for the computer.

**video bandwidth**  The maximum display resolution of a video screen, generally measured in MHz and calculated by multiplying horizontal resolution times the vertical resolution times the refresh rate per second.

**video BIOS**  The BIOS on the video card that provides a set of video-related functions that are used by programs to access the video hardware. This is much the same way the system BIOS provides the functions that software programs use to access the system hardware.

**video card**  A printed circuit board that converts images created in the computer to the electronic signals required by the monitor. Sometimes called *video adapter* or *video board*.

**video chipset**    The logic circuit that controls the video card. It almost always includes an internal processor that performs various video calculation functions before the RAMDAC chip outputs to the monitor.

**video display monitor**    Another term for *monitor*, *display monitor*, or *video monitor*.

**video driver**    Software that functions between the video card and other computer programs. It works with the video card to help draw Windows objects on the monitor.

**video memory**    The amount of RAM on the video card used by the video chipset to draw the requested screen display.

**viewable area**    A monitor's display area that is usable for a screen image. This differs from a monitor's screen size, due to the black border around the perimeter of each monitor that is unusable.

**virtual memory**    Memory made available by borrowing space from a computer's hard disk. It allows the computer to run programs larger than the system would ordinarily have the RAM to support.

**virus scanning and repair disk**    A disk used to start a virus detection program. It is usually bootable, and it may also have an **fdisk** utility to run tests and repair the hard disks.

**VM (virtual machine)**    An abstract program that runs a computer that doesn't exist physically, yet operates independently as a fully functional unit.

**VM manager**    The interpreter that executes commands for the VM.

**voice coil actuator**    The device that moves the head actuator assembly with read/write heads across the hard disk platters by electromagnetic attraction or repulsion of its wire coils against a magnet. This positions it precisely over the required track.

**voltage inverter**    A device that converts DC voltage from the battery to AC voltage that can be used by the power supply.

**voltage switch**    A lever located on the back of the power supply unit that allows the user to switch between 120v and 220v electrical power.

**volume**    A fixed amount of storage on a disk, created by formatting a partition. It contains the actual file-management system used by an operating system.

**volume boot code**    The bootstrap loader that launches the operating system.

**VPN (virtual private network)**    A means by which to set up private networks on the World Wide Web, using encrypted transmissions.

**VRAM (video RAM)**    A specialized DRAM memory chip on video boards designed for dual port access; it helps provide two access paths so information can be written to and read from simultaneously.

# W–Z

**wait state** A clock tick during which nothing happens. It occurs between cycles and is used to ensure that the processor does not get ahead of the rest of the computer.

**WAN (wide-area network)** A communications network that connects clients both countrywide and worldwide.

**warm boot** To start up a computer by using the restart button or by pressing Ctrl + Alt + Del.

**.wav** The file extension for sound files stored as waveforms.

**waveform** A representation, usually graphic, of a wave's shape. It indicates the wave's frequency and amplitude.

**wavetable synthesis** State-of-the-art sound synthesis using actual instrument sound rather than recorded instrument sound.

**Web (World Wide Web)** A huge internetwork that consists of all the documents on the Internet. Written in HTML, the Web locates documents by their uniform resource locator (URL) addresses. Routers are able to decide on data's best pathway across networks.

**Web site** A server that contains Web pages and other files that is online to the Internet 24 hours per day.

**wide SCSI-2** A variant of SCSI-2 that utilizes the 16-bit bus standard over a 68-pin connector.

**wildcard** A character such as an asterisk or question mark that takes the place of a letter or word. It allows the user to conduct a broad search for files that share common characteristics and/or extensions.

**win.com** Also called the *loader*, the **win.com** file starts Windows and contains the **win.cnf**, **lgo**, and **rle** files.

**win.ini** A Windows 3.1 file that stores information about the appearance of the Windows environment.

**win_root** A folder in which the Registry Editor is stored.

**Win32** An application interface that is common to all of Microsoft's 32-bit operating systems.

**window** A display area where a program or utility can function.

**windowed display** One of the separate viewing areas on a display screen in a system that allows multiple viewing areas as part of its GUI.

**Windows** The Microsoft family of software programs, including Windows 3.1, 95, 98, NT, and 2000.

**Windows 2000**    The latest generation of Windows NT.

**Windows 95**    Microsoft's successor to the Windows 3.1 operating system for PCs. Released in 1995, Windows 95 ushered in a new level of GUI sophistication and ease of use for PC users.

**Windows 95 Resource Kit**    Microsoft's definitive guide to Windows 95.

**Windows 98**    The newest generation of Windows 95.

**Windows Explorer**    The file manager in Windows that helps users find and manipulate system files and folders.

**Windows NT (New Technology)**    Microsoft's 32-bit operating system designed for high-end workstations, servers, and corporate networks.

**Windows NT security**    Measures taken to protect the NT network against accidental or intentional loss, usually in the form of accountability procedures and use restrictions.

**WINS (Windows Internet Name Service)**    A part of the Windows NT Server that manages and assigns IP addresses to workstation locations without any user or administrator being involved in the configuration.

**word**    A computer's natural storage unit, typically consisting of 8 bits, 16 bits, 32 bits, or 64 bits.

**workgroup**    A group of network users who share network resources.

**workstation**    A computer intended for individual use, but faster and having more functionality than a PC.

**WRAM (window RAM)**    A modification of VRAM that improves performance, reduces cost, and is designed specifically for use in graphics cards to allow for higher-performance memory transfers.

**wrap plug**    Another term for *loopback connector*.

**write multiple**    An ATA-2 enhanced BIOS drive command that enables the controller and drive circuitry to support multiple-sector disk reads concurrently.

# Notes

**Notes**

**Notes**

# Notes

# Notes

# Notes

# Notes

# Notes